KU-236-232

The Later Foucault

Politics and Philosophy

edited by

Jeremy Moss

SAGE Publications
London • Thousand Oaks • New Delhi

Editorial arrangement, Introduction and Chapter 9 ©
Jeremy Moss 1998
Chapter 1 © David Couzens Hoy 1998
Chapter 2 © Wendy Brown 1998
Chapter 3 © Barry Hindess 1998
Chapter 4 © Paul Patton 1998
Chapter 5 © Barry Smart 1998
Chapter 6 © Jana Sawicki 1998
Chapter 7 © William Connolly 1998
Chapter 8 © Duncan Ivison 1998
Chapter 10 © Barry Allen 1998

All rights reserved. No part of this publication may be
reproduced, stored in a retrieval system, transmitted or utilized
in any form or by any means, electronic, mechanical,
photocopying, recording or otherwise, without permission in
writing from the Publishers.

 SAGE Publications Ltd
6 Bonhill Street
London EC2A 4PU

SAGE Publications Inc
2455 Teller Road
Thousand Oaks, California 91320

SAGE Publications India Pvt Ltd
32, M-Block Market
Greater Kailash – I
New Delhi 110 048

British Library Cataloguing in Publication data

A catalogue record for this book is
available from the British Library

    ISBN 0 8039 7675 5
    ISBN 0 8039 7676 3 (pbk)

Library of Congress catalog card number 97–062170

Typeset by M Rules
Printed in Great Britain by Redwood Books,
Trowbridge, Wiltshire

UNIVERSITY OF HERTFORDSHIRE
HATFIELD CAMPUS LRC
HATFIELD AL10 9AD 309994

BIB 0803 97 6763

CLASS 320.092 LAI

LOCATION FwL

BARCODE 44 05111846

44 0511184 6

The Later Foucault

WITHDRAWN

For Tristan

Contents

Part III   Political Traditions

Contributors' Notes

Barry Allen teaches philosophy at McMaster University, Ontario, Canada. He is the author of *Truth in Philosophy* (1993). His contribution to this volume is part of a work in progress entitled *Knowledge and Civilization.*

Wendy Brown is Professor in Women's Studies and Legal Studies at the University of California, Santa Cruz, USA, and Visiting Professor in Political Science at the University of California, Berkeley, USA. Her most recent book is *States of Injury: Power and Freedom in Late Modernity* (1995).

William Connolly teaches political theory at the Johns Hopkins University where he is a professor. His recent publications include *Identity\Difference: Democratic Negotiations of Political Paradox* (1991), *The Augustinian Imperative* (1993) and *The Ethos of Pluralization* (1995).

Barry Hindess is Professor of Political Science at the Australian National University in Canberra. His most recent book is *Discourses of Power: From Hobbes to Foucault* (1996).

David Couzens Hoy is Professor and Chair of Philosophy at the University of California, Santa Cruz, USA. He is the author of *Critical Theory* (with Thomas McCarthy, 1994), *The Critical Circle* (1978) and editor of *Foucault: A Critical Reader* (1986). A forthcoming book is entitled *Critical Resistance.*

Duncan Ivison is Lecturer in Political Theory in the Department of Politics at the University of York, UK. He has published articles on the history of political thought and contemporary political theory. He is the author of *The Self at Liberty: Political Argument and the Arts of Government* (1997).

Jeremy Moss teaches in the Philosophy Department at the University of Melbourne, Australia. He teaches and writes on European philosophy and political theory.

Paul Patton is Associate Professor of Philosophy at the University of Sydney, Australia. He has published numerous articles on contemporary European philosophy, and recently translated Gilles Deleuze's *Difference and Repetition* (1994). In addition, he has edited *Nietzsche, Feminism and Political Theory* (1993), and *Deleuze: A Critical Reader* (1996).

Jana Sawicki is Professor of Philosophy and Women's Studies at Williams College, USA. She is the author of *Disciplining Foucault: Feminism, Power and the Body* (1991), and 'Foucault, Feminism and Questions of Identity' in *The Cambridge Companion to Foucault* (ed. Gary Gutting, 1994).

Barry Smart is Professor of Sociology at the University of Portsmouth, UK. He has published two monographs on the work of Foucault – *Foucault, Marxism and Critique* (1983) and *Michel Foucault* (1985). He is also the author of *Modern Conditions: Postmodern Controversies* (1992) and *Postmodernity* (1993). He is the editor of *Michel Foucault: Critical Assessments:* I and II (3 volumes, 1994; 4 volumes, 1995) and *Facing Ambivalence: Modernity and Moral Responsibility* (1998).

Acknowledgements

This collection grew out of a conference I organized on the tenth anniversary of Foucault's death in 1994. The collection has since expanded to include a number of other contributors whose work I thought provided original insights into Foucault's often-overlooked later thought. Along the way many people have provided both intellectual and practical help with the task of turning the many good intentions into a book. Tony Coady, Marion Tapper and Len O'Neill were especially helpful both in their comments on my own work and with their worldly advice on the book itself. John Rundell of the Ashworth Centre for Social Theory was also an invaluable source of advice. I would also like to acknowledge the generous support of the Ashworth Centre for Social Theory, the Philosophy Department, the Centre for Philosophy and Public Issues at the University of Melbourne, for providing help with the original conference. The Buckland Foundation was also generous in its initial support for the book. At later stages Steven Tudor gave invaluable advice on a number of chapters. Also, to my editor Robert Rojek and production editor Pascale Carrington at Sage, I owe thanks for the patience and care with which they saw the project through.

Introduction: The Later Foucault

Jeremy Moss

For those interested in some of the political implications of Foucault's work, the controversies generated by his work of the 1970s posed serious problems. As the chapters in this collection testify, Foucault's claim that power is all pervasive in society led many to object to Foucault's work on two separate grounds. Perhaps the most common concern was that Foucault could produce no independently justified norms on which to base not only his own critiques, but any other critical enterprise.[1] In addition, Foucault was thought to have overstated the extent to which individuals could be 'subjected' to the influence of power, leaving them little room to resist. To some extent, Foucault's later works on government and ethics provides an opportunity to go beyond some of these questions, as they contain better accounts of concepts such as freedom, agency and domination. While I do not think Foucault's later works provide answers to all of the questions circulating around the issues of power and subjectivity, his thoughts were naturally better articulated than when he initially began to explore these topics consciously in *Discipline and Punish*. In the light of these new developments, the chapters in this collection attempt to respond to some of the problems standardly associated with Foucault's thought.

One of the reasons that Foucault's work has been so controversial is because it offers new insights into how we should understand some of the key issues in political thought. Much of value has been written about the new ways of looking at politics that Foucault's work opens up. The politicization of areas of everyday practices and the significance of subject formation are two of the most obvious. Yet I think the fruitful use of Foucault's work is not exhausted in these discussions. A great deal of what is discussed in political philosophy in the English-speaking world in the last 30 years has been left untouched by the sorts of insights that Foucault offers. I am thinking here of topics in political philosophy such as the law, liberalism or the question of justice as well as some of the more foundational ideas such as freedom, responsibility and the scope of the political. Power, for instance, has long been a subject that has interested political philosophers of both the left and the right, and yet, if there is one thing that Foucault might be said to have achieved, it is the redefinition of how we think about power in contemporary society. Foucault's elucidation of something so fundamental as the phenomenon of power has the potential to alter a multitude of other political ideas, ranging from how we think of citizens to the nature of the political itself. Far from being a domestication of Foucault into the traditional sphere of political philosophy, I see the chapters in this collection as sharing the theme of *using* Foucault's later work to contribute to a range of issues that present themselves in contemporary discussion of political thought. But before introducing the individual chapters collected here, it would be appropriate to say a few words about the scope and periodization of Foucault's later work, because, while I think there is a significant shift in his understanding of key terms such as 'power' and 'subjectivity' in the later work on government and ethics, some of the moves are prefigured in the earlier work on power and the subject. The interest in government, for instance, was certainly present in the work on sexuality, as the material on biopower attests.

Government

Foucault's work on government represents his 'mature' stance on power and, as with much of his later work, is a refinement of and response to his thinking about power in *Discipline and Punish* and, to a lesser extent, *The History of Sexuality Vol. 1*. The account of power which he gave in *Discipline and Punish*, while still in my view his most empirically impressive account of how power functions, glossed over the important role of the subject in power relations and the more general strategies of power. As Colin Gordon has pointed out,[2] some of Foucault's Marxist critics were quick to note that this emphasis on the micro-physics of power ignored its global operation. Foucault had already sought to address many of these problems by the time he wrote *The History of Sexuality*. Indeed, the phenomenon of biopower as discussed in Part V of *The History of Sexuality* was the name for a new form of power concerned with managing the processes of life itself on both an anatomical and a social level. The first of these levels resembles disciplinary power, as analysed in *Discipline and Punish*, in that it operates on the body and its forces in an attempt to mould individuals so that they fit into various institutional structures. The second pole around which this power developed, according to Foucault, was more general, with a focus on the population. Here Foucault had in mind the explosion in the seventeenth and eighteenth centuries of discourses concerned with demographics, in particular, 'economics' and 'health sciences'.

While biopower afforded Foucault a better view of the general or global character of power, his interest in governmentality allowed a clearer vision still. In his courses at the Collège de France in the late 1970s, Foucault pursued a research programme on what he called the 'arts of government'.[3] In these studies Foucault tried to outline the specific political rationality of the modern state. The arts of government were a new form of pastoral power, which in turn had its origins in the institution of the Catholic Church. Unlike ancient forms of power, pastoral power was concerned with the salvation of everyone in 'the flock' on an individual level, requiring, ideally, a thorough knowledge of the subject's 'soul' and officials who could monitor and account for each and every individual. It was an individualizing power in that it sought, through supervision, to structure the life of the individual, both through confessional technologies and techniques of self mastery. As the ecclesiastic institutions declined as the modern period began, Foucault argues, the function of pastoral power spread from the monastery to the state and its institutions.

Though the Christian pastorate never functioned effectively as a governor of subjects, Foucault argues, the modern state came to resemble a form of pastoral power through its use of various arts of government. Two of the arts of government which Foucault had in mind here were what he called the doctrines of *reasons of state* and the *theory of police*. The former doctrine marked a concern with the state not as a fief of its ruler but as a complex of 'things and men', to be administered for its own sake. The theory of police, or science of administration, on the other hand, held that the arms of government should intervene to ensure the flourishing of all aspects of the individual: body, soul, wealth, in short, their 'happiness'. What Foucault saw in the discourses on the state in the early modern period was the genesis of a political rationality gradually and imperfectly put into place in the form of the modern state and its regulatory institutions. The state resembled pastoral power in that it was an individualizing form of power which substituted the worldly happiness of its citizens for spiritual aims of the pastorate. This was carried out through an ever-increasing range of officials, institutions and, finally, through the development of knowledge and the application of techniques of power that were both total – involving the population – and individual, directed towards the body and its capacities. Foucault's observations about the individualizing nature of pastoral power also signalled a closer attention to individuals' own role in their constitution, which I will discuss below. As Barry Allen in his chapter in this collection points out, 'Governmentality' was the term Foucault coined to identify both the way in which power guides the conduct of individuals and the modern rationality which demands that everything and everyone be 'managed'.

Had he lived, Foucault would no doubt have had more to say about power and taken the study of government in different directions. However, while the later work on government constitutes an unfinished programme, it still furnishes us with a valuable account of power as Foucault understood it. What interested Foucault was the way in which the arts of government, as they were put into practice by the state, represented an attempt to guide individuals' conduct where this is, as he puts it, to 'structure the possible field of action of others'.[4] I will say more about the conceptual significance of this formulation below. For now it is enough to note that Foucault's interest in the conduct of individuals, as influenced by the state and its institutions, integrated Foucault's analysis of the micro-techniques of power with more general phenomena of the development of the modern state. As many of the chapters here argue, the later work on power also appreciated that government of conduct usually involved a degree of self-government, which brings us to Foucault's work on ethics.

Ethics

Foucault notes that the original plan for *The History of Sexuality* was to study sexuality as an experience understood as the correlation of fields of knowledge, types of normativity and forms of subjectivity as they are found in contemporary culture.[5] He found that a theme common to the study of sexuality was that of the desiring person. One could not study the experience of sexuality without looking at the idea of the desiring person. And so, 'the idea was to investigate how individuals were led to practise, on themselves and on others, a hermeneutics of desire, a hermeneutics of which their sexual behaviour was doubtless the occasion, but certainly not the exclusive domain'.[6] Thus Foucault sought to study how sexuality became a domain of moral experience for both Ancient Greek and Roman cultures through a particular 'problematization'. He was interested in how and why these cultures came to see sexuality as a moral problem that had quite a different framework from those cultures which succeeded them. Of particular interest to Foucault were the practices which helped shape the problematization of sexuality, the 'techniques of the self' or 'arts of existence' employed by individuals to transform themselves.

While sexuality was one of the domains in which individuals sought to constitute themselves, what Foucault was primarily interested in was the activity of self-constitution itself, which he called ethics. By defining techniques of the self and the moral problematization of sexuality as the object of his study and not the moral codes of the time, Foucault wanted to broaden how we understand morality and ethics. What he brings out in the ethical writings is the role individuals themselves play in implementing or refusing a particular type of subjectivity. To be ethical is thus not to be 'right' or 'moral', it is rather to engage in 'a process in which the individual delimits that part of himself that will form the object of his moral practice, defines his position relative to the precept he will follow, and decides on a certain mode of being that will serve as his moral goal'.[7] This process of care for the self, so central to Greek and Roman morality, involved ethical work in so far as there was an attempt to transform oneself into a particular type of subject, a process which involved decisions, goals and a certain amount of freedom to choose between different alternatives.

Foucault made it clear that Greco-Roman ethics, as a whole, could not simply be grafted on to modern moral problems. However, in the idea of work on the self Foucault thought he had found something that he could use in a modern version of ethics. This development of an ancient idea finds a parallel in Foucault's understanding of the ethos of the Enlightenment which he identifies in Kant.[8] Foucault finds in Kant's understanding of the 'maturity' humans need to show in their use of reason the basis for a modern question centred around a critical ontology of ourselves. What is common to ancient ethics and the Enlightenment ethos is the necessity of a critical attitude towards the self that both is aware of the contingency of the self's traits and displays a willingness to rework them. Interestingly, Foucault's version of this question combines both archaeological and genealogical critique to sift through the layers of a subject's identity. However, the most important feature of Foucault's understanding of Kant's question is that it recognizes the significant role played by human freedom, in this case the freedom to reflect on and potentially change aspects of the self. We should note, though, that the freedom that subjects have to shape their own identities is not the kind of human freedom that Sartre proposed in *Being and Nothingness*, but a freedom born out of interaction with relations of power.[9] Foucault saw the freedom that subjects have to work on themselves not as an abstract freedom, but as dependent on the resources they had at their disposal, both in terms of their own capacities and the structures of society. The ethical component of critical ontology also adds a crucial counterweight to the understanding of power and its impact on the subject by pointing out how subjects shape their own government through technologies of the self.

Conceptual Changes

As was invariably the case with Foucault, the motion back and forth between his empirical and theoretical positions produced new formulations of the domain in which he was interested. Thus Foucault's interest in government allowed him to better integrate more successfully how power functioned at both the local and the general level, providing him with a broader understanding of power in a way which the conceptions of discipline and biopower did not. While there is not the space here to discuss all of the changes to the conception of power wrought by the later work, it would be useful to mention two changes in particular as they relate to the standard objections raised against Foucault mentioned at the beginning.

The first of these changes concerns Foucault's ontology of freedom. A defining feature of power for the later Foucault is that subjects have the possibility of not just reacting to power, but of altering power relationships as well. Foucault moved away from the rhetoric of *Discipline and Punish* where power seemed to constitute individuals, without there being much opportunity to resist power, to a position where individuals have the scope to refuse the regulation of apparatuses of power. He describes how at the heart of the power relationship there lies what he calls the 'intransigence of freedom'.[10] By writing of freedom in this way, Foucault emphasized that power relationships always operate against a background of subjects whose capacities for resistance are ever a factor in determining the outcome of a clash of forces. Thus subjectivity in the later Foucault is a far more active constituent of power relations. Moreover, not only did Foucault conceptualize to a greater degree the possibility of resistance, his later work on ethics turned almost exclusively to documenting active intra-subjective relationships. We can see how the concern with ethics ties in with the work on government, in that it represents one form of the exercise of a subject's freedom – the freedom to work on the self. Ethics, in this sense, functions as an antidote to forms of power which seek to limit individuals in the choices they have for exercising their capacities and powers.

Secondly, this change in his ontology of power also enabled Foucault to give a clearer account of the scope for a normative evaluation of power. What we find with the essay on the Enlightenment and some of the later interviews is a concern with promoting 'practices of liberty'. Here Foucault seems to suggest that, as a bare minimum, subjects need to be able to reflect on and, ultimately, to 'work on' their own capacities so as to have the potential to reject unwanted forms of identity. While on the face of it, such an approach is fraught with problems surrounding how one should treat other subjects' autonomous desires to become different types of subject, it at least places the autonomous choices of a subject near the centre of political evaluation. Thus Foucault's studies of ethics allowed him to integrate normative notions such as autonomy and freedom. As Paul Patton suggests below, when these ethical concerns are added to the conceptualization of power as government, this provides a minimal standard against which to measure whether a form of power involves domination.

The Chapters

Genealogy and the Scope of the Political

One of the most disturbing things for many political philosophers interested in Foucault is the perceived 'Nietzscheanism' in his work. The problems concerning Foucault raised by Jürgen Habermas, Nancy Fraser and Charles Taylor are well known[11] and, interestingly enough, they all attribute some of the blame to the baneful influence of Nietzsche, whose genealogical and critical histories had an obvious impact on Foucault. A common response to Foucault's Nietzscheanism is that his genealogical method relies on the very assumptions that it seeks to criticize. On this score Habermas has argued that Foucault is involved in what he calls a 'performative contradiction'. A further response to Foucault's perceived Nietzscheanism made by Taylor has been to argue that, although Foucault's genealogies disrupt certain understandings of ourselves, they leave no room for an alternative set of normative assumptions. Foucault's confusion on this issue emanates from a lack of a vocabulary of liberation and freedom in his thought.[12]

While Foucault is indebted to Nietzsche, his Nietzscheanism is not a carbon copy of Nietzsche, nor are the Nietzschean elements simply pessimistic and without any positive normative application. It is a common mistake in understanding Foucault to treat his essay on Nietzsche, 'Nietzsche, Genealogy, History', as a straightforward statement of Foucault's own views. There are many points at which Foucault diverges from Nietzsche both politically and philosophically. Moreover, Foucault is not simply a Nietzschean. Indeed, one could just as well point to Foucault's interest in Kant as an influence on his work. It was, of course, Foucault's interest in Kant which led to the long project which culminated in *The Order of Things*. It is no surprise, therefore, that in his last writings there is a return to Kant in and around the study of the Enlightenment. However, it is not just that Foucault maintained an interest in Kant that we should find noteworthy, but also the Kantian-inspired themes that permeated the later work. For instance, Foucault's conception of critical philosophy owes much to Kant. Foucault credits Kant with founding the two critical traditions between which modern philosophy is divided: one stemming from the Kant of the three critiques, which he calls the 'analytics of truth', and the other from the Kant of the essay 'What is the Enlightenment?', called an 'ontology of the present'. For Foucault, providing an ontology of the present involves articulating the processes that have led to what we are now so as to allow space for the possibility of ethical transformation. Foucault sees the modern version of this Kantian question as involving not just a critique of the present, but a critique attached to specific programmes of transformation. What is more, these transformations take place with the political goal of *increasing* our freedom. As some of the chapters in this section demonstrate, the Kantian-inspired theme of an ontology of the present with its ethical values provides Foucault both with an antidote to some of the criticisms of the Nietzschean 'nihilism' that supposedly inhabited his work and a concrete contribution to political philosophy.

David Couzens Hoy's chapter discusses some of these major Kantian and Nietzschean themes in Foucault's work while providing a defence of Foucault's genealogical method. He begins by looking at the much discussed connection between Foucault and politics. As Hoy notes, Foucault has contradictory statements on the connection between philosophy and politics, asserting in different places both that there is a connection and that there is not. However, Hoy argues that Foucault's considered conception of the connection is a type of critical philosophy drawn from Kant, where the role of philosophy is to 'keep watch over the excessive powers of political rationality'. This is a return to a type of philosophy which is politically concrete and engaged.

Habermas has been very critical of Foucault's efforts to pursue his brand of critical philosophy through his genealogical studies. Interestingly, Hoy argues that although Habermas is the modern inheritor of the early critical theorists, Foucault is, in fact, a truer representative of that tradition. Hoy contends that Foucault's genealogical method shares some of the characteristics of other 'critical philosophies' that have questioned the value of the Enlightenment idea of rationality. Thus, unlike Habermas, both the critical theorists and Foucault refuse to succumb to the 'blackmail' of the Enlightenment by avoiding being either simply 'for' or 'against' reason. Instead, Foucault insists on the historical nature of reason and the contradictions and counter-traditions that are to be found within the history of reason. This brings out the central question of the debate between Habermas and Foucault, according to Hoy: whether there is a need for Foucault's genealogical studies to be backed by an abstract theory of reason.

Hoy is critical of Habermas's objection that the genealogist needs some sort of external standard to conduct criticism. For instance, Habermas claims that the preference for pluralism expressed by Foucault and others is just that – a *preference*, which itself cannot escape the idea that there is still a choice involved in the liking for pluralism. Thus, he argues, if this pluralism is not to involve a vicious relativism that allows all forms of social practices no matter how destructive, there will have to be some standards which transcend the plurality of different communities. What this approach to genealogy fails to appreciate is the sense of genealogy as a version of 'internal critique', not unlike modern forms of cultural anthropology. Hoy argues that on this interpretation, a genealogical analysis might serve to highlight the hidden assumptions operating in a social practice, thereby opening up a space to question that practice. For this reason the genealogist does not have to deny some sort of consensuality in the face of Habermasian objections (that would be blackmail). Quoting Foucault, Hoy argues that it is not a matter of being '. . . *for consensuality*, but one must be against nonconsensuality'. The genealogist is thus not committed to the values of consensuality and community on the basis of there being universal values which underlie the communicative competence of community members. The values of community and solidarity have a moral grip on us for contingent and not universal reasons.

Wendy Brown also takes up the issue of Foucault's relation to politics through an analysis of the way genealogy refigures political life. She argues that many of the negative responses to Foucault's politics come from a distinctly modernist political camp, whereas genealogy displaces some of the key modernist approaches to political life. Foucault's method performs this task for politics by being an historically conscious form of philosophy. Brown looks to Foucault's essay on Nietzsche to trace Foucault's reorientation of interpretation towards the contingent twists and turns of history, especially the history of the body. History, according to this description, becomes 'a field of openings – faults, fractures and fissures', which opens a space for political possibility by disrupting the patterns of the past. Reminding us of how cross-disciplinary Foucault's work is, Brown points out that the ontology of the present is something which crosses the roles of philosophy and history and reorients them both to the political task of understanding who we are and the processes that have formed us.

Although the disruption of the older conception of history is a negative process, Brown locates positive transformations of political life in the fall-out from the genealogical method as it is applied to history and political theory. The first of these, a fracture of history, is, for Brown, Foucault's single most distinctive contribution to politics. His historical/philosophical studies make the present less ossified than we are accustomed to assume. This in turn allows us to appreciate the contingency of the present and thus the possibilities of other ways of approaching our historical situation. The focus of critique for Foucault is 'political rationality'. Whether this is the norms and assumptions that govern a regime of power, or the particular form of government to be found in modern societies, political norms and tactics, argues Brown, will flow from the need to respond to the terms of a rationality. In addition, the politics appealed to on this interpretation stem less from transcendent values than from the opportunities and limits with which we are presented. Here Brown argues that, as the genealogical approach has shown, if there are no laws to history then there are, consequently, no transcendent values either and no essential link between a critique of power and a normative prescription. So, too, with strategies for resistance; they will be a matter of 'political taste and timing'.

The outcome of the genealogical contribution to politics is that there is no one set of values or practices which flow from the investigation of the history of the present. Brown puts it nicely when she says that the 'ontology of the present' is not the same thing as an 'ontologically grounded politics'. This, of course, raises the question of Foucault's own political positions, which are often taken as examples of how one might construct a politics from his own work. However, they, too, should be seen as personal preferences of Foucault and not as something which flows from the genealogical method itself. Overall, the value for us in Foucault's work, claims Brown, lies in what it opens up and not in what it proscribes.

Barry Hindess's discussion of the political takes a different route from Brown's. In a perceptive scrutiny of Foucault's statements on the political, he explores the different senses of the political that Foucault adopts and relates them to the more traditional uses of the term derived, ultimately, from the metaphor of the *polis*. Hindess notes that it should come as no surprise that Foucault both resembles and diverges from past ideas of the political, as all political discourse is fundamentally mimetic. While there is no one basic meaning of politics to which all definitions refer, there are several common elements that Foucault drew upon in developing his own account, an account which reflects its varied inheritance.

Hindess locates two quite different uses of the concept of the political in Foucault's work. The first is the well-known identification of the political with the governmental. For Hindess, this understanding of government, centred on the state and its institutions, is to be criticized because it is too narrow a conception of the political. He argues that while it might be true that this is a legitimate account of a new idea of the political that arose in the early part of the sixteenth century, it does not take into account the sense of the political introduced by Weber which covers sectional interests and action. What Weber's notion of the political introduces to Foucault's account is action that is not government (seen as the state), but action that is conducted to some extent outside government control. The importance of this broader view of politics is that it contests the idea that politics is tied to the operation of governments and opens up a field in which interests other than those of the government are deemed to be important. It is this process of the emergence of the political, argues Hindess, which Foucault neglects.

Foucault's other use of the term 'political' located by Hindess is a 'politically' more radical one. Here the emphasis is anti-governmental. Hindess argues that this conception of government can be understood in two contexts: Foucault's comments on emancipation, and his discussion of technologies of the self. Foucault's own version of emancipation is one which rejects any sort of universalism and replaces it with 'specific transformations' that minimize domination. Along with Hoy, Hindess notes the similarity of some of

Foucault's concerns with challenging domination to those of the critical theorists. Part of this more radical idea of the political is finding new techniques of the self which do not repeat a Christian hermeneutics or Enlightenment idea of the self but which allow us to increase our own liberty. Hindess concludes that Foucault's politics holds out an ideal of self-government shorn of the normalizing practices of power as domination, but which nonetheless has its utopian leanings.

Ethics and the Subject of Politics

The chapters in this section of the book tackle the two long-standing concerns about Foucault's work that I mentioned at the beginning. The first of these objections centres around the claim that Foucault owes us an account of how subjects are able to operate as agents in the face of disciplinary mechanisms which normalize their behaviour. No doubt this objection has much to do with the account of agency and power to be found in *Discipline and Punish*, which, at least rhetorically, gave the impression that agency virtually ceased to exist in the face of the onslaught of power. The second major concern about Foucault's work dealt with here stretches across almost the entire range of Foucault's output from the 1970s onwards. It concerns the contrast between the obvious normative engagement of Foucault's texts and the lack of any clearly articulated normative framework in which to place and justify that engagement. Nancy Fraser is perhaps the clearest exponent of this line of attack. She argues that while Foucault is a staunch enemy of humanism and its values, he nonetheless appears to appeal to traditional humanist values to give his work normative force.[13]

Paul Patton's contribution takes up both of these criticisms of Foucault's work. Patton's answer to Foucault's critics is that Foucault does, in fact, provide us with an account of the subject and power which allows for a means of distinguishing between different forms of power. Patton argues that Foucault's subject must be understood primarily in terms of power, in the sense of the capacity to be or do various things. On the basis of this account of power as capacity, Patton uses Foucault's later work to make some distinctions concerning power and domination. He argues that if power is seen as the ability to perform a range of actions, then, power is exercised over B when A has succeeded in modifying the range of actions open to B. Described in such a way, the exercise of power is neither good nor bad. However, when there is an asymmetrical relationship between subjects, such that B has limited capacity to act, we can say that there is a state of domination. While Foucault's works have been geared towards exposing such asymmetrical power relations, relations that define and limit subjects' capacities, Patton points out that domination always supervenes on a primary field of power in the above sense.

In answering the charge of finding a criterion of judgement sufficient to distinguish between power and domination in Foucault, Patton finds an initially unlikely ally in C.B. Macpherson. He discusses Macpherson's appeal to the ideal of the conscious use and development of human capacities as a measure of whether a society is democratic. This opportunity to develop one's capacities (and invent new ones) is what Macpherson calls 'developmental' power, and is to be contrasted with a notion of 'extractive' power, which refers to the ability one group has to employ the capacities of others. According to Patton, the conscious control of the development of human capacities is exactly what Foucault appeals to in some of the later work on the Enlightenment. Indeed, it is an appeal to autonomy which allows Foucault to provide an answer to his critics' scepticism concerning his normative assumptions. In so far as a system of power prevents the autonomous use of a subject's capacities, argues Patton, there will be grounds for condemnation. Patton's interpretation of Foucault here functions both as an account of how resistance is possible and as an answer to how we might condemn some forms of power as domination. Unlike Kant, however, the Foucaultian appeal to autonomy is neither universal nor metaphysical. Instead, Patton argues that it is based on an 'historical' rather than 'transcendental' understanding of autonomy as that which is the precondition of politics and ethics. Autonomy, in this sense, is something that is present or not present by virtue of a subject's place in a grid of power.

If Patton's chapter helps us to understand the way domination can be determined using Foucault's conception of the subject, Barry Smart turns his attention to a different question regarding Foucault's subject: in what sense is responsibility towards others possible within Foucault's late concern with the subject? Smart argues that while Foucault is able to clarify the possibility of resistance in the later work, as well as in his earlier thoughts on power, this still sheds little light on the way in which subjects might be said to be responsible for their actions. The technologies of the self which Foucault looked at in Ancient Greek society opened up new ways for him to understand the subject as an active subject. Yet, while Foucault admits that these practices are transmitted through social interaction, he does not, according to Smart, address the issue of the responsibility the subject has for this creation of itself and the necessity of the relationship with others that accompanies self-formation. Moreover, Smart argues that Foucault's analyses of the practices of the self ignore the context in which these practices occur.

One sense of ethical responsibility that has been attributed to Foucault is an ethic of responsibility which applies to the intellectual. While Smart acknowledges that this is a sense of responsibility present throughout Foucault's work, he claims it is still too narrow. A wider sense of responsibility was present in Ancient Greek ethics, where care for the self was linked to essential exchanges with others, though Foucault goes some way towards acknowledging the links between care for the self and care for others in his remarks on Hebrew notions of duty, ultimately these themes are left undeveloped. Where Foucault's work leaves us with a underdeveloped sense of our relation to others, the work of Levinas places responsibility to others at the heart of ethics. Ultimately, Smart concludes, Levinas is a better place to look for an ethics of responsibility specific to late modernity.

One of the most productive encounters between Foucault and political theory has occurred in the uses of his work in feminist theory. Foucault, of course, has been roundly criticized by feminists on the grounds that he is both unable to provide an adequate epistemology and because he has a politically inadequate account of resistance. However, as Jana Sawicki suggests of Sandra Lee Bartky's work, which traces the effects of the practices of the fashion and beauty industry on creating women's subjectivities, there is room within an account of disciplinary power for an account of agency and resistance too. Indeed, this is also one of the interesting features of Judith Butler's work on Foucault. For Sawicki, the strength of Butler's account of the subject is that it attacks the idea of a foundational subject while at the same time acknowledging the possibility of adopting subject positions in a consciously political way. There are clear affinities with Foucault here, in particular, his preference for a type of politics which focuses on the partial transformation of subjectivities. Sawicki also notes how Donna Haraway's work provides an appropriation of Foucault's ideas, through the central figure of the 'cyborg', which enables Haraway to construe resistance in a non-utopian way.

As Sawicki points out, many of the faults that feminists find with Foucault are mirrored across the spectrum of political responses to Foucault's work. So while feminists such as Nancy Fraser lament the lack of normative foundations in Foucault's work, critics like Habermas and Charles Taylor also worry that much of Foucault's normative commitment is without warrant. In response to this line of thinking, Sawicki notes that much of Foucault's later work can be seen as a tacit answer to these sorts of criticisms, particularly the work on the Enlightenment. In common with David Hoy's contribution, Sawicki observes that Foucault refuses the blackmail of the Enlightenment, whereby one is either 'for' or 'against' reason, and instead positions himself in part of the Enlightenment tradition by identifying with aspects of Kant's work. Another of the useful elements of Foucault's thought for feminists that Sawicki identifies is the vision of work on the self, as it is presented in *The Use of Pleasure* and the work on the Enlightenment. Sawicki connects this emphasis on self-constitution with Haraway's desire for a politics which consciously creates marginal subjects which can resist oppression. This modern version of ethics recognizes that the subject relies on the cultural patterns for the material of self constitution. While Sawicki shows that there is much that deserves criticism in Foucault by feminists and others, she nonetheless provides a forceful account of how elements of Foucault's insights and method, especially in the later work, can be usefully employed to broaden our understanding of what it is to engage in emancipatory politics.

William Connolly's chapter also tackles the link between ethics and politics in the course of his exploration of Foucault's ethical sensibility. He argues that, while Foucault's ethics attempts to move beyond the morality of good and evil, it does not remove the need for an ethics. Though Foucault's genealogical attacks on modern political rationalities threaten received patterns of identity and morality, Connolly points out that Foucault's work also enjoins us to engage in a 'generous sensibility'. Indeed, these two seemingly paradoxical features of Foucault's work are closely linked. Foucault's attempt to uncover the contingent origin of modern identities and the moral assumptions that surround them, also directs us to the inevitable plurality of identities and moral standpoints. In recognition of this state of affairs, Connolly argues that the ethical sensibility which emerges from Foucault's work is one where individuals should both cultivate a generous approach to alternative identities, and contest accounts of morality which fail to appreciate the contingent nature of identities. As Connolly conceives it, this approach involves a certain sort of universalism, in that it recognizes a need to affirm permanently the contingent character of being, what he labels an 'on*ta*logical' universalism, in recognition of the alogical character of history.

Connolly's understanding of Foucault's ethical sensibility merges the critical side of Foucault's work with the ethical. His approach also draws attention to the political implications of Foucault's ethical sensibility when he suggests that there are correspondences between Foucault's ethical work and political involvement, and an account of democracy. He argues that a democratic ethos should not neglect the contingency of identities – and the uncertainties this may entail – for the role of efficient government or state security. Instead, the territorial state must strike a balance between these two competing demands. The nature of the identities and affiliations which emerge in the late modern era may well cross territorial boundaries. Thus, Connolly argues that the democratic ethos needed to respond to this phenomenon will not necessarily limit itself to the boundaries of the modern nation state, but respond instead to the global pressures which shape identity. While these observations of Connolly's show some of the possible implications of Foucault's work for politics, he also notes that the attempt to transport an ethical sensibility into the political sphere, where general policies are required, risks reducing the complexity of the situation. Connolly's sensitivity to the limits of ethics constitutes a timely reminder of the problems associated with using Foucault's work in a political way.

Political Traditions

Foucault's involvement with political issues is well known. Throughout the 1970s he was active in a number of high-profile campaigns ranging from prison reform to support of Cambodian boat people. His support for groups engaged in particular issues mirrored his commitment to piecemeal transformation in the political sphere, which in turn flowed from his understanding of the nature of modern power. To some extent, Foucault's understanding of not only power but also the evolution of thinking about power was shaped by his engagement with key figures of the Western political tradition, such as Hobbes and Machiavelli. The interest in Machiavelli, for instance, stemmed from his place as a key figure against whom the 'reasons of state' theorists reacted. Foucault's engagement with political thought also extended to topics such as the traditions of nineteenth-century liberalism, the law and, as we have seen, the theory of government. Yet, as I mentioned above, much of the work that has been done on Foucault and political philosophy and theory has been dismissive of terms such as 'rights' or 'justice'. No doubt Foucault's own attitude serves as an explanation here. Foucault was loath to be put in a political tradition or camp and was especially hostile to some of the French organized left.[14] Yet when we ask what difference Foucault's work makes to key concepts in political theory we can see that much of his work, whether it is on power or the subject, is relevant to understanding many of the important elements in contemporary political philosophy. The chapters in this section undertake to relate Foucault to some of the traditions of political thought and its contemporary variants.

Duncan Ivison's chapter on Foucault and rights takes up the complicated issue of the relationship between Foucault's work and the rule of law. Ivison points out that Foucault's remarks on law, especially those concerning the juridical conception of law as a model of power, usually serve to emphasize the obsolete character of this model. Not only does it fail to capture the nature of power, but it is in fact a mask for the disciplinary techniques which regulate individuals. However, Ivison's chapter seeks to show that Foucault does have a conception of law cashed out in terms of a theory of rights, despite his apparent hostility to liberal humanism. One influential position in the liberal tradition is that of H.L.A. Hart, who claims that rights ('natural' or 'human') are something that we have *qua* being human, and which are logically independent of the particular forms of social arrangements in which we find ourselves. Ivison argues that, fundamentally, the types of rights postulated in liberal political theory are connected to respect for persons as potential makers of claims. These rights are, of course, ideal and not actual. While Foucault's discussion of rights is quite different from Hart's, Ivison cites instances in Foucault's later work where Foucault engages in 'rights talk' which, for all intents and purposes, is an appeal to a new theory of right.

The key to understanding the place of rights is to see that the subject of rights is not a juridical subject but a subject formed in 'battle'. As such, any appeal to rights will not base itself on a juridically conceived subject, but on one that is a product of particular struggles. Unlike the conception of the subject handed down to us from traditional political theory, Foucault's version is one where particular traits are gained through an 'agonistic' relation to power. Ivison points out that Foucault's attitude towards the political goals of subjects formed in this type of power can be seen as rejecting forms of individuality imposed on us and creating new forms through new practices of liberty. Thus a particular right might be supported in so far as it fosters a practice of liberty. This would be a tactical and not universal support for rights, based on its usefulness for the fostering of freedom in Foucault's sense. As Ivison puts it, this is to invoke a juridical concept in a unjuridical way.

My own chapter tackles Foucault's contribution to political philosophy from another angle. Despite the obvious differences between the two thinkers, Foucault and Rawls seem to share a similar idea of freedom and autonomy, which are constitutive values of both their positions. In his later work, Rawls is careful to place these values at the centre of his system. Likewise, Foucault's later work also places great emphasis on autonomy and freedom. However, Foucault's use of autonomy is connected to power in ways that Rawls fails to recognize. Rawls argues in his recent work, *Political Liberalism*, that principles of justice should be worked out in terms of the basic structure of society and include, so far as possible, no reference to any particular moral doctrine. He also argues that there ought to be a specifically 'political' approach to questions of justice. However, Foucault's conception of governmental power and his later idea of the subject, dramatically alter the political landscape by forcing new elements into the view of the 'public reason'. Specifically, the threats that are placed in the path of autonomy and freedom in Foucault's sense come not just from lack of access to political institutions, but from normalizing practices throughout the fabric of society. If an account of justice is to model the values of autonomy and freedom as Foucault conceives them, then it will have to take these threats into account. Hence one of the consequences of Foucault's work on government is a redefinition of the scope of the 'political'.

Barry Allen's chapter provides a fitting conclusion to the volume as it maps Foucault's contribution to political philosophy through outlining his position in relation to some of the main tendencies of modern political thought. He argues that while Foucault's own summaries of the traditions of political philosophy are often too broad and sweeping, Foucault himself is best seen as a representative of what Allen calls the modern 'ethos of individuality'. The ethos of individuality can be characterized by a concern to guarantee the liberty of individual conduct, while the ethos of authority, the second of the two reactions to what it is to govern that have emerged in the modern era, is characterized by an additional concern with the collective good. Allen locates the development of modern political thought in conjunction with major changes in the social, economic and political nature of modern societies, such as the globalization of the economy and the weakening of the nation-state. Foucault's thought was in part an attempt to respond to the changed conditions that modern society brought about and it is in his analytics of modern power that Allen takes Foucault's greatest contribution to political philosophy to lie.

Allen dwells on the historical context of the key elements that shape Foucault's idea of governmental power: pastoral power, the *theory of police* and *reasons of state*. Each of these elements serves to shape Foucault's 'mature' concept of power, the idea of power as government. Of course, Foucault's investigation of government, suggestive as it is, stops short of articulating the function of government in the latter half of the twentieth century. Here Allen provides a number of useful links between Foucault's work and the analysis of contemporary power. In an interesting final section, Allen gives some form to what Foucault's contributions to modern political philosophy might amount to. One thing Allen rules out is the interpretation of Foucault as positing an ethics of self-creation. He thinks that the work on ethics is better cast as a reminder that a political rationality that puts politics above all else is a danger precisely because it leads us to forget that politics might be better seen as opening up a space for new subjectivities. Yet, while politics needs ethics, ethics also needs political government and self-restraint, and it is one of Foucault's achievements, Allen tells us, to have given us the tools to elucidate the nature of the present in which this is the case.

Conclusion

In general, then, what are we to make of the contribution of Foucault's later work to our understanding both of his own work and to some of the key ideas in political thought? First, one of the most refreshing things about the later work is the way it builds on and clarifies some of the central ideas of Foucault's research. Not only does the later work entail a new understanding of these ideas, they also find expression in new fields of inquiry whose legacy is only just beginning to be explored. Moreover, whatever remaining problems and gaps there are in Foucault's thought, in his later work there is at least a productive answer to some of the more pressing challenges of earlier approaches to his work. The clarification of power and subjectivity that Foucault achieves through his research into ethics and government provides a clear response to his earlier efforts to analyse the relation of the subject and power through his understanding of disciplinary power. What many of the chapters collected here underscore are the varieties of productive ways of answering some of the standard concerns with Foucault's work: problems surrounding his philosophical method, his lack of normative justification, and the active role of the subject.

When we ask about Foucault's contribution to political thought, it is interesting to note that part of Foucault's contribution comes through his unique way of answering a very old question. Foucault's critical ontology poses the question of who we are in the present and how we have become who we are, in order to provoke new ways of thinking about ourselves. In thinking of the task of philosophy in this way, Foucault identifies himself not just with Kant, but also with the philosophers of antiquity who sought to understand who they were through their ethical and social relations. Through his critical ontology of the present, Foucault furthers our understanding of one of the most important questions in political philosophy: the relation of the self to those broader structures of power which surround us. In doing so, Foucault perhaps shares a common concern with much of what is interesting in philosophy in the English-speaking world in recent years. I am thinking here of the renewed attention in political philosophy to the significance of the relationship of the individual to the community and to the broader power structures of which they are a part. Witness both the communitarian and feminist attacks on liberalism, which centre on liberalism's lack of concern for the processes whereby individuals are shaped by their embeddedness in power relations. Whatever the merits of these approaches, they are part of a modern concern with understanding who we are. What the chapters in this collection tell us is that Foucault's unique approach to this question is full of possibilities, both for understanding contemporary society and for providing new approaches to how to free ourselves from some of its constraints. As a modern version of the question about who we are, Foucault's work deserves our careful attention.

Notes

1 N. Fraser, 'Foucault on modern power: empirical insights and normative confusions', in *Unruly Practices* (University of Minnesota Press, Minneapolis, 1989).

2 G. Burchell, C. Gordon and P. Miller (eds), *The Foucault Effect: Studies in Governmentality* (Harvester Wheatsheaf, Brighton, 1991), p. 4.

3 Michel Foucault, 'Governmentality', in Burchell et al. (eds), *Foucault Effect*.

4 Michel Foucault, 'The subject and power', in H.L. Dreyfus and P. Rabinow (eds), *Michel Foucault: Beyond Structuralism and Hermeneutics* (Harvester Wheatsheaf, Brighton, 1982), p. 221.

5 Michel Foucault, *The Use of Pleasure*, trans. R. Hurley (Penguin, Harmondsworth, 1991), p. 4.

6 Ibid., p. 5.

7 Ibid., p. 28.

8 Michel Foucault, 'What is Enlightenment?', in P. Rabinow (ed.), *The Foucault Reader* (Penguin, Harmondsworth, 1986).

9 Michel Foucault, 'On the genealogy of ethics: an overview of work in progress', in Rabinow (ed.), *Foucault Reader*, p. 3.

10 Foucault, 'Subject and power', p. 222.

11 See, for instance, C. Taylor, 'Foucault on freedom and truth', in *Philosophy and the Human Sciences* (Cambridge University Press, Cambridge, 1992).

12 Ibid.

13 Fraser, 'Foucault on modern power', pp. 17–35.

14 Michel Foucault, 'Politics and reason', in L. Kritzman (ed.), *Michel Foucault: Politics, Philosophy, Culture* (Routledge, London, 1988), p. 46.

Part I

GENEALOGY AND THE SCOPE OF THE POLITICAL

1

Foucault and Critical Theory

David Couzens Hoy

Although Foucault died over a decade ago, he still continues to influence our ongoing theoretical debates. His texts continue to intrigue us, and they remain difficult for us to interpret, to digest, or to accept. My goal here is to raise some of the more pressing critical objections to Foucault's genealogical method. I should stress that I will be focusing on his method, and not on the details of his analyses. Undoubtedly there are many historical details about which he was not correct. But the genealogical method itself still stands as a distinctive approach to social theory and historical analysis. My specific interest here is in trying to see whether genealogy can be defended philosophically.

A crucial philosophical issue generating heated debate today is one that plagues our readings not only of Foucault but of other thinkers as well. That is the issue of the relation of philosophy and politics. This issue is focused most poignantly when theorists like Martin Heidegger and Paul de Man appear to have made some degree of concrete political commitment to fascistic movements. The case of Foucault strikes me as being different from that of Heidegger, however. It is at once more promising and more difficult. More promising because Foucault was personally active in some political causes that were not as obviously reprehensible as fascism, however controversial they may have been. More difficult because although his writings seem to be politically engaged, exactly how they generate this effect is not clear. The ethical and political principles that motivate his social critique are hard to discern.

The line of criticism against Foucault that I will be discussing is often labelled his *Nietzscheanism*. That is, Foucault's theoretical descriptions (for instance, of power) do not suggest definite directions for resistance or change. To liberal pragmatists and leftist activists alike, Foucault's strategy of saying 'everything is dangerous', and therefore never identifying anything as unequivocally *good* or *evil*, seems too indirect, too 'Nietzschean'. In what follows I will explain some respects in which Foucault is indeed a Nietzschean, but I will show how his strategy of genealogy can respond to such criticism. First, however, I turn to how this strategy forces us to confront the general question of the relation of philosophy and politics, of ontology and ethics.

Philosophy and Politics

My initial suggestion for approaching this question is the simple but often unappreciated point that the connection between philosophy and politics depends on the conception of philosophy that is at issue. For instance, Bertrand Russell argued that there was absolutely no connection between epistemology and politics. I believe that he was right about philosophy as he conceived it, but not about all conceptions of philosophy. Foucault, for instance, is not doing epistemology as Russell was. In Foucault's hands genealogy is a more concrete and empirical conception of philosophy, one that is less obviously disconnected from concrete social, political and ethical norms. To begin my investigation of this problem, however, I would first like to ask what the later Foucault's own philosophical view about politics is. Does he believe that philosophy and politics are separate from each other? Or does he believe that they are not separable?

Looking for evidence of his attitude in interviews that he gave during the last year or so of his life, I find evidence that he asserted *both* of these things, that is, *both* that philosophy and politics are profoundly linked, and that they are not linked. So is he being inconsistent, or is there a complex but coherent position he could be holding?

Let's look at the statements in the interviews. In the 'Politics and Ethics' interview from April 1983, Foucault seems to be agreeing with Bertrand Russell that there is really no logical entailment between philosophy and politics. At best, Foucault says,

> there is [only] a very tenuous 'analytic' link between a philosophical conception and the concrete political attitude of someone who is appealing to it; the 'best' theories do not constitute a very effective protection against disastrous political choices; certain great themes such as 'humanism' can be used to any end whatever.[1]

Foucault then points out that in the French Resistance one philosopher who was active, and indeed was killed, was Cavaillès, a historian of mathematics who would not have been expected to be politically active. In contrast, 'None of the philosophers of *engagement* – Sartre, Simone de Beauvoir, Merleau-Ponty – none of them did a thing'.[2]

Similar statements can be found a year later in the May 1984 interview, 'Polemics, Politics and Problemizations'. Here again Foucault repeats a point that he had made a year earlier, namely, that he has been criticized from every conceivable position on the political checkerboard. He delights in this and admits, 'It's true that I prefer not to identify myself and that I'm amused by the diversity of the ways I've been judged and classified'.[3] He adds statements like,

'I don't think that in regard to madness and mental illness there is any "politics" that can contain the just and definitive solution'.[4] Or: 'I have never tried to analyze anything whatsoever from the point of view of politics. . . . [For example,] I am neither an adversary nor a partisan of Marxism.'[5]

In contrast, however, in different interviews around the same time one can find statements like the following (in an interview from 20 January, 1984): 'I think that the relationships between philosophy and politics are permanent and fundamental.'[6] To go back to the April 1983 interview, we see this contrasting attitude at the very same moment that he distanced philosophy from politics:

> I do not conclude from this [very tenuous link between philosophy and politics] that one may say just anything within the order of theory, but, on the contrary, that a demanding, prudent, 'experimental' attitude is necessary; at every moment, step by step, one must confront what one is thinking and saying with what one is doing, with what one is. I have never been too concerned about people who say: 'You are borrowing ideas from Nietzsche; well, Nietzsche was used by the Nazis, therefore . . .'; but, on the other hand, I have always been concerned with linking together as tightly as possible the historical and theoretical analysis of power relations, institutions, and knowledge, to the movements, critiques, and experiences that call them into question in reality. . . . The key to the personal poetic attitude of a philosopher is not to be sought in his ideas, as if it could be deduced from them, but rather in his philosophy-as-life, in his philosophical life, his ethos.[7]

While this quotation still seems to disconnect the *private* life of the philosopher from philosophy itself, the last word, 'ethos', provides an important clue to Foucault's stance on the political. In the interview from 20 January, 1984 Foucault says of the Greek meaning of *ethos*:

> *Ethos* was the deportment and the way to behave. It was the subject's mode of being and a certain manner of acting visible to others. One's *ethos* was seen by his dress, by his bearing, by his gait, by the poise with which he reacts to events, etc. For them [the Greeks], that is the concrete expression of liberty. That is the way they 'problematized' their freedom.[8]

Foucault thus thinks of the *ethos* as personal, but not as private. The *ethos* is publicly observable, and it is visibly permeated by social norms and political codes. So Foucault has no intention of using a distinction between the public and the private to distinguish the philosophy from the politics of an intellectual. In the *ethos* the political is personal and the personal is political.

Foucault can be read as applying this sense of *ethos* to present debates, for instance, as a response to Habermas's theory of the 'ideal speech situation' presupposed by any rational attempt to transcend power arrangements and arrive at uncoerced agreement. Foucault finds this theory too utopian:

> The thought that there could be a state of communication which would be such that the games of truth could circulate freely, without obstacles, without constraint and without coercive effects, seems to me to be Utopia. It is being blind to the fact that relations of power are not something bad in themselves, from which one must free one's self. I don't believe there can be a society without relations of power, if you understand them as means by which individuals try to conduct, to determine the behaviour of others. The problem is not of trying to dissolve them in the utopia of a perfectly transparent communication, but to give one's self the rules of law, the

techniques of management, and also the ethics, the *ethos*, the practice of self, which would allow these games of power to be played with a minimum of domination.[9]

Foucault is thus interested in returning to a form of philosophy where theory and *ethos* are not disjoined or differentiated. He sees philosophy itself as embedded in an *ethos*, and thus as always critically involved in minimizing domination.

Being interested in ethics does not get Foucault off the hook entirely, however, since one can be a specialist in moral philosophy and still be apolitical. Foucault, however, gives 'ethics' a special meaning, one that is not equivalent to 'moral philosophy'. Being interested in the *ethos* will help meet the charge that he is a nihilist (in the sense alleged by those who brand him with 'Nietzscheanism'), since he recognizes the necessity of values. The general method for investigating the *ethos* is genealogy. Foucault is not doing a genealogy of *morals*, since Foucault believes that the moral principles that people espouse are fairly constant throughout history. He is doing a genealogy of *ethics*, which involves describing what people *do* more than what they *say*, with *patterns of action* more than with *ostensible, conscious principles*.

What is the later Foucault's answer, then, or at least, what *should* his answer be, to the question of the relation of philosophy and politics? The idea of doing genealogy, and especially a genealogy of ethics, is developed as a method precisely to compensate for his earlier detached, disengaged, neutral method of archaeology. Genealogy is an emancipatory 'anti-science' or counterscience.[10] By this Foucault does not mean that genealogy is opposed to science and reason, but rather that genealogy undermines the blindness of mainstream social science to social asymmetries in the supposedly scientific acquisition and application of knowledge (for example, the doctor–patient asymmetry in psychiatry, and the Western–non-western asymmetry in ethnography). Genealogy intends to diagnose such asymmetries (or anomalies), even if it cannot offer a favourable prognosis. Genealogy recognizes its own involvement in this asymmetry, and its own contingency and temporariness: if the asymmetry is removed, if the anomaly is resolved, the genealogical analysis itself will no longer be applicable.

So genealogical knowledge claims to be only contingently true, not necessarily true. Also, genealogy is a form of philosophy that is intended to be ethically and politically concrete. Thus, it would not want to be defended by Russell's sharp separation of politics and epistemology. Instead, Foucault thinks of genealogy as a form of 'critical philosophy'. This phrase echoes a sense of philosophy that goes back to Kant, but not to the main works of Kant – not to the three *Critiques*, but instead to a little essay called 'What is Enlightenment?'. By critical philosophy Foucault means not so much the Kantian understanding of the role of philosophy as preventing reason from going beyond the limits of experience. Instead, Foucault draws our attention to the less well-known Kantian view that the role of philosophy is also 'to keep watch over the excessive powers of political rationality'.[11] Philosophy is critical in this other sense in that it diagnoses the present by raising 'the problem of the present time, and of what we are, in this very moment'.[12] The

Foucaultian twist that distinguishes him from Kant, however, comes when he adds immediately that '[m]aybe the target nowadays is not to discover what we are, but to refuse what we are'. But whether we are to discover or refuse ourselves, philosophy has the duty of sounding a warning about the danger of power. Foucault affirms that 'On the critical side . . . philosophy is precisely the challenging of all phenomena of domination at whatever level or under whatever form they present themselves – political, economic, sexual, institutional, and so on'.[13] I note that he does not hesitate to include the political among these forms of domination that are to be revealed and resisted. Of the later Foucault's two answers on the connection of philosophy and politics, then, this second one that sees them as intertwined appears to be his more considered view. I shall now go on to defend Foucault's efforts to capture this connection between philosophy and politics, between ontology and *ethos*, in the method that he calls genealogy.

Critical Theory

Foucault's description of philosophy as the critical challenge of domination might make us wonder whether genealogy is not directly reminiscent of a more recent development than Kant, namely, the 'critical theory' of the Frankfurt School.[14] The direct inheritor of the early critical theorists Horkheimer and Adorno is, of course, Jürgen Habermas. But what I wish to argue is that French poststructuralism is an alternative way of continuing the tradition of critical theory.

To make a case for the continuation of critical theory in poststructuralism is difficult since the connections are not obvious. From the perspective of history there is no direct tutelage between the founders of the Frankfurt School and the French, as there is between Adorno and Habermas. In an interview with Gérard Raulet, published in 1983 in *Telos*, Foucault comments on his own intellectual path and wishes that there had been direct historical connections. 'Now obviously', he says, 'if I had been familiar with the Frankfurt School, if I had been aware of it at the time, I would not have said a number of stupid things that I did say and I would have avoided many of the detours which I made'. But he is certain that the Frankfurt School did not have an influence on French thought, although he is puzzled as to why it did not:

> Now, the striking thing is that France knew absolutely nothing – or only vaguely, only very indirectly – about the current of Weberian thought. Critical Theory was hardly known in France and the Frankfurt School was practically unheard of. This, by the way, raises a minor historical problem which fascinates me and which I have not been able to resolve at all. It is common knowledge that many representatives of the Frankfurt School came to Paris in 1935, seeking refuge, and left very hastily, sickened presumably – some even said as much – but saddened anyhow not to have found more of an echo. Then came 1940, but they had already left for England and the US, where they were actually much better received. The understanding that might have been established between the Frankfurt School and French philosophical thought – by way of the history of science and therefore the question of the history of rationality – never occurred. And when I was a student,

I can assure you that I never once heard the name of the Frankfurt School mentioned by any of my professors.[15]

What Foucault sees in 1983 as the virtue and promise of the Frankfurt School stands in direct contrast to what Habermas sees there. What Foucault values in the earlier critical theorists is that they avoided the 'blackmail' involved in traditional theory's conception of reason. According to the traditional conception of theory, one must be either for reason or else be irrational. Foucault calls this 'blackmail' since it seems to make a 'rational critique of rationality' impossible. The Frankfurt School projected, and Foucault has tried to work out in historical detail, a similar endeavour. The shared task is to show that the Enlightenment conception of rationality, which appeared to be the only possible form of reason, has a history. Showing that this history of Reason has a beginning can lead to the thought that it might have an end, with the effect that it becomes 'only *one* possible form' of reason among others.[16] In contrast to Habermas, then, Foucault does not think that to undertake a rational critique of rationality one must either construct a theory of what rationality really is or fall into deep irrationality. For Foucault, 'reason is self-created', which means that humans develop forms or conceptions of rationality as part of their larger project of evolving an understanding of themselves given specific historical conditions.

Whereas Foucault is thus interested in the *historicity* of reason, Habermas is interested in the *theory* of reason. Each sees his question as the only possible way out of what Horkheimer and Adorno called the dialectic of enlightenment. That is, the modern search for knowledge promised enlightenment and freedom but has produced domination and barbarism as well. Habermas sees Foucault then as a postmodern, as a defender of irrationality, and Habermas himself wishes to defend reason and modernity.

The question is, however, whether this 'casting' is correct, both in respect to Foucault's own philosophical *ethos* and to the genealogical method as well. The interview with Raulet shows that even as late as a year or two before his death Foucault does not really understand the talk about a conflict between moderns and postmoderns. Foucault seems not even to have heard of postmodernism and he admits that he does not understand what the Germans like Habermas mean by the problem of modernity. The interview suggests that the strategy of contrasting modernism and postmodernism is a mistake. Foucault can make no sense of the thought of a 'collapse of reason': he maintains that 'there is no sense at all to the proposition that reason is a long narrative which is now finished, and that another narrative is under way'.[17] Foucault's initial reaction to the confrontation between a modern like Habermas and a self-avowed postmodern like Lyotard, before Foucault really knows much about the details of the controversy, is thus to say that both are guilty of 'one of the most harmful habits in contemporary thought: . . . the analysis of the present as being precisely, in history, a present of rupture, or of high point, or of completion or of a returning dawn, etc.' While he admits that he has been guilty of this habit himself earlier, he now thinks that the analysis of the present must be undertaken 'with the proviso that we do not allow ourselves the facile, rather theatrical declaration that this moment in which we exist is one of total perdition, in the abyss of darkness, or a triumphant daybreak, etc. It is a time like any other, or rather, a time which is never quite like any other.'[18]

What he means is that the present is always like any other present in being problematic, but it is always different in that it involves different problems. Genealogy is the investigation of the unique but problematic present. In Foucault's hands, I would suggest, genealogy lacks the apocalyptic tone sometimes heard not only in Nietzsche but also in Adorno. The point of Foucault's genealogical historiographies is not to destroy reason, but to remind us that reason's assumption of its own necessity and universality may be an illusion that ignores its historical formation in the past, its precariousness in the present, and its fragility in the future. Correlatively, genealogy analyses practices that were instituted in the name of reason but that threaten to harden into unquestioned but oppressive necessity. The genealogical diagnosis itself implies that there is still room for thinking about the possibility of transforming these practices. Foucault puts this point succinctly by suggesting that the value of the genealogical approach is that it 'serves to show how that-which-is has not always been'; it thereby shows as well 'why and how that-which-is might no longer be that-which-is'.[19] That is to say, by 'following lines of fragility in the present', genealogy helps us to see how what we take as necessary was not always the case. The point is not to show that historical forms of rationality are in fact irrational, or what an ideal form of rationality would be. Instead, the goal is to realize that since these forms of rationality have been made, they can be unmade. So genealogy does not deny rationality as such; instead, it investigates rationality not as abstract theory, but as enmeshed in the background web of concrete practices. Foucault's focus on different, historically changing forms of rationality is thus a preference for inquiry that is substantive, concrete and specific instead of abstract, general and purely procedural.

Critical History

The question for us now is whether Foucault's substantive genealogical histories need to be supplemented by an abstract, universal and procedural conception of reason that is validated solely by arguments (presumably transcendental ones) instead of by historiographical and sociological data. This is the central question posed by the opposition between Habermas and Foucault. In contrast to Foucault, Habermas sees as the essential task of philosophy today the construction of a single, systematic theory of reason. He thinks that philosophy can avoid metaphysical accounts of reason by showing how rationality is embedded not in metaphysical principles, but in the assumptions embodied in the activity of discursive communication. Whereas Habermas tries to salvage the rational kernel of modern philosophy through his linguistic turn, he thinks that French philosophers like Derrida and

Foucault abandon this kernel. Whereas Habermas takes the linguistic turn to restore and legitimate reason and philosophy, he sees the French poststructuralists' version of the linguistic turn as threatening the pre-eminence of both reason and philosophy.

Part of this picture of the poststructuralists as painted by Habermas is correct. They do abandon historical teleology, including both the hope in the progress of the species and any nostalgia for the ideals of the past. Their affinity is no longer exclusively with the modern tradition of enlightenment running through Kant and Hegel and Habermas, but also admittedly with a 'postmodern' current going back to Nietzsche's practice of 'effective' or 'critical history'. Although Nietzsche is not the first to abandon belief in the ultimate rationality of human endeavours and the teleology of human history, he exemplifies the counter-enlightenment, postmodern belief that the human species is only a temporary accident in an uncaring universe. The following 'fable' occurs in an early fragment from 1873:

> In some remote corner of the universe, poured out and glittering in innumerable solar systems, there once was a star on which clever animals invented knowledge. That was the haughtiest and most mendacious minute of 'world history' – yet only a minute. After nature had drawn a few breaths the star grew cold, and the clever animals had to die.[20]

Thus, Nietzsche is incredulous about Kant's belief that the human species could not be temporary, and we are now only too aware that Kant was wrong to think that humanity could not destroy itself.

Similarly, the recent French neo-Nietzscheans abandon the optimism of the Enlightenment and its rationalist projection of standards of universal commensurability. For Habermas, however, the price they pay is too great. The enlightenment assumption is that without universal standards, criticism of the past and present seems impossible. Also, without the deliberate transformation of such standards into optimistic aspirations guiding moral, social, and political action, the most that could be expected would seem to be a losing battle to preserve the *status quo*. From Habermas's enlightenment perspective, the likely outcome of the neo-Nietzscheans' pessimistic assessments of human action could even be that the gloomy prognosis would be self-fulfilling. Despairing resignation to sickness is likely to make the sickness worse, whereas there seems to be a better prognosis for those who somehow manage not to give in to disease emotionally.

Yet I would point out in response that Nietzsche's position is not nihilistic or despairing, and his writings are certainly not uncritical. So perhaps criticism is possible on different assumptions from the Enlightenment's rationalistic ones. Nietzsche's early writings work out a programme he calls 'critical history', and his later writings describe and defend a method of critical cultural and moral analysis labelled genealogy. In what follows I shall therefore try to paint a different picture from Habermas's of the critical potential of genealogy.

Habermas's stronger evolutionary model implies that once a later theory emerges, a logical justification independent of the accidents of the historical emergence of the theory also becomes possible. Habermas admits that the evolution of nature is a matter of mutation and chance, and he explicitly ascribes the idea of developmental evolution only to the human level. His model for the evolution of society is the organic individual, with its growth from youth to maturity, such that it seems natural to say that the learning process leads to progress and advance that we cannot imagine wanting to reverse, or to order in any different way.

The neo-Nietzscheans go beyond Habermas in rejecting a Whiggish story altogether. By 'Whiggish' I mean a story that sees the past as culminating in the present, which is then asserted to be necessarily superior to the past. The neo-Nietzscheans could maintain that Habermas's distinction between the evolution of nature and the evolution of humanity preserves the quintessentially metaphysical distinction between nature and spirit. For the Nietzscheans, if the evolution of nature (instead of the organism) is the model, and if evolutionary changes are the result of sudden genetic mutations or environmental accidents, then the 'ranking' of species has a different effect from that which the modern rationalist expects. While some species may be 'cleverer', it is difficult to say in what sense they are 'better' than other species. Conceivably, most species might have been better off if the most clever species had not emerged (especially as that species gradually annihilates most other species and perhaps all life on the planet). Furthermore, there is no reason to think that the clever species itself had to be as it is, for it could have been much better off lacking certain abilities it has or possessing abilities it lacks. The neo-Nietzscheans might argue that just as dogs lack the ability to do mathematics, or some species lack the desire to harm members of their own or other species, so humans may lack certain cognitive abilities, and they certainly could have had a more kindly disposition.

I doubt that there is a fact of the matter about which of these evolutionary models is true. The question is which of them is more useful, and for what purposes. I suggest that the neo-Nietzschean model has some advantages over the Whiggish one. The neo-Nietzschean model is not nihilistic. Instead, it challenges us not to be arrogant about the superiority of the present over the past, or of our own point of view in contrast to competing contemporary points of view. Instead of stressing the convergence of other viewpoints with our own, it holds open the difference between our viewpoint and other possible ones. Whereas the Whiggish model suggests that there are features of ourselves we could not imagine wanting to be any different, the neo-Nietzschean model challenges us to imagine ourselves as having different features from those we normally take for granted both in ourselves and in others.

Critical Philosophy

I have been arguing that Foucault's genealogical method is *internal critique* in a sense common to both Frankfurt School 'critical theory' and Nietzschean 'critical history'. Genealogy interprets and criticizes contingent social formations from the inside, without positing a transcendent perspective or transcendentally necessary universal standards. Let me now go on to test Foucault's genealogical programme against the charge that it is needlessly paradoxical.

One such charge is that the genealogist is caught in what Habermas calls a *performative contradiction*. The genealogist tries to observe the social phenomena from the inside, much as a cultural anthropologist does from the outside. The genealogist may thus be trying to practise a contradiction, and to occupy a standpoint that is simultaneously inside and outside. From Habermas's standpoint, the genealogist's social critique would seem to be positing its own critical claims as valid from the outside at the same time that it tried to get inside by suspending the very idea of validity. Genealogical critique would be asking for everyone's agreement that its critical claims were justified at the same time that it was putting the idea of social agreement and consensus into doubt.

My response to this objection to genealogy is that it misunderstands the practice of cultural anthropology when practised by ethnographers on their own culture. The techniques of anthropological observation are being used more and more by modern society on itself. This research shows that people are often unaware of their behaviour and motivation, as they are frequently surprised when they are questioned about why they said or did certain things. The genealogist thus tries to see as strange what the culture takes to be familiar. 'Insiders' reading a genealogical investigation come to see for the first time subliminal aspects of their social behaviour. Simply becoming conscious of social practices that were previously unconscious often leads to difficulty in continuing to engage in those social practices. Even if one did not reject such practices, one might still feel awkward about them, and be less skilful at engaging in them. So genealogy is not performing a contradiction by trying to estrange itself from *within*. Becoming aware of social behaviour that is normally unconscious often does lead to the insiders' becoming critical of that behaviour.

Furthermore, the genealogist need not believe that this process of critical self-estrangement from certain social practices is possible or valid only because of some ideal outside where everyone would agree that the social practice should be abandoned. Finding one's own previous behaviour to be strange simply means that one cannot engage in it any longer in the same way, not that one thinks that no rational being should engage in it. Those who are sceptical about consensus and social agreement being able to serve as the universal arbitrators of validity often point to the pluralism of society, its many different, contingent points of view. Genealogical pluralists are not only sceptical about achieving consensus between these points of view, they may think that it would be wrong to do so. They see plurality as a social good. Correlatively, any attempt to eliminate social difference or to promote a homogeneous culture would represent a social evil.

Habermasians are not impressed by the pluralist's meta-theory. They see it as caught in the self-contradiction whereby the pluralist cannot be a pluralist about pluralism itself. That is, the pluralist must think that pluralism is the correct view, and universally valid in so far as society really ought to be pluralistic. This contradiction shows up in a crucial practical problem: how pluralistic can a society be? There will be some groups with some values that could not be allowed if other groups are to be able to pursue their ends. So in the very effort to be pluralistic a society would undoubtedly have to draw limits on pluralism and to forbid certain possibilities. This practical problem points out, according to Habermasians, the need for some standards transcending any particular plurality. The presupposition, at least ideally, of a single community seems required for the particular groups to be able to pursue their particular ends. The charge is thus that pluralists cannot really oppose the ideal of social consensus since there must be an implied consensus on how much dissent is allowed. According to a noted interpreter of Habermas, 'The affirmation of pluralism' leads to a paradox since it 'implies the idea of a community wherein *everyone agrees to disagree*'.[21]

Foucault need not respond by denying this point. Instead, he professes *agnosticism* about Habermas's consensus model. When asked in a late interview about this model, Foucault remarked, 'The farthest I would go is to say that perhaps one must not be for consensuality, but one must be against non-consensuality'.[22] His point here, I believe, is that being for consensuality is a stronger position than merely being against nonconsensuality. In other words, the *for* and the *against* here do not represent a simple case of either *p* or *not-p*. Being for consensuality connotes for him the danger of an intolerance of difference. He probably believes that normally when one states what one believes to be true, one does not add the claim that others must agree. One simply says 'p'. Saying 'you must agree that p is true' suggests a stronger claim. Conceptually, analysing truth (or the assertion *that p*) as consensus (or the assertion that *everyone must agree that p*) seems misguided. Practically, Foucault may also be wary that being explicitly for consensuality may mean that in so far as one needs to insist that one's own position is right, one will be unable to believe that anyone could hold an opposing position rationally.

In contrast, being *against nonconsensuality* means only that when we encounter others who seem to have radically different views from our own, we should try to find out why this difference obtains, and whether there is any mutual ground for discussion. But this negative concession does not entail granting the stronger positive claim that all discussion presupposes necessarily that understanding between the two parties will result in agreement. Pluralists believe that they can enter discussion in good faith without necessarily believing that the discussion of social problems will result in a unanimous, univocal assessment of the empirical situation and consensus on the best solution.[23]

Has Foucault thus avoided the charge of paradox? To answer this let me restate the charge. The practical problem arises when social pluralism seems to presuppose that the community will agree to and permit the disagreement and the social plurality that the pluralist prefers. The Habermasian 'universalist' infers that the pluralist tacitly presupposes a higher, single community that allows for the possibility of dissent between various groups and cultures in that community. The universalist believes that there is a tension between, on the one hand, the pluralist's supposed picture of society as irrational and as always at war with itself, and on the other hand, the pluralist's tacit appeal to a more rational society that tolerates dissent and agrees to disagree. Universalism believes itself to be on stronger moral and political ground than pluralism in so far as it recognizes the need for rational community and solidarity. Pluralism's denial of consensus seems to entail a picture of society as consisting of hungry hordes in competition with one another, with no redeeming legitimation of any of the competing political strategies.

The important thing to say in response is that genealogical pluralism certainly should not oppose the possibility of social solidarity and community. Pluralism will have to grant that these values might well trump any attempt to destroy them. But it does not thereby have to grant that these values are eternal or universal. Solidarity and community mean little as universal abstractions, and are not simply meta-procedural idealizations. They rest on substantive conceptions of the social good, and are binding not in the abstract, but only in so far as they are practised concretely. Solidarity and community are thus not the imaginary focal points of an evolutionary learning process, but are binding only for contingent, historical moments. These values may be the highest achievements of these contingent moments, and they may serve as inspiration for later moments. But they cannot be repeated, and slavish imitation by a later moment may only lead to a reactionary blindness to the new problems that a later moment faces.

This answer, I believe, is one towards which Foucault was working in his last writings. Contrary to Habermas's reading, Foucault did not see himself as a counter-enlightenment thinker attacking 'the essential kernel of rationality'. Foucault suggests that this kernel 'would have to be preserved in any event'.[24] The implication that I draw from this remark is that for Foucault, Habermas's project of generating a meta-theory of rationality is not what is needed. Instead, what is needed is the more concrete practice of critical *history*, that is, genealogical critiques of the specific, concrete ways in which we have been socialized subliminally.

Foucault's late studies of changes in *ethos* between Greek, early Christian and modern times suggest that we can learn that our present self-understanding is not universal and eternal. These earlier self-understandings are not *alternatives* for us, since we cannot now go back to them. But they are also not *inferior* to ours, as a Habermasian evolutionary model would imply. The Habermasian model would suggest that the earlier self-understandings learned from their mistakes and 'matured' into the present one. Foucault's genealogies suggest in contrast that these different self-understandings are different *interpretations*. Seeing that other peoples lived successfully with different self-interpretations from our own should suggest that we can criticize regrettable aspects of ourselves that might have seemed universal and eternal. Seeing our own self-understanding as an interpretation instead of as the best or most highly evolved self-representation allows us to begin to criticize it. Self-criticism is more likely as the result of concrete genealogical histories than abstract, utopian projections of ideal uncoerced consensus.

Foucault's genealogy of ethics is part of a general project of writing a history of problematizations. That is, he does not see problems as eternal, or as questions that are to be solved if thought is to progress. What the problems are will change, and not necessarily because they have been solved. In the ethical sphere, Foucault wants to chart the shift in what he calls 'ethical substance' – a central term of Hegel's. The history of ethics will thus be the history of the changes in ethical substance (and other aspects of *Sittlichkeit*, including the '*mode d'assujettissement*'). The moral code, the standard or 'universal' principles, does not change much, on Foucault's account. However, contrary to Kantians, he thinks that this lack of change does not give the code 'binding force'. On the contrary, that it does not change even though the meaning of what it is to be ethical (the 'ethical substance') changes, suggests that the real ethical 'glue' must be found at the more concrete level that a genealogical 'critical history' investigates.

The genealogical critical history of ethical substance thus shifts the methodological focus away from the postulation of a single meta-community. In contrast, genealogy sees human beings as participating in multiple communities at once, with each of these communities arising from different concrete contingencies. To criticize one community or set of social practices, we do not need to imagine some ideal standpoint that is independent of any contingent concrete standpoint. More substantively, we may judge that community, not from outside our own standpoint (since there is no such outside), but from the standpoint of other communities, or other self-understandings, that we know to be, or to have been, viable. Alexander Nehamas makes this 'Nietzschean' point against Habermas especially clearly:

> We acquire our beliefs, our desires, our values at different times, in different circumstances, from various sources. Each one of us belongs to a number of distinct but overlapping communities, and each community has its own but overlapping standards of rationality – or, if you prefer, standards of communicative competence. We don't need to stand outside *everything* in order to criticize and evaluate the standards and practices, the 'reason', of any particular community. All we need is a position outside *it*. This position is provided by the many other communities of which we are all members.[25]

Conclusion

If genealogy is a viable version of critical theory, there will be some differences from the way that theory is construed traditionally. Inquiry is no longer conceived as the search for certainty, nor even as the search for transcultural, context-independent validity. Instead, inquiry is the reinterpretation of what is always already an interpretation. Methodologically, then, these critical interpretations are explained too abstractly if they are said to be mainly a matter of coming up with the best arguments, as if all that is involved is procedural argumentation from premises to conclusions. Argumentation will be involved in genealogical research, but the goal is more substantive, namely, to find new descriptions of ourselves that locate new possibilities in our situation. These reinterpretations may even change what the premises are. So while formal validity alone is always a necessary condition of good interpretation, it is not a sufficient condition, since good interpretation can alter our conception of what is to be argued and what our premises mean.

Critical theory conceived genealogically may unmask substantive injustice, but it need not justify this unmasking through the methodological picture of inquiry presented by traditional theory. It need not construe itself only as seeing through illusions and constructing a timeless, context-transcendent theory of rationality from which we can then measure present society. Instead, when practised genealogically, critical theory can present itself as offering new interpretations. Along the way it may be unmasking previous interpretations. Since what is unmasked is self-interpretation, this unmasking through genealogical critical history can now be seen not simply in traditional epistemological terms as 'revealing reality', but also modally as 'deconstructing necessity'. That is, genealogical research will show that self-understandings that are taken as universal, eternal and necessary have a history, with a beginning, and therefore, possibly, an end. Genealogy thus shows that self-understandings are interpretations, and it can bring us to suspect that conceptions of ourselves, which we have taken to be necessary, are only contingent. In making this contingency manifest, genealogy makes it possible for people to see how they could want to be different from how they are. In genealogy, therefore, politics and philosophy are no longer entirely irrelevant to each other, but instead, they become mutually reinforcing activities.

Notes

This paper was delivered at a conference, 'Foucault: Freedom and Politics', organized by Jeremy Moss in 1994 at the University of Melbourne for the tenth anniversary of Foucault's death.

1 Paul Rabinow (ed.), *The Foucault Reader* (Pantheon, New York, 1984), p. 374.

2 Ibid.

3 Ibid., p. 384.

4 Ibid.

5 Ibid., p. 385.

6 Michel Foucault, 'The ethic of care for the self as a practice of freedom', *Philosophy and Social Criticism*, XII (1987), p. 124.

7 Michel Foucault, 'Politics and ethics: an interview', in Rabinow (ed.), *Foucault Reader*, p. 374.

8 *Philosophy and Social Criticism* XII, p. 117.

9 *Philosophy and Social Criticism* XII, p. 129.

10 See 'Two lectures' in Michel Foucault, *Power/Knowledge* (Pantheon, New York, 1980), pp. 83–5; p. 83 for the phrase 'anti-science' and p. 85 for the claim that genealogy is emancipatory. For an illuminating discussion of the 'countersciences', see Gary Gutting, *Michel Foucault's Archaeology of Scientific Reason* (Cambridge University Press, Cambridge, 1989), pp. 214–24.

11 Michel Foucault, 'The subject and power', Afterword in Hubert L. Dreyfus and Paul

Rabinow, *Michel Foucault: Beyond Structuralism and Hermeneutics*, 2nd edn (University of Chicago Press, Chicago, 1983), p. 210.

12 Ibid., p. 216.

13 *Philosophy and Social Criticism* XII, p. 131.

14 Portions of what follows also appear in various places in Chapters 5 and 6 of David Couzens Hoy and Thomas McCarthy, *Critical Theory* (Basil Blackwell, Oxford and Cambridge MA, 1994), and are reprinted with permission.

15 Michel Foucault, 'Interview with Gérard Raulet', *Telos* 55 (Spring 1983), p. 200. Similar remarks can be found in the 1978 interview on 'Adorno, Horkheimer, and Marcuse' in Michel Foucault, *Remarks on Marx: Conversations with Duccio Trombadori*, trans. R. James Goldstein and James Cascaito (Semiotext(e), New York, 1991), pp. 115–29.

16 Ibid., p. 201.

17 Ibid., p. 205.

18 Ibid., p. 206.

19 Ibid.

20 F. Nietzsche, 'On truth and lie in an extra-moral sense', in *The Portable Nietzsche*, trans. Walter Kaufmann (Viking Press, New York, 1954), p. 42.

21 David Ingram, 'The postmodern Kantianism of Arendt and Lyotard', *The Review of Metaphysics* XLII (1988), p. 52 (emphasis added).

22 Foucault, 'Politics and ethics', p. 379.

23 In *Power/Knowledge*, p. 82, Foucault maintains that criticism works by recovering 'differential knowledge incapable of unanimity and which owes its force to the harshness of everything surrounding it'.

24 Michel Foucault, 'What is enlightenment?', in Rabinow (ed.), *Foucault Reader*, p. 43.

25 Alexander Nehamas makes this point against Habermas while reviewing Habermas's book, *The Philosophical Discourse of Modernity* in the 30 May, 1988 issue of *The New Republic* 198, 22, pp. 34–5.

2

Genealogical Politics

Wendy Brown

Discontent about Foucault's failure to develop a politics according to which one can make judgements and interventions generally attaches to one of the following elements of his thought: his theorization of power as ubiquitous and his sundering of power from oppression; his critique of sovereignty (and hence sovereign accountability); his critique of modernist liberation politics as tending to extend regulatory productions of identity; his formulation of the normatively constrained and constraining character of all discourse; his insistence that subjects come into being only through subjection; his emphasis on local struggles and local knowledge; and his concomitant rejection of global political claims and universal political truths.

The political complaint derived from each of these is proffered through a distinctly modernist philosophical and political grammar. If power is ubiquitous, so the grievance goes, then hierarchies of dominant and subordinate, oppressor and oppressed are rendered invisible, and there is no place 'beyond power' where justice and freedom might prevail. If sovereign states or subjects are not sites of political power, then there can be neither political accountability nor addressees for political demands. If there is no pre-discursive subject and no subject without subjection, then neither political agency nor political freedom are possible. If there is no Truth external to discourse, then there are no fixed norms by which we can judge or according to which we can act, nor are there any prospects for a global or millenarian movement of political transformation. The grammar of these complaints is modernist not only because of the 'if/then' rationality in which the truth that refuses to be unsettled appears as a conclusion that masquerades as a consequence, but also because these tacit precepts all subscribe to and are linked in a common (modernist) understanding about what constitutes politics: Truth, legitimacy, agency, sovereign subjects and institutions, accountability, revolution. It is politics in a modernist mode that Foucault aims to undo with genealogy by locating power and its cousin, contingency, at the centre of political life.[1]

Indeed, Foucault hardly rushes to reassure readers and interviewers sceptical of his 'politics' by conventional standards that their scepticism is misplaced. In interviews, his responses to expressly political questions are frequently vague, oblique, deflective, or simply bland. Much of his writing also bears an unpolitical tenor: the questions that preoccupy him – about Truth, power, body, soul, rationality, the subject, or ethics – while of obvious relevance to politics, are often posed in strikingly unpolitical fashion. His chosen objects of historical and political study – madness, prisons, sexuality, medicine, technologies of the self – reside, at best, in the margins of political life. His studies on 'governmentality' are notably dry; there is absence of political agenda or urgency in most of his writing; and his insistence on non-millenarian political perspectives is paralleled by the absence of a moral or a prescriptive note in his own genealogies, by his refusal to talk about the good – or even the bad. Foucault is inclined instead to identify the 'danger-ousness' of every discourse or strategy, an inclination which even he admits can be discouraging, yielding at most a 'pessimistic activism'.[2]

While these features of Foucault's intellectual habit combined with his explicit political remarks suggest, at first brush, a certain wariness towards political engagement, they may be read as part of his effort to reconfigure the relation between intellectual and political life. This effort, I shall argue, deploys genealogy to *displace* four conventional approaches to scholarly engagement with political questions: (1) *historical analyses* in which history is cast either as progress or as a panoply of alternatives to our own time;[3] (2) *philosophical critique*, or what he sometimes calls 'a general analytics of truth', that is, critique bound to metaphysics rather than oriented towards historically specific formations; (3) *policy* advocacy – specific reforms and leg-islative proposals centred on the state; and (4) *political position-taking* on various conflicts, policies and events. With genealogy, Foucault intends to pose a set of questions quite different from those afforded by these four approaches. He seeks to ask, on the one hand, what is the nature of our time, what is our 'political ontology', and on the other, what are the logics of power that have produced this condition and within which we operate? In derailing conventional political–intellectual postures with such questions, and espe-cially in deposing unitary logics of history with multiple logics of power as the foundation of political analysis, Foucault aims to craft a different kind of political space within which critics can operate. This space does not privilege particular political values or projects even as it radically denaturalizes ele-ments of the present, calls the present into question, calls the question of the present. This is the space – harbouring no particular political aims but replete with challenging exposures and destabilizations – of genealogical politics.

In 'Nietzsche, Genealogy, History', Foucault's most sustained discussion of genealogy, he does not say what genealogy is but rather what it defines itself against, what conventions of history and metaphysics it aims to disrupt. This apparently *indirect* articulation of genealogy itself exemplifies the practice of genealogy. 'Nietzsche, Genealogy, History' is an account of contemporary values – in particular, progressive history and metaphysical critique – as prob-lematic fictions; it is an alternative story of our commonplaces that aims to reveal their fictive, hence fragile character. It is a production that reveals the terms by which we live through rupturing them, by doing violence to their ordinary ordering and situation. Foucault's account of genealogy in 'Nietzsche, Genealogy, History' also mirrors genealogical practice in its emer-gence through conflict and through its tracing of forces – not groups, individuals, or concepts – in battle. Foucault explains genealogy not by systematically articulating the coherent method it entails, but as an embattled 'emergence' – something that must fight for place, something that must displace other conventions of history, in order to prevail.

In the simplest terms, genealogy emerges in opposition to progressive history on one side and metaphysics on the other. Yet it also tenders a genealogical critique of what it opposes in so far as it reveals how each of these practices is implicated in the other: the emergence of genealogy exposes the metaphysics in progressive historiography and the historical unconscious of metaphysics. This in turn serves the positive task of developing a philosophically self-conscious historiography (a historiography loosened from or at least made conscious of the historical meta-narratives it invokes) and a historically conscious philosophy, both of which contribute to the re-figuring of political space Foucault achieves with genealogy. To see the grounds for this positive turn, we must first examine in closer detail the negative programme of genealogy, what ground it seeks to disrupt, what denaturalizations it aims to perform.

*

'The genealogist needs history to dispel the chimeras of the origin, somewhat in the manner of the pious philosopher who needs a doctor to exorcise the shadow of his soul.'[4]

Genealogy, according to Foucault's reading of Nietzsche, is not to be confused with a quest for origins, nor, however, will it 'neglect as inaccessible the vicissitudes of history' and eschew the problem of beginnings. Rather, genealogy will 'cultivate the details and accidents that accompany every beginning; it will be scrupulously attentive to their petty malice . . . await their emergence . . . not be reticent in "excavating the depths"'.[5] Foucault contrasts the genealogical emphasis on 'beginnings' as a domain of accident, disparity, conflict and haphazardness, with conventional history's pure, or 'distant ideality of the [idea of] origin'. And history as a 'concrete body of a development' is contrasted with a notion of history as the travels of pure soul.

Just as genealogy metaphorizes history as body – 'with its moments of intensity, its lapses, its extended periods of feverish agitation, its fainting spells' – it also features the body itself as historical. The body is 'the inscribed surface of events' as well as 'a volume in perpetual disintegration'.[6] But neither the corporeality of history nor the historicity of the body can be brought into relief without challenging a belief in the purity of origins and the attendant notion of linear, teleological development. Similarly, neither the extent to which history is composed of feelings, sentiments and power, nor the historicity of feelings, sentiments and power – their non-essential and mutable character – can be discerned until they are grasped as mutually constitutive, until the supra-historical perspective that denies them a place in history is supplanted by genealogical analysis. For Foucault, '"effective" history [genealogy] differs from traditional history in being without constants'.[7]

*

> 'Genealogy does not resemble the evolution of a species and does not map the destiny of a people.'[8]

As the study of 'stock' or 'descent' rather than development, as that which reverses the direction in which historians conventionally proceed, genealogy permits 'the dissociation of the self, its recognition and displacement as an empty synthesis'.[9] By historicizing everything, yet inverting the directionality of historical vision to regard the scenes of conflicts and accidents as constitutive of the present, genealogy deconstructs essentialist notions of the body and the self; it disrupts coherent identities, both individual and collective. Foucault's emphasis upon 'accidents', 'errors' and 'faulty calculations' as that which 'gave birth to those things that continue to exist and have value for us', aims to replace the notion that 'truth or being [lies] at the root of what we know or what we are' with an appreciation of contingency.[10] If everything about us is the effect of accident rather than will or design, then we are, paradoxically, both more severely historical and also more malleable than we would otherwise seem. We are more sedimented by history, but also more capable of intervening in our histories, than is conceivable through historiographies that preserve some elements of humans and of time as fixed in nature. 'Nothing in man . . . is sufficiently stable to serve as the basis for . . . understanding other men.'[11]

Thus one of the most important aims of genealogy is to denaturalize forces and formations in excess of what either conventional history or metaphysical criticism can achieve, to take that which appears to be given and provide it not simply a history but one which reveals how contingently it came into being, how non-inevitable its existence is. This kind of history is precisely the opposite of teleological history, indeed is in a permanent quarrel with teleological history, in so far as it treats the present as the accidental production of the contingent past, rather than treating the past as the sure and necessary road to the inevitable present. Moreover, the heritage traced by genealogy is not an 'acquisition' or a 'possession that grows and solidifies' but rather, 'an unstable assemblage of faults, fissures, and heterogeneous layers that threaten the fragile inheritor from within or from underneath'.[12] This formulation, too, in supplanting an evolutionary with a geological image, metaphorically recasts the weight of history as something that works not through linearity or pure temporality, not as a force moving through time, but through spatial accretion – 'heterogeneous layers'. This weight is partly a consequence of the paradoxical fact that the genealogist treats time more gravely – is more attentive to its power as a field of forces in space – than the historian guided by a supra-historical perspective which 'finds its support outside of time'.[13] Yet again, even as the weight of history is multiplied by this perspective, so also is its inconsistency and contingency brought into relief: 'the search for descent . . . disturbs what was previously considered immobile; it fragments what was thought unified; it shows the heterogeneity of what was imagined consistent with itself'.[14]

Through these transformations in the objects and movement of history, genealogy reorients the relationship of history to political possibility: even as the field of political possibility is bounded by the histories of the present, these histories are themselves tales of improbable emergence, and thus offer openings for disturbance. In place of the lines of determination laid by laws of history, history is cast as a field of openings – faults, fractures and fissures. Conversely, rather than promising a certain future, as progressive history does, genealogy is deployed to *incite* possible futures. Openings along fault lines, and incitements from destabilized (because denaturalized) configurations of the present comprise the stage of political possibility. But in so doing, these openings and incitements dictate neither the terms nor the direction of political possibility, both of which are matters of imagination and invention, themselves limited by what Foucault terms the 'political ontology of the present'. 'As it is wrong to search for descent in an uninterrupted continuity, we should avoid thinking of emergence as the final term of a historical development . . .'[15]

Just as the histories of emergent phenomena are tales of conflicts and accidents, the phenomena themselves are cast by genealogy as 'episodes' rather than 'culminations'. The metaphysics of conventional histories, in placing present needs at the origin, fail to grasp the subjugating forces that constitute the dynamic of history; they substitute 'the anticipatory power of meaning' for 'the hazardous play of dominations'.[16] Genealogy promises dirty histories, histories of power and subjection, histories of bids for hegemony waged, won and vanquished, the 'endlessly repeated play of dominations', rather than histories of reason, meaning or higher purpose.[17] Genealogy traces continual yet discontinuous histories, histories without direction yet also without end, histories of varied and protean systems of subjection. 'Humanity does not gradually progress from combat to combat until it arrives at universal reciprocity . . . humanity installs each of its violences in a system of rules and thus proceeds from domination to domination.'[18] The content, the lived modality of 'effective history', is politics and the moving force of this history is power. Put the other way around, there are no non-political moments in genealogical history. With genealogy, we can no longer speak of an 'engine' of history because genealogy makes clear that history is not propelled; it does not lead forward but is rather the retrospective record of conflicts yielding an emergence. History is no longer 'moved' because it does not harbour direction, ends, or end, even while it bears 'generative processes'.[19]

*

'[N]o one is responsible for an emergence; no one can glory in it since it always occurs in the interstice.'[20]

The space of this dirty history is what Nietzsche and Foucault both call a non-place, a 'pure distance', a 'place of confrontation'.[21] It is a non-place because in the confrontation or battle that genealogy seeks to document, in the site of emergence, contestants do not oppose each other in an order that houses them both, but rather, fight to bring into being an order (Foucault sometimes recurs to the infelicitous language of 'system') in their respective images. Thus genealogy does not feature individuals, parties or even purposes as agentic or accountable. Instead, it documents 'the entry of forces . . . their eruption, the leap from the wings to centre stage'.[22] Moreover, these forces are not identical to themselves over time: 'the isolation of different points of emergence does not conform to the successive configurations of an identical meaning'. Part of what must be documented in order to disrupt a narrative that essentializes historical forces is 'substitutions, displacements, disguised conquests, and systematic reversals'.[23] Only then can a metaphysics committed to the 'slow exposure of the meaning hidden in an origin' be supplanted with an understanding that eschews a supra-historical perspective.[24] And only through such an understanding can a politics animated by the moral accountability of persons for political conditions be replaced by an *effective politics*: a politics of contesting forces that demands projects and strategies rather than moral righteousness; a politics of bids for power rather than remonstrances of it.

*

> History becomes 'effective' to the degree that it introduces discontinuity into our very being – as it divides our emotions, dramatizes our instincts, multiplies our body and sets it against itself. 'Effective' history deprives the self of the reassuring stability of life and nature, and it will not permit itself to be transported by a voiceless obstinacy toward a millennial ending.[25]

The measure of genealogy's success is its disruption of conventional accounts of ourselves – our sentiments, bodies, origins, futures. It tells a story that disturbs our habits of self-recognition, poses an 'us' that is foreign: this is the disconcerting effect of Nietzsche's *Genealogy of Morals* as well as Foucault's *Madness and Civilization*, *The History of Sexuality*, or *Discipline and Punish*. Each begins with an account by which our epoch commonly recognizes itself – morally good, intrinsically reasonable, sexually liberated, politically humane – and asks not only whether these stories are 'really true' but what function of power each purported Truth serves, what each particular fiction conceals and, even more importantly, produces.

Genealogy not only achieves its disruptions through disturbing popular narratives but microcosmically as well. Where there is narrative logic or continuity, genealogy assaults it with the introduction of counter-forces and revelations of discontinuity; an 'event' is deconstructed as 'the reversal of the relationship of forces'; 'destiny' is upset by insistence upon 'the singular randomness of events'; 'profound intentions and immutable necessities' are forced into a relationship with 'countless lost events, without a landmark or a point of reference'; reason is revealed as only contingently so, neutral (scientific) knowledge is exposed as a massive exercise in power, the unique individual is rewritten as a messy historical production.[26]

Is genealogy, then, only perverse in its disruptions and confabulations? Does it only negate? Knowledge is 'made for cutting', Foucault insists, and the political landscape genealogical knowledge dissects is the monolith of the present, a landscape that genealogy converts into a series of questions: Who are we? What is the nature of our time? And what kind of subjects has this time made of us? What is the 'ontology of our present'?[27]

*

> What is happening today? What is happening now? And what is this 'now' within which all of us find ourselves; and who defines the moment at which I am writing? [it] seems to me that the question Kant is answering [in 'What is Enlightenment?'] . . . is not simply . . . what is it in the present situation that can determine this or that decision of a philosophical order [but rather] what is it in the present that produces meaning now for philosophical reflection?[28]

What does Foucault intend through the odd philosophical–historical locution, 'ontology of the present?' He credits Kant both with this formulation of the task of philosophy and with its opposite, the development of 'an analytics of truth'.[29] Against the metaphysical reach of the latter, an ontology of the present asks, 'What is our present? What is the present field of possible experiences?' These are the questions Foucault understands Kant to have posed about the Enlightenment not by defining the elements of the age but through recognition of the elements of its *coming into being*, through the struggles and partial successes of its emergence.[30] Foucault elaborates:

> . . . the function of any diagnosis concerning the nature of the present . . . does not consist in a simple characterization of what we are but, instead – by following lines of fragility in the present – in managing to grasp why and how that-which-is might no longer be that-which-is. In this sense, any description must always be made in accordance with these kinds of virtual fractures which open up the space of freedom understood as a space of concrete freedom, i.e., of possible transformation.[31]

In the easy substitution of the terms 'ontology', 'nature' and 'diagnosis', Foucault hints at the function of an ontology of the present. The point is to grasp ourselves as 'ill' in some way that exceeds the symptom without pretending to an objective standpoint or even one external to the discourse in which the illness transpires, and without subscribing to notions of root or foundational causes.

Foucault's desire for a 'diagnosis' or 'ontology' of the present reconfigures the relationship of philosophy to history and the relation of philosophy and history to politics. The task of philosophy becomes curiously historical: in apprehending the nature of ourselves in the present, philosophy must recognize us as historical beings and our time as a time in history. Conversely, history is subjected to philosophical critique in so far as it must be divested of reason and direction at the same time it is tethered to a conventionally philosophical question: 'how can we know our time and ourselves when we cannot move beyond or outside of them?'. Foucault describes genealogy's resolution of this problem thus: 'Effective history studies what is closest, but in an abrupt dispossession, so as to seize it at a distance . . .'.[32]

Since even genealogical 'histories' cannot be divested of projects by which they are inevitably inflected, philosophical self-consciousness is required to keep track of such projects. But these kinds of histories also require philosophy to call into question the terms of its object of study, even as philosophy requires genealogy – the radical historicization of its terms – to do the same. Genealogy or 'effective history', Foucault reminds us, 'differs from traditional history in being without constants'.[33] It 'emphatically excludes the 'rediscovery of ourselves' and 'becomes "effective" to the degree that it introduces discontinuity into our very being'.[34] History bound to the task of creating an ontology of the present is thus consonant with the Socratic charge to philosophy to expose the familiar as an illness – 'its task is to become a curative science'.[35]

In this strange locution of mixed genres, 'ontology of the present', genealogy effectively *crosses* philosophy and history, undercutting the premises by which each ordinarily excludes the other in its self-definition. At the same time, in posing the diagnostic question, 'Who are we?' genealogy attaches both history and philosophy to a political task, that of knowing who we are, knowing our ill body and bodies. Thus, for example, in his own genealogy of contemporary 'governmentality', Foucault traces the unlikely imbrication of 'pastoral power' and *raison d'état* to bring into view the contemporary political rationality that not only rules but produces us: 'Our civilization has developed the most complex system of knowledge, the most sophisticated structures of power: what has this kind of knowledge, this type of power made of us?'.[36] Again, the notion of subjects produced by historically and culturally specific configurations of knowledge and power confounds the boundaries conventionally drawn between philosophy and history.

Importantly, however, while genealogy attaches thinking to the apprehension of political conditions, it does not thereby *politicize* intellectual inquiry. Rather, genealogy's refiguring of philosophy and history extends to a refiguring of the political which directly opposes this term to conventional understandings of politicization on one side and policy on the other.[37] While genealogy is saturated by a political impetus, while it is deployed to replace 'laws of history' with exposures of mechanisms of power and relations of force, while it is carried out in the name of denaturalizing the present in order to highlight its malleability, genealogy neither prescribes political positions nor specifies desirable futures. Rather, it aims to make visible why particular positions and visions of the future occur to us, and especially to reveal when and where those positions work in the same register of 'political rationality' as that which they purport to criticize.

Foucault pejoratively links 'politicization' with 'totalization' and contrasts his own genealogical studies with such closures. This does not mean that he opposes politics as such, nor that he naively believes his intellectual endeavours to be independent of politics. Rather, he intends his inquiry to call into question certain political truths and commitments, and hence to open an otherwise closed political space:

> I have especially wanted to question politics, and to bring to light in the political field, as in the field of historical and philosophical interrogation, some problems that had not been recognized there before. I mean that the questions I am trying to

ask are not determined by a pre-established political outlook and do not tend toward the realization of some definite political project.

This is doubtless what people mean when they reproach me for not presenting an overall theory. But I believe precisely that the forms of totalization offered by politics are always, in fact, very limited. I am attempting, to the contrary, apart from any totalization – which would be at once abstract and limiting – to open up problems that are as concrete and *general* as possible, problems that approach politics from behind and cut across societies on the diagonal . . . [38]

While Foucault invests genealogy with the possibility of emancipating intellectual inquiry from certain kinds of position taking, and deploys it to question certain conventional Left positions (for example, those of Marxism, Maoism, social democracy and liberation politics bound to social identity), he is equally concerned to separate such inquiry from policy concerns. In his genealogy of 'pastoral power', Foucault provocatively links policy with policing (and policy studies with the aims of a police state) through a study of the emergence of *Polizeiwissenschaft*, a term connoting both policy science and police science.[39] Through this genealogy, Foucault casts the very preoccupation with policy – formulating it, influencing it, studying it – as less the limitations of reformist politics (the conventional Left critique) than a symptom of a contemporary political rationality that renders quite normal the state administration of everyday life. Foucault's genealogy of the political rationality which fuses *Polizeiwissenschaft* with *raison d'état* shows how

reason of state's problem of calculating detailed actions appropriate to an infinity of . . . contingent circumstances is met by the creation of an exhaustively detailed knowledge of the governed reality of the state itself, extending (at least in aspiration) to touch the existences of its individual members. The police state is also termed the 'state of prosperity'. The idea of prosperity or happiness is the principle which identifies the state with its subjects.[40]

Thus, the proliferation of policies that 'constitutes a kind of omnivorous espousal of governed reality, the sensorium of a Leviathan', *is* intricately linked to the tacitly but ubiquitously policed order that is both disciplinary society and the society saturated with *policy*.[41] Indeed, disciplinary society is the policy-bound society; it is one with the public policy state. According to Foucault, 'what [the seventeenth- and eighteenth-century authors of *Polizeiwissenschaft*] understand by 'police' isn't an institution or mechanism functioning within the state, but a governmental technology peculiar to the state; domains, techniques, targets where the state intervenes'.[42] These interventions deal with everything concerning 'life' – health, highways, public safety, workplaces, poverty – in short, all that today traffics under the rubric of 'public policy'.

The *police* includes everything. But from an extremely particular point of view. Men and things are envisioned as to their relationships: men's coexistence on a territory; their relationships as to property; what they produce; what is exchanged on the market. It also considers how they live, the diseases and accidents which can befall them. What the police sees to is a live, active, productive man.[43]

Political–intellectual concern with influencing policy would appear to further subject intellectual life to the political rationality inclusive of

Polizeiwissenschaft, indeed to abet this rationality with the very instrument – intellectual critique – that could be used to 'cut' it ('knowledge is made for cutting . . .'). Thus Foucault's turn away from policy recommendations, or from the use of intellectual inquiry for purposes of policy reform, is not simply a matter of intellectual indifference or radical disdain for political reformism. Rather, this turn converges with the larger project of genealogy as well as with the specific genealogy of governmentality proffered in his lectures on 'Politics and Reason' and 'Governmentality'. That larger project is to identify the discourses and political rationalities constitutive of our time such that they are brought into relief as historical, contingent, partial, and thus malleable, such that 'that-which-is' can be thought as 'that-which-might-not-be'.

*

Thus far I have suggested that Foucault's reformulation of the political, tendered as opposition to politicization on the one hand and to policy on the other, is the effect of genealogy's displacements of conventions of history and philosophy and especially the displacement of their conventional disidentification with one another. Against what he argues the political is not, we may now consider in closer detail three aspects of Foucault's reformulation of the political: (1) the emphasis on fracture; (2) the emphasis on political rationality; and (3) the sundering of genealogical discoveries from political prescription through the interruption of 'logics of history'.

Fracture   Genealogy, Foucault argues, reveals the present to be the 'consequence' of a history fraught with accidents, haphazard conflicts and unrelated 'events' which are themselves 'singularly random' and nothing more than 'the reversal of a relationship of forces'. Notwithstanding frequent misreadings of Foucault's thought on this point, the randomness and discontinuity of history makes the past *and* present more rather than less difficult to understand as it makes the present more heavily weighted by an infinitely complex history, a history that conforms neither to temporal lines nor to spatial structures. 'The world we know is not this ultimately simple configuration where events are reduced to accentuate their essential traits, their final meaning, or their initial and final value. On the contrary, it is a profusion of entangled events.'[44] Foucault continues, citing Nietzsche:

> If it appears as a 'marvellous motley, profound and totally meaningful,' this is because it began and continues its secret existence through a 'host of errors and phantasms.' We want historians to confirm our belief that the present rests upon profound intentions and immutable necessities. But the true historical sense confirms our existence among countless lost events, without a landmark or a point of reference.[45]

The significance for political thinking of history's composition by accidents and unrelated events is that it subjects the apparent totality of the present to this non-linear, discontinuous history, and thereby breaks apart the present. In this, genealogy potentially articulates politically exploitable fissures and fractures in 'the present'; it produces openings and interstices as sites of political agitation or alternatives. Genealogy thus reduces the political *need* for progressive history as the only source of a motion away from the present even as it eliminates the grounds for such history. Similarly, genealogy reduces the *need* for 'total revolution' even as it eliminates the possibility of it by depriving the present of the status of totality, revolution's critical object. Hence Foucault's insistence that the question 'What is the nature of our present?' does not consist in 'a simple characterization of what we are', but rather 'follows lines of fragility in the present'.[46] Fractures in history become the material of political possibility in the present to the extent that they signify weaknesses or openings in the structure of the present – 'virtual fracture[s] . . . open up the space of freedom'.[47]

In Foucault's view, the project of making the present appear as something that might not be, or that might not be as it is, would seem to constitute *the* distinctive contribution of intellectual work to political life. It should now be clear why genealogy – which aims to reveal the wholly constructed character of the present even as it reveals discontinuities and fissures in that construction – rather than polemic or general critique, is the venue of this offering.[48] Put another way, Foucault's oft-rehearsed argument on behalf of the 'specific' rather than 'universal' intellectual appears now as an argument rooted in the singular powers of genealogy to bring into relief critical dimensions of the present. Foucault's jettisoning of metaphysical critique in favour of local genealogical criticism seems, then, less hinged to the dominations metaphysical critique reiterates than to the distance such critique fails to achieve from the constitutive terms of its own time. Recall that for Foucault, political efficacy is 'not a matter of emancipating truth from every system of power (which would be a chimera . . .) but of *detaching the power of truth from the forms of hegemony* – social, economic and cultural – within which it operates at the present time'.[49]

Political Rationality   This term in Foucault's work is related to what he first named 'episteme' and then 'discourse' yet it also functions differently from both. Rationality, as Foucault reworks it from Weber, designates the legitimating discursive structure of any political order; governmental rationality is precisely that which releases governments from the need to use instrumental violence. Thus, political rationality does not, as for Weber, legitimize or 'cover' violence, but replaces violence as a mode of governance; rationality *is* itself a modality of power. 'The government of men by men . . . involves a certain type of rationality. It doesn't involve instrumental violence.'[50] As we saw in the discussion of *Polizeiwissenschaft*, 'policing' – conventionally understood as an instance of explicit state violence – is reconfigured by Foucault as a mode of rationality. *Polizeiwissenschaft* involves detailed application of detailed knowledge to specific relationships, and is quite different in character from the brute threat of a nightstick.

It is because Foucault opposes rationality and power to force and violence that he speaks of *rationality* rather than rationalization, of *governmentality* rather than government: 'The main problem when people try to rationalize something is not to investigate whether or not they conform to principles of rationality, but to discover which kind of rationality they are using.'[51] Thus, 'the criticism of power wielded over the mentally sick or mad cannot be restricted to psychiatric institutions; nor can those questioning the power to punish be content with denouncing prisons as total institutions. The question is: how are such relations of power rationalized?'.[52]

While Foucault sometimes uses political rationality to refer to the discursive logics legitimating all regimes of power, from asylums to schools to monarchies, he also uses the term to specify a particular form of government prevailing in the modern West which 'first took its stand on the idea of pastoral power, then on . . . reason of state'.[53] In this second usage, political rationality names the unique political form yielding the simultaneous processes of individualization and totalization that is Foucault's signature critique of modernity. This political form has its roots in the historical accident of an imbrication of emerging state power with pastoral power: 'If the state is the political form of a centralized and centralizing power, let us call pastorship the individualizing power.'[54] Foucault does not mean to suggest that the individualizing and totalizing mechanisms comprising modern state power were easily woven together. Rather, his genealogy of modern political power is intended in part to show the initially antagonistic relationship between the evolution of the state's centralizing powers and 'the development of power techniques oriented towards individuals and intended to rule them in a continuous and permanent way'.[55] 'Political rationality' marks the resolution of this antagonism into the governmental form of the policing or policy-state: 'Just to look at nascent state rationality, just to see what its first policing project was, makes it clear that, right from the start, the state is both individualizing and totalitarian'.[56]

Regardless of whether Foucault is speaking of political rationality as a proper or improper noun, he deploys it to call attention to the limited effect of any resistance or critique that attacks the effects of a particular rationality rather than the scheme as a whole. In this regard, political rationality may be seen as replacing the notion of 'the system' in political thinking which seeks to reach beyond epiphenomenal injustices in order to criticize the grounds of those injustices:

> . . . Those who resist or rebel against a form of power cannot merely be content to denounce violence or criticize an institution. Nor is it enough to cast the blame on reason in general. *What has to be questioned* is the form of rationality at stake. . . . Liberation can only come from attacking . . . political rationality's very roots.[57]

Yet it is precisely the difference between a 'rationality' and a 'system' that is significant in Foucault's reformulation of the political and that prevents this seemingly foundational account from being so. For unlike the coherently bounded, internally consistent (or internally contradictory) and relatively ahistorical figure of a system, a rationality cannot be apprehended through empirical description or abstract principles, nor can it be falsified through general critique. Political rationalities are orders of reason, not systems of rule; hence what must be captured for them to be subject to political criticism is their contingent nature, a contingency that can only be articulated through genealogy. Similarly, the exploitable weaknesses in a political rationality are not systemic contradictions, but rather, effects of fragmented histories, colliding discourses, forces that prevailed without triumphing, arguments insecure about themselves. Such weaknesses cannot be exploited through philosophical critique that remains internal to or unaware of the terms of a particular rationality. Genealogical critique aims to reveal various rationalities as the ones in which we live, to articulate them *as* particular forms of rationality. This articulation allows us to call into question the terms of political analysis from outside those terms as well as discern the historically produced fissures in their construction. Hence Foucault's remark, 'the history of various forms of rationality is sometimes more effective in unsettling our certitudes and dogmatism than is abstract criticism'.[58]

Sundering Genealogical Discoveries from Political Prescription Where modernist conventions of radical political critique are oriented towards systems and their contradictions, Foucault argues for articulating the political rationalities constitutive of the present. Similarly, where modernist conventions of radical political normativity consult history either for images of alternatives to the present (what Foucault disparagingly terms 'a history of solutions') or to discern 'laws of history' that determine the present and future, Foucault argues for discerning political possibility – 'the space of freedom' – in 'lines of fragility in the present'. In refusing totalizing logics to history and political life, in replacing logics of history with notions of randomness, accident and battle, and in replacing a notion of political systems with political rationalities, Foucault refigures the relationship between the history of the present, the nature of the present and political possibilities in the present. History is figured less as a stream linking past and future than as a cluttered field of eruptions, forces, emergences. As discontinuities lack of directional laws in history are pressed to the foreground, history is spatialized – conceptually wrenched from temporal ordering – and the political possibilities of the present are thereby expanded.

In his effort to locate power in space and not only in time, Foucault both highlights space as the domain of battle and brings into focus the organization of space as itself a tactic of power, for example, the Panopticon. Put another way, Foucault seeks to interrupt analyses of the transformations of discourse that operate in the vocabulary of time (and their invariable anthropomorphizing of history according to a model of individual human development) with a *geography* of power.[59] 'Anyone envisaging the analysis of discourses solely in terms of temporal continuity would inevitably be led to approach and analyse it like the internal transformation of an individual consciousness. Which would lead to his erecting a great collective consciousness as the scene of events.'[60] In this formulation, Foucault explains why teleology rather than, for example, devolution attends historiographies attached to time as a prime-mover. By contrast,

> . . . to trace the forms of implantation, delimitation, and demarcation of objects, the modes of tabulation, the organisation of domains mean[s] throwing into relief . . .

processes – historical ones, needless to say, of power. The spatialising description of discursive realities gives on to the analysis of related effects of power.[61]

Foucault's 'ontology of the present' is not merely a different way of casting the historical conditions in which contemporary practices transpire, but a different way of casting those conditions as the stage for potential political invention and intervention. If history does not have a course, it does not bear a prescriptive relation to the future; the 'weight' and contours of history establish limits but not norms for political action. '[Genealogy's] designation or description of the real never has a prescriptive value of the kind, "because this is, that will be . . .".'[62] If history is without logic, it bears no logical entailments; there is no inference to be made from it about what is to be done or what is to be valued. As history is emancipated from metaphysics and so becomes radically desacralized, so also does politics become a matter of opportunity, limits and judgement rather than unfolding historical schemes and transcendent ideals. Politics must grapple with logics of power rather than logics of history; it must develop strategies to combat entrenched regimes of rationality rather than orders of reason.

As genealogy severs the links between 'origins' and contemporary aims and purposes, so also does it aim to sever critique from prescription.[63] (This is not the same as the impossible project of de-linking critique and norms.) The radical political value of genealogy is its effect in calling into question the most heavily naturalized features and encrusted relations of the present, its effect in exposing as a consequence of power what is ordinarily conceived as divinely or naturally ordained. Yet while genealogy aims to render as an effect of power what hides behind timelessness for its legitimacy and unassailability, what is done with that *exposé* is a matter of political taste and political timing. Hence Foucault's general unwillingness to say what is to be done about punishment, sexual regulation or the treatment of the mentally ill at the conclusion of his studies of these issues. Put another way, Machiavelli becomes the exemplary theorist of political alliance and political action in the discursive political space opened by genealogy. For Machiavelli, history teaches how to recognize political openings, but what is done with those opportunities is a matter of desire, imagination, skill and luck.

*

> . . . there is a very tenuous 'analytic' link between a philosophical conception and the concrete political attitude of someone who is appealing to it; the 'best' theories do not constitute a very effective protection against disastrous political choices . . .[64]

In suggesting that the politics of Foucault's thinking are the politics enabled by genealogy, I am challenging the notion that his particular political positions (variously termed anarchist, libertarian, conservative or neo-liberal) and enthusiasms (May 1968, prison reform, sexual de-regulation, the Cambodian 'boat people', the Iranian revolution) are the necessary outcome of genealogical studies or genealogical consciousness. A genealogical politics has no necessary political entailments; rather, it affords a particular kind of discursive space for political thought and judgement, and for political interventions, which is precisely a space free of the notion of necessary entailments. Often considered a failing from a perspective in which legitimate political positions must flow directly from the endpoint of 'objective' or 'systematic' political critiques, genealogy refuses this ruse and features instead the forthrightly contingent vehicles of desire, attachment, judgement, and alliance as the spirit of political positions and positioning.

Genealogy thus carves features of political space in an image parallel to its critique of conventional political and historical premises. Just as it is opposed methodologically to progressive accounts of history, unitary engines of history and essential subjects of history, it affords a post-progressivist politics, a post-unitary politics and a post-identity politics, yet does so without prescribing their replacements. This is especially the case since genealogy does not oppose these things on moral or political grounds, but rather, generates a discursive political space in which they are called into question.

In so far as genealogy contests a linear, progressive historical narrative, genealogical politics cannot deduce any necessary perspectives or future outcomes from any condition in the present. Rather, the present and its genealogy are grasped as the limiting conditions of political intervention and invention, not the governors of it. Similarly, as genealogy contests a unified course of history with a map of 'haphazard conflicts' and a 'profusion of entangled events', genealogical politics abandons the notion of a single party and a single direction for political opposition or political envisioning. And, as genealogy problematizes essentialized feelings, sentiments, bodies and subjects by insisting that everything has a history, by reading all of these as historical effects, genealogical politics eschews any tight connection between the production of particular identities on one hand and particular political positions or values on the other. An 'ontology of the present' does not confuse itself with ontologically grounded politics. Indeed, an ontology of the present could be precisely that which productively disrupts or 'cuts' the tight relation between constructions of identity and normative political claims within a contemporary political rationality.

The politics of Foucault's body of political, philosophical and genealogical studies, I am suggesting, should not be linked to or infered from Foucault's explicit political values, views or attachments. The latter are a matter of contingent predilection; the political work his philosophical thinking can be made to do is relatively detachable from that predilection and could be attached to others. Should this be a source of political anxiety for Left intellectuals? To the contrary: once the radical contingency of political views and judgements is avowed, it is possible to depoliticize the theoretical enterprise without thereby rendering it apolitical. It becomes possible to distinguish between the political possibilities that a certain body of theory affords, the political uses to which it can be put, the political positions of the theorist, and a particular political deployment of the theory. *Political* truth is then no longer sought within a particular theory, but is, rather, that which makes an explicit bid for hegemony in the political realm. And theory may be allowed a return to its most productive place as, *inter alia*, an interlocutor of that domain.[65]

Notes

1 By 'modernist', I mean to circumscribe features of modernity in the West that contrast not merely with what has been attributed to that which is problematically declared 'after' it, but 'before' and culturally 'outside' it as well. The politics of the Age of Enlightenment might be a more precise nomenclature for this act of circumscription, except for its tendency to accent Reason.

2 Michel Foucault, 'On the genealogy of ethics: an overview of work in progress', in P. Rabinow (ed.), *The Foucault Reader* (Pantheon, New York, 1984), p. 343.

3 In 'Genealogy of ethics' Foucault argues: '. . . you can't find the solution of a problem in the solution of another problem raised at another moment by other people. You see, what I want to do is not the history of solutions, and that's the reason why I don't accept the word *alternative*. I would like to do the genealogy of problems, of *problematiques*' (p. 343).

4 Michel Foucault, 'Nietzsche, genealogy, history,' in Rabinow (ed.), *Foucault Reader*, p. 80.

5 Ibid., p. 80.

6 Ibid., p. 83.

7 Ibid., p. 87.

8 Ibid., p. 81.

9 Ibid.

10 Ibid.

11 Ibid., p. 87.

12 Ibid., p. 82.

13 Ibid., p. 87.

14 Ibid.

15 Ibid., p. 83.

16 Ibid.

17 Ibid., pp. 85.

18 Ibid.

19 'Prison talk', *Power/Knowledge: Selected Interviews and Other Writings 1972–1977*, trans. C. Gordon (Pantheon, New York, 1980), p. 50.

20 Foucault, 'Nietzsche, genealogy, history,' p. 85.

21 Ibid., p. 85.

22 Ibid., p. 84.

23 Ibid., p. 86.

24 Ibid.

25 Ibid., p. 88.

26 Ibid., p. 88–9.

27 'The art of telling the truth', in L. Kritzman (ed.), *Michel Foucault: Politics, Philosophy, Culture* (Routledge, London, 1988), p. 95.

28 Ibid., p. 87.

29 'Critical theory/intellectual history' and 'The art of telling the truth', both in Kritzman (ed.), *Politics, Philosophy, Culture*, p. 36 and p. 95.

30 In 'What is Enlightenment?' Kant writes, 'If we are asked "Do we now live in an enlightened age?" the answer is "No", but we do live in an *age of enlightenment*. As things now stand, much is lacking which prevents men from being, or easily becoming, capable of correctly using their own reason in religious matters with assurance and free from outside direction. But, on the other hand, we have clear indications that the field has now been opened where men may freely deal with these things. . . .'. *Foundations of the Metaphysics of Morals*, 2nd edn, trans L.W. Beck (Macmillan/Library of Liberal Arts, New York, 1990).

31 Foucault, 'Critical theory/intellectual history', p. 36.

32 Foucault, 'Nietzsche, genealogy, history', p. 89.

33 Ibid., p. 87.

34 Ibid., p. 88.

35 Ibid., p. 90.

36 Foucault, 'Politics and reason', in Kritzman (ed.), *Politics, Philosophy, Culture*, p. 71.

36 Colin Gordon, 'Governmental rationality: an introduction', *The Foucault Effect* (University of Chicago Press, Chicago, 1991), p. 10.

38 Foucault, 'Politics and ethics: An Interview', in Rabinow (ed.), *Foucault Reader*, p. 375.

39 Foucault, 'Politics and reason', pp. 77–9.

40 Colin Gordon, 'Governmental rationality', p. 10.

41 Ibid.

42 Foucault, 'Politics and reason', p. 77.

43 Ibid., p. 79.

44 Foucault, 'Nietzsche, genealogy, history', p. 89.

45 Ibid.

46 Foucault, 'Critical theory/intellectual history', p. 36.

47 Ibid.

48 Foucault, 'Polemics, politics, and problematizations', in Rabinow (ed.), *Foucault Reader*, p. 381.

49 'Truth and power', in *Power/Knowledge*, p. 133 (emphasis added). For his general argument on behalf of the 'local' or 'specific' intellectual, see pp. 126–33.

50 Foucault, 'Politics and reason', p. 84.

51 Ibid., p. 59.

52 Ibid., p. 84.

53 Ibid., p. 85.

54 Ibid., p. 60.

55 Ibid.

56 Ibid., p. 84.

57 Ibid., pp. 84–5 (emphasis added).

58 Ibid., p. 83.

59 On Foucault's effort to spatialize power, see, of course Michel Foucault, *Discipline and Punish* (Vintage Books, New York, 1979), but also 'Questions on geography', pp. 69–71, and 'The eye of power', pp. 149–51, both in *Power/Knowledge*.

60 Foucault, 'Questions on geography', p. 69.

61 Ibid., pp. 70–1.

62 Foucault, 'Critical theory/intellectual history', p. 37.

63 In *The Genealogy of Morals*, trans. Walter Kaufmann (Vintage Books, New York, 1989), Nietzsche writes, 'the cause of the origin of a thing and its eventual utility, its actual employment in a system, lie worlds apart; whatever exists, having somehow come into being, is again and again reinterpreted to new ends, taken over, transformed, and redirected . . .' (p. 77).

64 Foucault, 'Politics and ethics', p. 374.

65 I have elaborated this point in 'Toward a genealogy of political moralism', in T. Keenan and K. Thomas (eds), *Democracy, Community, and Citizenship* (Verso, forthcoming).

3

Politics and Liberation

Barry Hindess

> Political rationality has grown and imposed itself all throughout the history of Western societies. It first took its stand on the idea of pastoral power, then on that of reason of state. Its inevitable effects are both individualisation and totalisation. Liberation can only come from attacking, not just one of these two effects, but political rationality's very roots.[1]

Here, in the final paragraph of Foucault's Tanner Lectures, the idea of liberation is invoked in opposition to that of political rationality, a counter-position in which the term 'political' could almost be replaced by 'governmental'. This usage, in which 'political' rationality refers to a rationality of government, appears throughout Foucault's discussions of government and its rationalities, and it is characteristic of the literature inspired by this aspect of Foucault's later work.[2] However, the term 'liberation' is not without political connotations of its own. Foucault's counter-position of liberation to political rationality can also be seen as expressing a 'political' standpoint which is opposed to the 'political' rationality of government in the modern West. A few lines before the passage quoted above, for example, Foucault invokes a 'political criticism' which condemns the state for both its individualizing and its totalizing effects. Thus, while he frequently uses 'political' in the sense of 'governmental', there are also passages in Foucault's later work in which 'political' is employed in a strongly anti-governmental sense.

This chapter examines these two contrasting usages of 'political' in Foucault's work and their relationships to his conception of liberation. Foucault's second, anti-governmental, usage of 'political' is particularly interesting in the light of his own critique of the utopian pretensions of much progressive politics. For all the force of that critique, we shall see that there are points at which Foucault's radical alternative displays utopian pretensions of its own. Indeed, I argue that there is a sense in which a certain utopianism is characteristic of political discourse. Thus, while it may be possible, as many of Foucault's comments suggest, for political critique to go beyond progressive utopias derived from the fantasies of the European Enlightenment, any such manoeuvre will rest on the implicit or explicit invocation of an utopia of another kind. There can be no 'political' critique of political reason that does not itself partake of the character of 'political' discourse.

Political as Governmental

I began this chapter with an extract from Foucault's Tanner Lectures, 'Omnes et Singulatim: towards a criticism of political reason'. The 'political reason' invoked here is clearly that of government, but it is a reason which is governmental in a very particular sense. First, and most obviously, the term 'political' refers us not to the government of oneself or of one's household, but rather to the government of a state or a community. But there is a second, more complex, qualification to the identification of the political with the governmental which should be noted here. A few pages before the passage quoted above, Foucault insists that Aquinas's 'model for rational *government* is not a *political* one'[3] – apparently on the grounds that Aquinas derives the order of government by analogy with the order of nature ordained by God. Aquinas's model is not *political*, it seems, because it recognizes no distinctive rationality of government. This suggests that 'political' refers not simply to a rationality of government, but rather to what Foucault sometimes describes as an 'autonomous' rationality of government – that is, a rationality which is thought to be intrinsic to the nature of the state, and which cannot therefore be derived from the interests and desires of whatever secular or spiritual figure happens to rule the state at any given time. Consider, for example, Foucault's comment on the anti-Machiavellian writers who aimed to distance themselves 'from a certain conception of the art of government which . . . took the sole interest of the prince as its object and principle of rationality'. In its place 'they attempted to articulate a kind of rationality which was intrinsic to the art of government, without subordinating it to the problematic of the prince and his relationship to the principality of which he is lord and master'.[4] Their aim, in other words, was to articulate a *political* rationality of government that was distinct from what, in a different usage of the term, might reasonably be called the *political* rationality of the Prince. It is the rationality of government here which Foucault identifies as political, not the rationality of the Prince. Foucault goes on to argue that, while the *idea* of an autonomous art of government is clearly present in this anti-Machiavellian literature, such an art could not be properly developed while 'the institutions of sovereignty were the basic political institutions and the exercise of power was conceived as an exercise of sovereignty'.[5] His claim is that the political rationality of the Prince, and of the various surrogates of the Prince, served as an obstacle to the development of an autonomous political rationality of government. For that development, Foucault maintains, we have to wait until the eighteenth century.

The dependence of this 'political reason' on the conception of an 'autonomous' art or rationality of government is significant here, first, because it focuses on the interests, or the welfare, of the state and of the community which is ruled by the state, and it seeks to understand those interests in their own terms. Political reason, in other words, addresses practical questions of how best to manage the population of the state and the institutions, organizations and processes which that population encompasses, without reference to overarching imperatives that might be thought to derive from the distinctive interests of a secular or spiritual ruler or indeed from requirements laid down by God.

Foucault claims that the development of such a rationality was initially blocked by a focus on problems of sovereignty. He also insists that such a focus has continued to inhibit the analysis of government in political theory. 'We need to cut off the King's head: in political theory that has still to be done.'[6] Foucault's own discussions of the political rationality of government pay particular attention to pastoral power and to liberalism. He presents pastoral power as involving a relationship between ruler and ruled which is more intimate, and more continuous, than would be allowed by any understanding of government in terms of the rights and obligations of citizenship.[7] Pastoral power is concerned more with the welfare of its subjects than with their liberty. Foucault's discussion of pastoral power in the Tanner Lectures, and especially his contrast between the discourse of pastoralism and that of citizenship, might seem to suggest that the former is particularly responsible for the individualizing aspects of the political rationality of government in the modern period. In fact, however, liberalism as Foucault describes it can also be seen as embodying individualizing tendencies, particularly as a consequence of its focus on the formation of 'free' subjects who can normally be relied on to govern their own behaviour in some appropriate manner.[8]

This political rationality's focus on the state and the community ruled by the state is significant, secondly, for its difference from what, in another common usage of the term, might be called the political rationality of individual or sectional interests. It is in this quite different sense of political, for example, that Weber proposes to identify action as 'politically oriented': 'if it aims at exerting influence on the government of a political organisation; especially at the appropriation, redistribution or allocation of the powers of government'.[9] Political action in Weber's sense is not always to be identified with the work of government itself. It might also be undertaken by those who regard themselves as having little or no influence on government and who aim, as they might see it, to improve their situation in this respect. To adopt this Weberian usage, then, is to say, contrary to Foucault's normal usage of these terms, that *political* rationality should not necessarily be identified as a rationality of *government*: it might also be concerned, for example, with the question of how best to influence the work of government or how best to take it over.

In addition to the political rationality of the Prince, Weber's proposal invites us to consider as 'political' the rationality of the party or the movement – and, of course, of the individuals who seek to lead or to influence them. The possibility of behaviour that might be regarded as political in this factional sense clearly requires that the persons concerned have some room for manoeuvre. Action or rationality which is *political* in Weber's extended understanding of the term, then, is something that can be attributed only to members of the political unit whose behaviour is in some important degree free from direct government control: political action, in this sense, is an activity of free persons.

I have discussed elsewhere the significance of Foucault's neglect of such political action for his account of the political rationality of government.[10] What should be noted here is that, just as the exponents of the art of government established a sense in which the rationality of the Prince could be seen as subverting the proper conduct of government, so they also established a legacy in which the political rationality of the party or movement could be represented in similar terms. Thus, the idea of an autonomous art or rationality of government prepares the ground for an influential view which sees politics as a threat to good government.[11] Whenever politics is thought to play an important part in the affairs of a community we should expect to find that the rationality of government is far from being regarded simply as 'autonomous' in Foucault's sense. It will also be seen as in danger of corruption by the political rationality of faction – if not as having already been corrupted.

Political as Anti-governmental

Now consider the more radical usages of the term 'politics' in Foucault's work. At one point in the interview 'Politics and the Study of Discourse' (originally published in 1968) Foucault raises a series of questions about the nature of progressive politics. Is it

> tied (in its theoretical reflexion) to the themes of meaning, origin, constituent subject, in short, to all the themes which guarantee in history the inexhaustible presence of a Logos, the sovereignty of a pure subject, the deep teleology of a primeval destination? Is progressive politics tied to such a form of analysis – rather than to one which questions it?[12]

The rest of the interview elaborates on Foucault's negative answer to these questions.

In practice, as Foucault's rhetorical questions clearly suggest, there is a strong case to be made for the contrary view. The greater part of what has been understood as progressive politics does seem to rest on exactly the positions which Foucault here explicitly rejects, and his work has often been criticized by progressive writers for precisely this reason.

This is not the place to consider the vicissitudes of the idea of progressive politics. Let me just note that, while the term itself hardly appears in Foucault's later work, echoes both of the 'progressive' ideas which Foucault appears to deny, and of his negative reaction to those ideas, can be heard at significant points in many of his essays, lectures and interviews. I have already referred to Foucault's invocation, in the penultimate paragraph of his Tanner Lectures, of a 'political criticism' which, he tells us, 'has reproached the state with being simultaneously a factor for individualisation and a totalitarian principle'.[13] Similarly, in 'The Subject and Power' he maintains 'that the *political*, ethical, social, philosophical problem of our days is not to try to liberate the individual from the state . . . but to liberate us both from the state and from the type of individualization which is linked to the state'.[14]

Given its bearing on the idea of liberation, it is clear that, in such passages, 'political' can hardly be read as meaning 'governmental'. What Foucault has in mind in this usage of the term has to be seen in two distinct but related contexts. One concerns his treatment of the ideal of emancipation from the effects of power, an ideal which has played such an important part in enlightenment thinking and in subsequent understandings of progressive politics. Foucault has little patience with that ideal. His account of power and its effects undermines any conception of a generalized human emancipation of the kind proposed by critical theory – and critical theorists have naturally picked on this issue as one of their major objections to Foucault's work.[15] If, as Foucault argues, power is unavoidable, there is no point in postulating an imaginary condition of emancipation from its effects as a viable normative ideal.

Emancipation from particular systems of power, or from the effects of the employment of particular techniques of power, is another matter entirely. Foucault certainly suggests that such limited and specific emancipations might well be regarded as desirable in some cases. For example, after insisting that 'the historical ontology of ourselves must turn away from all projects that claim to be global or radical', Foucault goes on to say:

> I prefer the very specific transformations that have proved to be possible in the last twenty years in a certain number of areas that concern our ways of being and thinking, relations to authority, relations between the sexes, the way in which we perceive insanity or illness; . . .[16]

The most that such reforms can hope to achieve is to substitute one set of powers for another. There is no sense in which they can be seen as participating in any universalistic process of emancipation from the effects of power as such. Nevertheless, in spite of his explicit refusal of the universalistic discourse of emancipation, there are significant passages, especially in his interviews and shorter essays, in which Foucault's treatment of states of domination – that is, 'what we ordinarily call power'[17] – seems to resurrect many of critical theory's traditional concerns. At the end of 'The Ethic of Care for the Self as a Practice of Freedom', for example, he identifies the critical function of philosophy with 'precisely the challenging of all phenomena of domination'. He goes on to claim that this function emerges from the imperative to 'Be concerned with yourself, i.e., ground yourself in liberty . . .'.[18] Now consider his comment earlier in the same interview that:

> relations of power are not something bad in themselves, from which one must free one's self. . . . The problem is not of trying to dissolve them in the utopia of a perfectly transparent communication, but to give one's self the rules of law, the techniques of management, and also the ethics, the *ethos, the practice of self which would allow these games of power to be played with a minimum of domination.*[19]

Foucault does not object to relations of power in which things could easily be reversed or to hierarchical practices of pedagogy based upon superior knowledge – provided, of course, that the pupils are not subjected to 'the arbitrary and useless authority of a teacher'.[20] In another of his interviews he distinguishes between the Greek view of friendship, which is a matter of reciprocity, and their ethics of pleasure . . . . linked to a virile society, to dissymmetry, exclusion of the other, an obsession with penetration, and a kind of threat of being dispossessed of your own energy and so on. All that is quite disgusting![21]

These and other such comments plainly suggest that Foucault regards domination as an evil to be avoided as far as possible. His concern is not only with the impact of domination on the liberty of the dominated, but also with the condition of those who seek to dominate. The problem, he insists, is to 'give one's self . . . the techniques of management' that will result in 'a minimum of domination'.[22] Without necessarily endorsing the classical Greek account of care for the self in its entirety, Foucault clearly sympathizes with the view that 'if you care for yourself correctly . . . then you cannot abuse your power over others'.[23] In fact, both the counter-position of liberty to domination and the idea that there are costs to oneself in the attempt to dominate others are familiar refrains in Western political thought. Foucault's sentiments in this area are ones that will be widely shared – especially by supporters of a more traditional style of progressive politics.

The second context in which Foucault's more radical usage of the term 'politics' has to be understood is that of technologies of the self. These have a history which goes back considerably further than the modern project of emancipation. This is the import of his claim in 'The Subject and Power' that 'we have to refer to much more remote processes [than the Enlightenment] if we are to understand how we have been trapped in our history'.[24] The *political* problem here is to help us to escape from the traps of our history, and especially from those that can be traced to the 'more remote processes' which Foucault goes on to consider in the later volumes of *The History of Sexuality*. Since the ways in which we have been trapped in our history also affect our understandings of politics, Foucault insists that

> I have especially wanted to question politics, and to bring to light in the political field, as in the field of historical and philosophical investigation, some problems that had not been recognized there before. . . . I am attempting . . . to open up problems that are as concrete and general as possible, problems that approach politics from behind . . .[25]

What is at issue in this problematization of politics 'from behind' is set out in the closing lines of Foucault's Dartmouth lectures:

> Maybe our problem now is to discover that the self is nothing else than the historical correlation of the technology built in our history. Maybe the problem is to change those technologies. And in this case, one of the main political problems would be nowadays, in the strict sense of the word, the politics of ourselves.[26]

The technologies referred to in this passage are those of the hermeneutics of the self. Foucault is concerned, first, with technologies which have emerged out of early Christianity, and in fact out of its transformation of earlier Greek and Roman technologies (mostly, he suggests, in connection with the Christian insistence on the sacrifice of the self). He is concerned, secondly, with later Western attempts to constitute an alternative ground for the subjectivity of the self. In Foucault's view, the desire to establish a positive hermeneutic of the self in place of the sacrificial hermeneutic invoked by Christianity has been 'one of the great problems of Western culture'.[27]

This desire is at the heart of the conception of 'progressive politics' which Foucault presents as insufficiently radical. Our problem as inheritors of Western culture is not primarily to develop an alternative to the technologies associated with Christian hermeneutics of the self – along the lines, say, of the Enlightenment and its successors. Indeed, the implication of Foucault's discussion is that, far from representing liberation from the effects of domination, the Enlightenment and post-Enlightenment ideal of individual human autonomy should be seen as one of domination's most influential effects. Our problem, rather, is to displace both Christian and secular technologies of the self, and the images of the self which they have generated, and in particular, 'to get rid of the sacrifice that is linked to those technologies'.[28]

The Metaphor of the *Polis*

The more radical but relatively infrequent usage of the term 'political' in Foucault's work, then, concerns a project of liberation, both from practices of domination which impose on the liberty of others and from technologies of the self which we have been taught to impose on our own liberty. How does this usage relate to the more conventional usages of the term identified above? I have argued elsewhere that most if not all modern conceptions of politics can be seen as based on metaphorical extensions or elaborations of the idea of politics as having to do with the affairs of the *polis*. It would take too long to develop this general argument here.[29] This section aims, instead, to show that the conceptions of politics involved in Foucault's various usages of the term are no exception to this general rule, thereby preparing the ground for a brief, concluding discussion of Foucault's relationship to Enlightenment and post-Enlightenment radicalism.

I begin by noting that the metaphor of the *polis* offers both a sense in which the 'political' and the 'governmental' should be regarded as equivalent and, at least under certain conditions, a sense in which they could be seen as distinct. For the Greek citizens of the independent city-states, politics simply is the affairs of the *polis*, and there is no place for a distinction between the activity of collective self-government and political action in the Weberian sense considered above. This identification of the political and the governmental clearly rests on the idea of the *polis* as a self-contained unit of a very distinctive kind – that is, as a unit consisting of individuals who are able to participate in the affairs of the *polis* as autonomous agents. However, it is not difficult to see how that same identification of the political and the governmental could be extended to other relatively self-contained units governed by laws (including 'customary' laws), whether or not they possess a *polis* or its equivalent. 'Politics' in this extended sense can then be seen as referring to the government or control of such units.[30] It is in something like this latter sense that Foucault writes of 'political reason'.

Adapting the metaphor in a somewhat different fashion, politics can also be seen, in the Weberian sense, as action oriented towards the conduct of government. I noted earlier that political action which is not itself governmental in this sense can be attributed only to members of a political unit whose actions are in some important degree free of direct control by government. Citizens of a *polis* will be free in the relevant sense. However, since the metaphor of the *polis* presents citizens as both governors and governed, it will not necessarily lead us to make any clear distinction between the governmental and the political. This further step requires a use of the metaphor which nevertheless allows a distinction between the collective actions of free persons and the actions of their government.

What makes this last distinction possible is the development of the modern conception of the state as a discrete set of institutions, distinct from the life of the ruler or rulers of the political community.[31] In particular, this development underlies the perception of *politics* as the distinctive activity of government, separable from other aspects of public life. This is precisely the sense of 'politics' in which Foucault can describe Aquinas's model of rational government as 'not political':[32] it is not political because, at least as Foucault presents it, Aquinas's model recognizes no distinctive rationality of government. Where the rulers of the state are its citizens, the conception of the state as a distinctive set of institutions suggests a sense in which the public life of citizens is nevertheless distinct from the work of government. In this respect, the development of the modern conception of the state as a discrete set of institutions gives rise to the more general understanding of *politics* as an activity of citizens which may or may not be directly governmental. This development also makes possible the subsequent emergence of the idea of civil society and of the economy as elements of public life distinct from both the governmental and political spheres. While Foucault's work on governmentality focuses on the emergence of these latter conceptions, there is an important sense in which he pays little attention to the emergence of politics itself.

On the other hand, this conception of the state as a discrete set of institutions also suggests a view of the ruled as comprising, at least in principle, a relatively stable population and territory – that is, as a territorial community existing independently of its subjection to some particular ruler or rulers. In this respect, the development of the concept of the state can be seen as a precondition of those new forms of political rationality which Foucault sees emerging in parts of Western Europe during the seventeenth century: the concern for the welfare and security of the population – as distinct from, and sometimes in contrast to, that of the ruler; the generalization of discipline throughout society; and the governmental adoption of the model of pastoral power.[33] Here, too, the combination of the metaphor of the *polis* with the modern conception of the state gives a distinctive character to the understanding of government: it is the government of a community consisting of (at least some) autonomous persons and having a political life that is not entirely subject to the government's (that is, the state's) control.

The second feature of the metaphor of the *polis* to be noted here is that the understanding of 'political' as referring to the affairs of the *polis* involves a corresponding view of the non-political. The boundaries of the political sphere distinguish the citizen from the non-citizen, and the public life of the individual as citizen from other aspects of the citizen's existence. The latter distinction implies that, while citizens may be subject to the laws and to other decisions of the *polis*, they also have a life which is not wholly determined by the *polis*. They have, in other words, an independent base in their non-public life which enables them to participate in the life of the *polis* as autonomous persons. Government of the *polis*, if it is not to appear to be tyrannical, must be experienced by such individuals both as a kind of *collective* decision-making and as a matter of *individual* self-government – with both the individual and the collective acknowledging the constraints imposed by the other. This, of course, is a familiar refrain in modern political thought.

This distinction between the political and the non-political is one source of modern demarcations, between public and private. The most important point to notice here is that this distinction also sustains a markedly ambivalent perception of the *polis* and consequently of politics itself.[34] Not only will there be different views as to where precisely the boundary between the political and the non-political should lie, but there will always be those who regard it as presently lying in the wrong place – and whatever boundary may be presumed to exist it can hardly be regarded as entirely secure.[35] On the one hand, this suggests that the autonomy of the citizen may be perceived as being in danger of subversion – if not as already having been subverted – by political action. This is the source of what Foucault describes as the political criticism of the state as a 'factor for individualisation'. It is always a criticism of an individualization which is seen as an imposition advanced in the name of another kind of individualization which is not seen as an imposition.

On the other hand, the political sphere may be perceived as being in danger of corruption by the invasion of concerns that properly belong elsewhere. The problem here is seen as arising, not so much from the existence of individual desires and interests, as from the intrusion of those desires and interests into public life. Such intrusion is often seen as tending in the direction of tyranny, that is, as leading to the expansion of governmental power beyond its proper limits. This perception of the state as involving a 'totalitarian' principle is the source of the other reproach which political criticism, as Foucault describes it, has directed against the state.

To the extent that either of these lines of criticism can be said to suggest the possibility of a remedy, it is one that can be found only in 'politics' itself: either in a politics which regards the defence of the citizen from undue governmental interference and the defence of politics against corruption as among the central responsibilities of government, or in anti-political politics which aims to purge public life of the corrupting effects of politics. This last view is often associated with the inversion of the traditional perception of politics as in danger of corruption to produce the materialist understanding of politics as the corrupt reality itself.[36] From this perspective, politics just *is* the pursuit of sectional interests and the claim of disinterest will itself be seen as just another kind of corruption.

My final point in this section concerns the mimetic character which is an ubiquitous, if insufficiently remarked, feature of all political discourse.[37] This means, in particular, that political unities are commonly treated as if they had the character of *representations* – that is, they are presented as reproductions of a model or ideal, which is often itself based directly or indirectly on some imagined past or present reality. Striking examples here are the use of classical models in the debates over the drafting of the American constitution and in the discourses of the French Revolution, the later uses of those events as sources of further models, and the use of remarkably idealized models of Western society in contemporary programmes of modernization or democratization. Here, too, it is interesting to refer to Aquinas's model of rational government, which Foucault presents as 'not political'. I have noted a sense in which Foucault's comment is entirely apposite. But there is another sense in which Aquinas's view, that the order of government should be modelled on the order of nature ordained by God, can be seen as an excellent example of the mimetic character of political discourse. Since I have emphasized the metaphorical significance of the *polis* for all modern conceptions of politics, perhaps I should also say that the mimetic character of politics should not be regarded simply as arising from the modern use of that metaphor. Politics in its earliest sense, as the affairs of the *polis*, also has a clearly mimetic character. The affairs of the *polis* include practices of inclusion and exclusion, both of persons and of behaviours – which is to say that a significant part of the life of the *polis* consists in the effort to make both the *polis* and its members conform to ideal images of what they should be. While the *polis* may not require the 'sacrificial hermeneutic' of the self, which Foucault locates particularly in the development of Christianity, it nevertheless involves its own images and technologies of the human individual. In this respect, the *polis* too can be seen as imposing its share of sacrifices, not only on women and slaves, but also on the citizens themselves.[38] As for the modern period, when, as Foucault tells us, 'political criticism has reproached the state with being simultaneously a factor for individualisation and a totalitarian principle',[39] we should remember that it has always done so in terms of alternative images of how things should be. In effect, one set of mimetic projects is disputed in the name of other mimetic projects which are regarded as superior.

Conclusion

These points have taken us somewhat away from the understandings of politics entailed in Foucault's own usages of the term, but they will, I hope, have shown something of the variety of distinct and sometimes conflicting usages of 'politics' and cognate terms to be found in the modern period. There is no core meaning of 'politics' to which all of the various usages should be expected to conform, and it is not always a sign of confusion on the part of an author if distinct and conflicting usages appear in the one text. The following usages are commonplace in modern political discourse:

> political as governmental or, as in Weber, pertaining to government – and, as a variation on this, politics as a threat to good government; politics as a corruptible if not already corrupted sphere of public life; politics as creative project aiming at the purification of society – and of politics in particular – usually through the reproduction of a model or ideal based directly or indirectly on some imagined past or present reality; and, especially for Enlightenment and post-Enlightenment intellectuals, politics as a project of purification through the creation of some approximation to a self-governing community of free persons.

The last of these is at the heart of most varieties of 'progressive politics', and even of Foucault's more radical usage of the term 'politics'. The fundamental difference here between Foucault and those who cling more directly to the Enlightenment heritage concerns the question of individualization. Foucault's questioning of Christian, and later Western, technologies of the self has the effect of portraying the free persons posited in Enlightenment radicalism as individuals who have internalized the means of their own domination. These autonomous persons have each learned to give the law to themselves while, as in Kant's imaginary social contract, they also give up their 'external freedom in order to receive it back at once as members of a commonwealth, i.e. of the people regarded as a state'.[40]

While Foucault's treatment of power undermines the utopian pretensions of much progressive politics, there are nevertheless points in his interviews and shorter essays which seem to propose an alternative critical standpoint. This critical politics offers the prospect of liberation both from the domination imposed on us by others and from the domination we have each been taught to impose on ourselves. As part of this project, Foucault regards it as necessary to free us also from the illusion of freedom under which the Enlightenment presents its favoured modes of domination. In many respects, this rejection of the Enlightenment view of freedom resembles Foucault's earlier, Nietzschean account of history as an 'endlessly repeated play of domination', each of which

> is fixed, throughout its history, in rituals, in meticulous procedures that impose rights and obligations . . . the law is a calculated and relentless pleasure, delight in the promised blood, which permits the perpetual instigation of new dominations and the staging of meticulously repeated scenes of violence. . . . Humanity does not gradually progress from combat to combat until it finally arrives at universal reciprocity, where the rule of law finally replaces warfare; humanity installs each of its violences in a system of rules and thus proceeds from domination to domination.[41]

And yet Foucault also seems to hold out a prospect of liberty.

I have insisted on the mimetic character of political discourse, and Foucault's occasional invocation of the absence of domination as an ideal on which to base a critical 'politics' is no exception. Relations of power will still be present under such conditions but, in the absence of domination to hold them in place, they will be unstable and reversible.

Foucault, of course, maintains that the Greeks should not be taken as a model, finding them neither 'exemplary nor admirable'.[42] Nevertheless, it is clear that, again like Nietzsche and so many others before him, Foucault does return to the Greeks in the hope of finding 'an original form of thought . . . outside of Christian phenomena'.[43] Those who return to the Greeks in this way have generally sought to appropriate the aspects of Greek society of which they approved, and to discard the aspects of which they did not approve. In this respect, Foucault follows a well-worn tradition. His anodyne portrayal of power relations in the absence of domination reproduces his equally anodyne account of the Greek ideal of friendship – according to which, in contrast to their ethics of pleasure, relations between individuals should be based on reciprocity. But it does without the appalling forms of domination on which the Greek citizens' cultivation of friendship so obviously depended.

The utopian character of such a project is clear enough. But, if my point about the mimetic character of politics is correct, we should be careful not to pretend, as Foucault sometimes does, that this utopianism is something that can be avoided. There can be no political critique which does not exhibit this most characteristic feature of political discourse.

Notes

1 Michel Foucault, 'Omnes et singulatim', *The Tanner Lectures on Human Values*, Vol. II, S.M. McMurrin (ed.) (Cambridge University Press, London, 1981), p. 254.

2 G. Burchell, C. Gordon and P. Miller (eds), *The Foucault Effect: Studies in Governmentality* (University of Chicago Press, Chicago, 1991); M. Dean, *The Constitution of Poverty. Toward a Genealogy of Liberal Governance* (Routledge, London, 1991); P. Miller and N. Rose, 'Political power beyond the state: problematics of government', *British Journal of Sociology*, 43, 2 (1992), pp. 173–205; A. Barry, T. Osborne and N. Rose (eds), *Foucault and Political Reason: Liberalism, Neo-Liberalism and Rationalities of Government* (University College of London Press, London, 1966).

3 Foucault, *Tanner Lectures on Human Values*, p. 244 (emphasis added).

4 Foucault, 'Governmentality', in Burchell et al. (eds), *Foucault Effect*, p. 89.

5 Ibid., p. 97.

6 Michel Foucault, 'Truth and power' in *Power/Knowledge* (Harvester Wheatsheaf, Brighton, 1980), p. 121.

7 Foucault, *Tanner Lectures on Human Values*. Cf. B. Hindess, *Discourses of Power: From Hobbes to Foucault* (Blackwell, Oxford, 1996).

8 B. Hindess, 'Liberalism, socialism and democracy: variations on a governmental theme', *Economy and Society*, 22, 3 (1993).

9 M. Weber, *Economy and Society: An Outline of Interpretative Sociology* (University of California Press, Berkeley, 1978), p. 55.

10 B. Hindess, 'Politics and governmentality', *Economy and Society*, 26, 2 (1997).

11 Consider, for example, the discussion of faction in *The Federalist Papers* #10: 'a number of citizens, whether amounting to a majority or minority of the whole, who are united and actuated by some common impulse of passion, or of interest, adverse to the rights of other citizens, or to the permanent and aggregate interests of the community'. Madison's aim in this paper is to show how government can be protected from the politics of faction.

12 Michel Foucault, 'Politics and the study of discourse', in Burchell et al. (eds), *Foucault Effect*, pp. 64–5.

13 Foucault, *Tanner Lectures on Human Values*, p. 254.

UNIVERSITY OF HERTFORDSHIRE LRC

14   Michel Foucault, 'The subject and power', in H.L. Dreyfus and P. Rabinow (eds), *Michel Foucault: Beyond Structuralism and Hermeneutics* (Harvester Wheatsheaf, Brighton, 1982), p. 216 (emphasis added).

15   The arguments here have been widely rehearsed, most clearly perhaps in Nancy Fraser, 'Foucault on modern power: empirical insights and normative confusions', in *Unruly Practices* (University of Minnesota Press, Minneapolis, 1989), T. McCarthy, 'The critique of impure reason: Foucault and the Frankfurt School', in T.E. Wartenberg (ed.), *Rethinking Power* (State University of New York Press, Albany, 1992) and C. Taylor, 'Foucault on freedom and truth', in *Philosophy and the Human Sciences* (Cambridge University Press, Cambridge, 1992). For excellent discussions of the issues here see P. Patton, 'Taylor and Foucault on power and freedom', *Political Studies*, xxxvii, 2 (1989) and P. Patton, 'Foucault's subject of power', *Political Theory Newsletter*, 6, 1 (1994).

16   Michel Foucault, 'What is Enlightenment?', in P. Rabinow (ed.), *The Foucault Reader* (Penguin, Harmondsworth, 1986), pp. 46–7.

17   Michel Foucault, 'The ethic of care for the self as a practice of freedom', in J. Bernauer and D. Rasmussen (eds), *The Final Foucault* (MIT Press, Boston MA, 1988), p. 19.

18   Ibid., p. 20. Compare his commentary on Kant's 'What is Enlightenment?' in which critique is described as 'seeking to give new impetus . . . to the undefined work of freedom' in Foucault, 'What is Enlightenment?'.

19   Ibid., p. 19.

20   Ibid. The implication here is that the 'useful' authority of the teacher is not to be classed among the practices of domination. For a sceptical view of this issue see my 'Great expectations: freedom and authority in the idea of a modern university', *Oxford Literary Review*, 17 (1995).

21   Michel Foucault, 'On the genealogy of ethics: an overview of work in progress', in Rabinow (ed.), *Foucault Reader*, p. 346.

22   Foucault, 'Ethic of care', p. 18.

23   Ibid., p. 8.

24   Foucault, 'Subject and power', p. 210. The same passage appears in 'Omnes et Singulatim' at p. 226. Notice that for Foucault, as for so many Western commentators, 'our history' is the history of 'our' civilization. It goes back, in other words, to the Romans and the Greeks.

25   Michel Foucault, 'Politics and ethics: an interview with Paul Rabinow, Charles Taylor, Martin Jay, Richard Rorty, and Leo Lowenthal', in Rabinow (ed.), *Foucault Reader*, p. 375.

26   Michel Foucault, 'About the beginning of the hermeneutics of the self', *Political Theory*, 21, 2 (1993), pp. 222–3.

27   Ibid.

28   Ibid., p. 227, n. 53.

29   B. Hindess, 'Polities without politics: anti-political themes in Western political discourse', in A. Schedler (ed.), *The End of Politics? Explorations into Modern Antipolitics* (Macmillan, Basingstoke, 1997); B. Hindess, '"The Greeks had a word for it": the *polis* as political metaphor', *Thesis Eleven*, 40 (1995).

30   The play between these two identifications of the political and the governmental underlies the somewhat disparaging perception of certain societies as political units which may nevertheless be regarded as pre- or non-political. What is thought to be missing in such cases is precisely the political life of the *polis*, collective self-government as an activity of free and more or less rational persons. Political units have been said to be without politics in this sense, either because their inhabitants are regarded as unfree or because they are thought to be governed by custom and tradition, rather than by the collective decisions of autonomous persons. Moses Finley's decision to exclude Rome under the emperors from his discussion of politics in the ancient world is an example of the first case. See M. Finley, *Politics in the Ancient World* (Cambridge University Press, Cambridge, 1983), p. 52. It is hardly necessary to give examples of the second.

31   For the emergence of this conception of the state, see Q. Skinner, 'The State', in T.J. Farr Ball and R.L. Hanson (eds), *Political Innovation and Conceptual Change* (Cambridge University Press, Cambridge, 1989).

32   Foucault, *Tanner Lectures on Human Values*, p. 244.

33   Michel Foucault, *Discipline and Punish* (Penguin, London, 1979); Foucault, *Tanner*

Lectures on Human Values; Foucault, 'Governmentality'.

34 In fact, the significance of these boundary relations between the political and the non-political is further complicated by the development of the modern idea of the state as a distinctive institutional form. I noted above that this development gives rise to a number of distinct understandings of politics and the political. In place of a simple distinction between the political and the non-political, we have to reckon with insecure demarcations between three spheres: the political or governmental; the civil or public; and the private – and therefore with a correspondingly greater variety of views as to the sources and consequences of corruption.

35 Farrar, for example, cites (and disputes) the Greek view that the *polis* boundary between citizen and non-citizen on the one hand and between the political and the non-political life of citizens on the other cannot ensure the exclusion of 'the primitive, the chaotic, the visceral (the slavish and womanish) from civic life', C. Farrar, 'Ancient Greek political theory as a response to democracy', in J. Dunn (ed.), *Democracy: The Unfinished Journey 508 BC to AD 1993* (Cambridge University Press, Cambridge, 1992), p. 29.

36 Compare the treatment of changing perceptions of politics in the early-modern period in M. Viroli, *From Politics to Reason of State: The Acquisition and Transformation of the Language of Politics, 1250–1600* (Cambridge University Press, Cambridge, 1992).

37 But see the treatment of political discourse by Miller and Rose as 'a domain for the formulation and justification of idealised schemata for representing reality, analysing it and rectifying it', Miller and Rose, 'Political power beyond the state', p. 178.

38 D.M. Halperin, 'The democratic body: prostitution and citizenship in classical Athens', in his *One Hundred Years of Homosexuality and Other Essays on Greek Love* (Routledge, New York, 1989); J.J. Winkler, 'Laying down the law: the oversight of men's sexual behaviour in classical Athens', in D.M. Halperin, J.J. Winkler and F. Zeitlin (eds), *Before Sexuality: The Construction of Erotic Experience in the Ancient Greek World* (Princeton University Press, Princeton NJ, 1990).

39 Foucault, 'Governmentality', p. 254.

40 I. Kant, extracts from *The Metaphysics of Morals*, in *Political Writings*, H. Reiss (ed.) (Cambridge University Press, Cambridge, 1970), p. 140.

41 Michel Foucault, 'Nietzsche, genealogy, history', in D. Bouchard (ed.), *Language, Counter-Memory, Practice: Selected Essays and Interviews by Michel Foucault* (Cornell University Press, Ithaca NY, 1977), pp. 150–1.

42 Michel Foucault, 'The return of morality', in L. Kritzman (ed.), *Michel Foucault: Politics, Philosophy, Culture* (Routledge, London, 1988), p. 244.

43 Ibid.

Part II

ETHICS AND THE SUBJECT OF POLITICS

4

Foucault's Subject of Power

Paul Patton

> Three centuries ago certain fools were astonished because Spinoza wished to see the liberation of man, even though he did not believe in his liberty or even in his particular existence. Today, new fools, or the same ones reincarnated, are astonished because the Foucault who had spoken of the death of man took part in political struggle.[1]

Criticism of Foucault returns constantly to two themes: first, his descriptive analyses of power provide us with no criteria for judgement, no basis upon which to condemn some regimes of power as oppressive or to applaud others as involving progress in human freedom. As Nancy Fraser puts this objection,

> Because Foucault has no basis for distinguishing, for example, forms of power that involve domination from those that do not, he appears to endorse a one-sided, wholesale rejection of modernity as such. . . . Clearly, what Foucault needs, and needs desperately, are normative criteria for distinguishing acceptable from unacceptable forms of power.[2]

Secondly, critics complain that he offers no alternative ideal, no conception either of human being or of human society freed from the bonds of power. The lack of recourse to any philosophy of the subject is often taken to explain the political weakness of Foucault's position: thus, Habermas argues that it is because there is no conception of the properly human subject in his work that Foucault is left with only the 'arbitrary partisanship of a criticism that cannot account for its normative foundations'.[3] For such critics, Foucault offers only a bleak political horizon on which the subject will always be an effect of power relations, and on which there is no possibility of escape from domination of one sort or another. For others, such as Ian Hacking, the problem is not so much that Foucault is pessimistic, it is that 'he has given no surrogate for whatever it is that springs eternal in the human breast'.[4]

Despite the anti-humanism of Foucault's approach, I wish to argue that his work does presuppose a conception of human being, and that he does offer a surrogate for hope. After all, his analyses of knowledge, power and sexual ethics are concerned with these modalities of cultural experience in so far as they affect *human* social being. These analyses are undertaken with the aim of producing critical effects upon present ways in which social reality is understood. In the absence of some such belief, Foucault's characterization of these studies as contributions to political struggles against individualizing technologies of power[5] would be paradoxical, along the lines suggested by Deleuze's remark quoted above. Foucault's analogue to the transcendental freedom which grounds Kant's belief in the possibility of human progress is an historical conception of human powers and capacities. Given what they have become, human beings will resist attempts to set limits to the autonomous use and development of their powers.

It is true that Foucault makes no use of the traditional humanist forms of critique. He argues that when philosophers invoke 'man' as the basis for their moral and political judgements, they invoke no more than their own or others concepts of human nature, which are themselves the products of particular, historically constituted regimes of truth. His refusal to rely upon concepts of an essential human nature is evident in his reluctance to use terms such as 'ideology' or 'liberation'. Nevertheless, his genealogies do presuppose a conception of the human material upon which power is exercised, or which exercises power upon itself. This human material is active; it is composed of forces or endowed with certain capacities. As such it must be understood in terms of power, where this term is understood in its primary sense of capacity to do or become certain things. This conception of the human material may therefore be supposed to amount to a 'thin' conception of the subject of thought and action: whatever else it may be, the human subject is a being endowed with certain capacities. It is a subject of power, but this power is only realized in and through the diversity of human bodily capacities and forms of subjectivity. Because it is a 'subject' which is only present in various different forms, or alternatively because the powers of human being can be exercised in infinite different ways, this subject will not provide a foundation for normative judgement of the kind that would satisfy Fraser or Habermas: it will not provide any basis for a single universal answer to the question, 'Why ought domination to be resisted?'.[6] However, the theory of power which frames this conception of the human subject does provide a means to distinguish domination from other forms of power. Moreover, given certain minimal assumptions about the nature of human being, and about the particular capacities which human beings have acquired, Foucault's conception of the subject does provide a basis on which to understand the inevitability of resistance to domination.

Foucault's Subject of Power

In *Discipline and Punish* and *The History of Sexuality Vol. 1*, Foucault describes strategies of power whose object or target is primarily the human body. Contrary to the view of critics such as Peter Dews, this body is no mere inert matter upon which power is exercised and out of which 'subjects' are created.[7] It is a body composed of forces and endowed with capacities. In *Discipline and Punish*, it is precisely in order to dress these bodily forces that the techniques of discipline are deployed. In *The History of Sexuality Vol. 1*, the body which has come to be constituted as the bearer of a sex, during the course of European history, is a body explicitly described as one capable of pleasures. The strategy of pedagogic control of children's enjoyment of such pleasures is one essential moment in the elaboration of the modern 'experience' of sexuality; the classification of adult pleasures into normal and pathological is another. The two other grand strategies which Foucault discusses involve specific capacities of the female body, chiefly those connected with reproduction and childbirth. The elaboration of what we have come to take for granted as human 'sexuality' thus may be understood to have involved a certain classification, ordering and finalization of this range of capacities for being and doing certain things. It is precisely because there is nothing natural about this construction, and because it was fabricated upon an active body, a body understood in terms of primary capacities and powers, that it was accompanied by resistance. The same is true of the disciplined body.

How did so many critics manage to overlook this conception of the body as subject of power? Perhaps because Foucault's writings during the 1970s tended to employ a neutral language of bodies and forces in place of the traditional terminology of political critique. Power relations were characterized in terms of conflict or alliance between forces, engendered on the basis of 'the moving substrate of force relations'[8] which constitutes the social field. Because it avoided any reference to human agents or agency, this language seemed to de-humanize the social field which it described. Nevertheless, Foucault sought to address the kinds of historical phenomenon which would ordinarily be regarded as the effects of human agency by means of an impersonal, non-subjectivist language of strategy and tactics. 'Strategy' referred to the operationalization of the social field in particular ways, such as the attempt to produce an orderly, obedient and productive population; 'tactics' referred to the disposition of forces employed to achieve strategic ends. In later discussions, such as 'The Subject and Power', Foucault appears to revert to a more familiar language of human agency: power relations are said to arise whenever there is *action upon the actions of others*.[9] In other words, power relations are conceived here not simply in terms of the interaction of impersonal or inhuman forces, but in terms of action upon the action of 'free' agents. However, 'free' means no more than being able to act in a variety of ways: that is, having the *power* to act in several ways, or not being constrained in such a fashion that all possibilities for action are eliminated. Here, too, the subject of power is a 'subject' in both senses of the term: a being endowed with certain capacities or possibilities for action and subjected to power relations.

Nor are these two ways of conceptualizing power relations as different from one another as they might at first appear. Ordinarily, what distinguishes an action from a mere bodily movement is the fact that it is voluntary rather than involuntary motion, and that it is intended to serve some purpose. Actions are intentional, goal-oriented movements or dispositions of bodily forces. Strategies are likewise intentional, goal-oriented movements or dispositions of forces. Strategies need not be the work of a single strategist, but can just as well be the product of more or less collective processes of calculation. Nothing that Foucault says about the subject of power suggests that human agency is in principle radically different. Nothing commits him to a voluntarist rather than a Hobbesian or a Nietzschean notion of the will.

But Foucault is committed to the view that social relations are inevitably and inescapably power relations. On his view, there is no possible social field outside or beyond power, and no possible form of interpersonal interaction which is not at the same time a power relation: 'to live in society is to live in such a way that action upon other actions is possible – and in fact ongoing. A society without power relations can only be an abstraction.'[10] This view is sometimes taken to imply that domination is inevitable, according to Foucault, or that there is no possibility of progress in human affairs in the sense that social relations may become less oppressive. Such conclusions are based upon misunderstanding Foucault's use of the concept of power. One source of confusion is the failure to make the necessary distinctions between power, power over and domination. In his later discussions of power, Foucault does make these distinctions explicit, and in doing so refutes the charge that his approach is incapable of distinguishing forms of power that involve domination from those that do not.

Power and Domination

In order to make sense of Foucault's use of the term, 'power' must be understood in its primary etymological sense, as the capacity to become or to do certain things. Power in this primary sense is exercised by individual or collective human bodies when they act upon each other's actions; in other words, to take the simplest case, when the actions of one affect the field of possible actions of another. In this case, where the actions of A have succeeded in modifying the field of possible actions of B, we can say that A has exercised power over B.[11] 'Power over' in this sense will be an inescapable feature of any social interaction. Moreover, characterized in these terms, with reference only to Foucault's thin subject of power, it is a normatively neutral concept. It involves no reference to action against the interests of the other party. After all, there are many ways in which agents can exercise power over other agents, only some of which might be detrimental to the 'interests' of the one over whom power is exercised: I can affect the actions of another by providing advice, moral support, or by passing on certain knowledge or skills. All of these will involve the exercise of power over the other, but not necessarily in ways that the other will find objectionable.

The exercise of power over others will not always imply effective modification of their actions. Precisely because power is always exercised between subjects of power, each with their own distinct capacities for action, resistance is always possible: 'where there is power, there is resistance'.[12] For this reason, it is only in exceptional circumstances that A can be sure of achieving the desired effect on B. Only when the possibility of effective resistance has been removed does the power relation between two subjects of power become unilateral and one-sided:

> A relationship of confrontation reaches its term, its final moment (and the victory of one of the two adversaries) when stable mechanisms replace the free play of antagonistic reactions. Through such mechanisms one can direct, in a fairly constant manner and with reasonable certainty, the conduct of others.[13]

In such cases, we have something more than the exercise of power over another, namely the establishment of a state of *domination*: in these cases, 'the relations of power, instead of being variable and allowing different partners a strategy which alters them, find themselves firmly set and congealed'.[14] Bentham's Panopticon provides a model of such mechanisms for controlling the conduct of others: the asymmetrical structure of visibility which is the key to the architectural design maps on to the fixed asymmetrical distribution of power which defines every system of domination. Traditional family relations provide Foucault with another illustration of the same structure of fixed and asymmetrical power relations. Within the eighteenth- and nineteenth-century institution of marriage the wife was not entirely deprived of power. She could be unfaithful to the husband, steal money or refuse sexual access: 'She was, however, subject to a state of domination in the measure where all that was finally no more than a certain number of tricks which never brought about a reversal of the situation.'[15]

Foucault is not the first to identify domination with stable and asymmetrical systems of power relations. His definition does, however, make it clear that such systems are always secondary results, achieved within or imposed upon a primary field of relations between subjects of power. Moreover, as with the definition of 'power over', his concept of domination is non-normative. Domination allows more or less predictable control of the actions of others. Beyond that, little is said about the purposes for which such states are established and maintained. One frequent purpose served by states of domination is to enable some to extract a benefit from the activity of others: economic exploitation in all its forms, from slavery through to the system of extraction of surplus value which Marx identified as the secret of capital, depends upon such systems of domination. C.B. Macpherson coined the useful term 'extractive power' in order to describe the capacity that some people acquire to employ or make use of the capacities of others. He argues that the system of private property and a free market in labour operates as a mechanism for the continuous transfer of part of the power of the class of non-owners to the class of owners.[16] In Foucault's terms, the exclusive ownership of means of production amounts to a system of domination which underpins the extractive power of a social class.

However, while extractive power may always presuppose some system of domination, states of domination may occur in situations where the flow of capacities or benefits is non-extractive. For example, Hobbes presents the relation of subjects to sovereign power as one of domination, since the sovereign must have 'the use of so much Power and Strength conferred on him, that by terror thereof, he is inabled to forme the wills of them all, to Peace at home and mutuall ayd against their enemies abroad'.[17] In Hobbes's account, the relationship of domination which obtains between state and citizens is a condition of maintaining the rule of law. In this case, the transfer of power precedes domination since it is the conferral of power by parties to the social contract which constitutes sovereign power. The purpose of this system of domination is not further extraction but the enhancement of the powers of its subjects.[18]

Pedagogic relations are another sphere in which a measure of domination may be acceptable, at least during some part of the educational process. Foucault uses this example in order to suggest that asymmetrical power relations are not in themselves evil: 'The problem is . . . how you are to avoid in these practices – where power cannot not play and where it is not in itself bad – the effects of domination which will make a child subject to the arbitrary and useless authority of a teacher, or put a student under the power of an abusively authoritarian professor, and so forth.'[19] The qualifying clauses attached to the objectionable cases of domination in these remarks suggest that other 'effects of domination' may not be objectionable. This indeed appears to be Foucault's general position: the exercise of power over others is not always bad, and states of domination are not always to be avoided.

Resistance, Autonomy and Freedom

Foucault does believe that the fact of widespread resistance to forms of individualizing power is evidence of the need for 'a new economy of power relations'.[20] But what is meant by this phrase, and what is the basis for such a recommendation? In global terms, to call for a new economy of power relations is to invoke the possibility of a different articulation of the forms of social and political domination, the forms of reversible or non-coercive exercise of power over others, and individual or collective capacities. It implies that, contrary to the experience of European modernity, the enhancement of collective capacities need not be linked to increase of domination. At the individual level, a person's power to do or be certain things will also be the result of a certain 'economy', comprising relations to oneself, relations to others, and relations to forms of discourse and modes of thought which count as truth. These are in effect Foucault's three axes of subjectification, and they serve to remind us that a minimal concept of persons should refer to a body that is trained or cultivated in certain ways (subject to 'power'), a set of relations to oneself and one's capacities (an 'ethics'), and a set of relations to modes of interpretation of one's relations to self and others ('truth'). Different powers may result from change along any of these axes, or from changes in the larger networks of social relations within which these personal capacities are exercised.

Recommendations such as this bring us back to the problem of the lack of normative criteria in Foucault's work. To suggest as he does that we need new forms of articulation of personal capacity, power over others and mechanisms of domination appears to imply the possibility of principles which might legitimize one 'economy' of power relations as better than another. Could Foucault adopt such principles while remaining consistent with his theoretical anti-humanism? In fact, as the critics have argued, he does not and cannot provide such criteria. By confining himself to the very thin notion of human being as a subject of power, Foucault deprives himself of the means to provide such normative criteria. However, it does not follow from this that he has no basis upon which to distinguish between forms of power that involve domination and those that do not. Nor does it follow that Foucault's thin conception of human being cannot be filled out in a manner which explains both resistance to domination and the possibility of transforming existing economies of power. I suggest that Foucault does employ such a robust conception of human being in his later work. However, far from providing universal criteria which would allow us to distinguish acceptable from unacceptable forms of action upon the action of others, his approach exposes the limitations of the demand for such criteria. In order to show how it does this, it is helpful to pursue the comparison with Macpherson.

Macpherson contrasts his concept of extractive power with another concept which he calls 'developmental power'. The latter refers to an individual's ability to use and develop his or her 'essentially human capacities'. He then uses this concept in order to define a truly democratic society as one which maximizes the ability of all to use and develop their essentially human capacities. Leaving aside the question what capacities are to count among the 'essentially human', it is clear that the concept of developmental power has a normative content. In effect, it provides Macpherson with an ideal standard by which to judge the 'democratic quality' of any society. For he argues that the degree of developmental power can be measured by reference to the presence or absence of impediments to the use and development of human capacities by all members of the society. On this basis, he is able to show that the structure of social relations which gives one class extractive power in relation to another class is incompatible with maximizing the developmental power of those who are exploited in this way. More generally, Macpherson's concept of developmental-power democracy provides a moral basis on which to reject any system of domination which sustains a form of extractive power. Any such system necessarily sets limits to the ability of some individuals to use and develop their own powers.

In fact, Macpherson's principle of maximizing developmental power excludes a wider class of systems of domination than those which sustain forms of extractive power. Consider his concept of 'essentially human capacities': while he does provide a list of human capacities likely to be included among the essentially human (capacity for rational understanding; for moral judgement and action; aesthetic creation and contemplation, etc.), Macpherson is reluctant to specify a determinate set of capacities which define human being. In part, this is because he has a conception of human being as essentially capable of development. The concept of developmental power refers to the ability of individuals to use *and develop* their capacities. This implies that new capacities might be developed, or that existing ones might be developed in ways that cause revisions in what is considered to be essentially human. Macpherson writes: 'the full development of human capacities, as envisioned in the liberal-democratic concept of man – at least in its most optimistic version – is infinitely great. No inherent limit is seen to the extent to which . . . human capacities may be enlarged.'[21]

Foucault's conception of human being in terms of bodies (differentially) endowed with capacities for action is similarly open-ended. Following Nietzsche, he allows that new human capacities may come into existence as effects of forms of domination, only to then become bases of resistance to those same forms of domination. Deleuze takes this Nietzschean thought a stage further in suggesting that the forces which defined 'man' have already begun to connect with new, non-human forces: 'Spinoza said that there was no telling what the human body might achieve, once freed from human discipline. To which Foucault replies that there is no telling what man might achieve "as a living being", as the set of forces that resist.'[22] However, Foucault's analyses of the different ways in which human beings are made subjects expose one further form of domination which Macpherson does not address, perhaps because of his focus upon extractive power. Determinate forms of subject may arise as a result of historical processes not directly connected with extractive power, as Foucault argues with regard to modern sexuality in *The History of Sexuality Vol. 1*. Once established, such forms of subjectivity, or at least the forms of knowledge, social relations, legal and other administrative arrangements which sustain them, may amount to more or less fixed modalities of power over individuals. As such, they constitute impediments to the ability of some individuals to use and develop their human capacities in particular ways, notably those identified as abnormal or deviant in a social, medical or psycho-sexual sense. In this manner, the ways in which certain human capacities become identified and finalized within particular forms of subjectivity – the ways in which power creates subjects – may also become systems of domination.

In order to see that Macpherson is equally committed to including impediments such as these among the limits to developmental power, we need only consider the further capacity that he adds to his list of the essentially human capacities, almost as an afterthought. He suggests that the exercise of human capacities, 'to be fully human, must be under one's own conscious control rather than at the dictate of another'.[23] The loss of an individual's ability to use his or her energies humanly, 'in accordance with his [or her] own conscious design',[24] plays a significant role in his account of the power which is lost when individuals are forced to work under the control of others in order to exercise their capacity for productive activity. In effect, the capacity for relatively autonomous use and development of one's capacities is a meta-capacity, a means of directing and experiencing the exercise of the other capacities of a particular body or determinate subject. Examples of its employment might include inventing and regulating one's use of a different economy of pleasures, or self-consciously acquiring the attributes necessary to operate effectively in a given political environment. As these examples suggest, there is no reason to expect that such degrees of autonomy will be developed by individuals acting alone rather than in the context of movements for change in certain aspects of social life.

Foucault invokes the same meta-capacity for autonomous use and development of human powers in his characterization of the *ethos* of modernity in 'What is Enlightenment?'. Drawing on Kant's characterization of Enlightenment as a process voluntarily embarked upon by some and aimed at the removal of limits to the exercise of the human power of rational self-determination, Foucault describes 'modernity' as involving a similarly self-critical attitude towards our present forms of social being. Moreover, just as Macpherson suggests that increases in developmental power may be negatively measured by the removal of limits to its exercise, so Foucault's account implies that progress in this critical task may be measured by the degree to which present limits to what it is possible to do or be have been overcome. Criticism, both theoretical and practical he says, 'will be oriented toward the "contemporary limits of the necessary", that is, toward what is not or is no longer indispensable for the constitution of ourselves as autonomous subjects'.[25]

Modernity, understood as an ethos of permanent self-criticism, presupposes the existence of possible subjects of such activity. Such subjects will necessarily be free in the sense that their possibilities for action will include the capacity to undertake this self-critical activity which Foucault calls 'work carried out by ourselves upon ourselves as free beings'.[26] So long as human capacities do in fact include the power of individuals to act upon their own actions, we can see that Foucault's conception of human being in terms of power enables us to distinguish between those modes of exercise of power which inhibit and those which allow the self-directed use and development of human capacities. To the extent that individuals and groups acquire the meta-capacity for the autonomous exercise of certain of their own powers and capacities, they will inevitably be led to oppose forms of domination which prevent such activity.

In this appeal to human autonomy, Foucault affirms a belief in human freedom which appears to contradict his suspicion of modern humanism. How then does his position differ from that of humanists such as Macpherson, who treats the capacity for autonomous action as a defining property of essentially human being, or the Critical Theorists who advocate the commitment to autonomy as a universal moral ideal? This apparent contradiction disappears once we take into account two features of Foucault's position: first, the fact that the suspicion of humanism is motivated above all by mistrust of the attempt to set limits to human freedom. 'What I am afraid of about humanism is that it presents a certain form of our ethics as a universal model for any kind of freedom.'[27] Secondly, the fact that Foucault's appeal to a principle of autonomy is not grounded in a metaphysical conception of human being as essentially free but in an analytics of power. From at least 'The Subject and Power' onwards, Foucault suggests that freedom is the ontological precondition of politics and ethics. However, this is an historical rather than a transcendental ontology. Freedom here is not the transcendental condition of moral action, as it is for Kant, but rather the contingent historical condition of action upon the actions of others (politics) and of action upon the self (ethics). Just as for Foucault political power exists only in the concrete forms of government of conduct, so freedom exists only in the concrete capacities to act of particular agents. As a result, the subject of freedom is a subject of power in the primary sense of that term.

In this perspective, autonomy must be understood as a capacity to govern one's own actions which is acquired by some people, in greater or lesser degree, and in respect of certain aspects of their bodies and behaviour. However it has been acquired and in whatever manner it is distributed, this capacity for autonomous action is sufficient to explain resistance to forms of domination. To the extent that domination enables the direction of the actions of others, or even simply establishes more or less fixed limits to the ways in which human capacities may be exercised, then states of domination will always constitute limits to the autonomy of those subject to them. In the attempt to exercise their capacity for autonomous action, those subject to relations of domination will inevitably be led to oppose them. It is not a question of advocating such resistance, of praising autonomy or blaming domination as respective exemplars of a good and evil for all, but simply of understanding why such resistance does occur. Foucault does not think that resistance to forms of domination requires justification. To the extent that it occurs, such resistance follows from the nature of particular human beings. It is an effect of human freedom.

Power and Agency

The fact that human beings have acquired this capacity at all presupposes the kinds of internal division within the self which Nietzsche saw as resulting from the human will to power turned back against its subject. The kinds of self-regulation of one's own body and its sexual relations with others described in *The Use of Pleasure* are evidence of the existence of such autonomy, however partial and restricted in scope. The freedom of the subjects of the Greek ethics of moderation and self-mastery was, Foucault suggests, more than just an emancipation from external or internal constraint: 'in its full, positive form, it was a power that one brought to bear on oneself in the power that one exercised over others'.[28] Here, as in many places, Foucault's language recalls the Nietzschean origins of his conception of human being in terms of power. On the basis of his theory of will to power, Nietzsche provides elements of a complex theory of human agency. Taking Nietzsche as a model therefore provides a useful guide to some background assumptions of Foucault's later writings on the subject and power, and suggests ways in which his thin conception of the subject of power might be expanded into a more robust theory of human agency.

Earlier, I suggested that the root concept of Foucault's concept of power is the notion of capacity. For bodies with the complexity and specific powers of human beings, power is the capacity for various kinds of *action* upon oneself and others. The kinds of action of which a human body is capable will depend in part upon its physical constitution, in part upon the enduring social and institutional relations within which it lives, but also upon the frameworks of moral interpretation which define its acts. Moral interpretations of phenomena are among the most important means by which human subjects act upon themselves and others: it is by such means that one can arouse pity in others, or experience one's own actions as cowardice or humility according to whether one lives in the moral culture of ancient Greece or European Christianity. By examples such as these, Nietzsche draws attention to the interpretative dimension of human action. The systems of knowledge and moral judgement which Foucault studied in relation to mental illness, punishment and sexuality are no less elements of the interpretative frameworks within which Europeans have acted upon the action of others. In this sense, Foucault's history of systems of thought involves a thought which 'can and must be analyzed in every manner of speaking, doing or behaving in which the individual appears and acts as subject of learning, as ethical or juridical subject, as subject conscious of himself and others. In this sense, thought is understood as the very form of action. . . .'[29]

However, the peculiarity of human action is that it is not only conscious but self-conscious: we are happy or sad according to whether our actions produce a feeling that our power is enhanced or a feeling that it is diminished. In other words, our own actions, and the actions of others upon us, produce affective states and these affective states in turn affect our capacity to act. In effect, there is a feedback loop between the success or otherwise of one's attempts to act and one's capacity to act. Nietzsche drew attention to the importance of this self-reflective dimension of human action in insisting upon the primacy of the 'feeling of power' in his analysis of willing in *Beyond Good and Evil*: 'he who wills believes with a fair amount of certainty that will and action are somehow one; he ascribes the success, the carrying out of willing, to the will itself, and thereby enjoys the increase of power that accompanies all success'.[30] On the basis of such remarks, Mark Warren argues that Nietzsche's theory of the will to power must be understood primarily as an account of the conditions of the human experience of agency. This is an historical rather than an a priori account: given the emergence of self-consciousness in the human animal, and given the relative weakness of this animal, Nietzsche claims that the striving to achieve the feeling of power has become humankind's strongest propensity: 'the means discovered for creating this feeling almost constitute the history of culture'.[31] Nietzsche's historical account of the human experience of power also functions as an argument for the overriding importance of this experience. As Warren suggests, 'In being conscious and self-conscious, humans increasingly strive less for external goals than for the self-reflective goal of experiencing the self as agent.'[32] This has important consequences for our approach to politics: if the experience of autonomy depends upon the larger networks of practice and social relations within which individuals act, but also upon the interpretative frameworks in terms of which they judge the success or failure of their acts, then maximizing autonomy requires practices of government of self and others which effectively enhance the feeling of power.

Foucault's reliance upon the experience of limits to freedom as an indicator of areas in which social change is possible may be understood against the background of the interpretative and affective dimensions of agency as these are defined by Nietzsche. In 'The Subject and Power', Foucault takes as the starting point for the analysis of power relations the existence of resistance to current structures of domination: 'opposition to the power of men over women, of parents over children, of psychiatry over the mentally ill, of medicine over the population, of administration over the ways people live'.[33] No doubt, the fact of resistance provides evidence that there is a capacity for relatively autonomous action by individuals with respect to certain areas of social life. However, Foucault's 'thin' conception of human being as a subject of power provides only the conceptual minimum required to describe the capacities of particular situated, corporeal subjects. These will result from the techniques of formation applied to the bodies of such subjects, as well as from the social relations within which they live and act. In order to account for the experience of these systems of power as forms of domination, as limits to individuals' capacities for action, Foucault must presuppose the existence of particular forms of self-interpretation and the existence of something like the feeling of powerlessness. In other words, he must suppose a fuller conception of human subjectivity which takes into account both the interpretative and the self-reflective dimensions of human agency. Such a conception is needed in order to explain the feeling of power and the lack of a sense of agency that is so often recorded as part of the experience of oppression.

Finally, we should note that expansion of Foucault's conception of human agency in this manner leads him away from rather than towards normative criteria for distinguishing acceptable from unacceptable forms of power. For if we accept Nietzsche's claim that forms of moral judgement are among the most important means of self-interpretation, and his view that what is important for human beings is the experience of the feeling of power, or what Warren calls experiences of agency, then it follows that effective moral values are dependent upon the conditions of such self-experience. In other words, values are internal to types of individual and social being, not independent of them. That is why Foucault does not seek to provide universal moral norms or criteria of evaluation, but instead offers a cautious recommendation of the

Greek practice of an 'ethics of existence'.[34] This might be read as a proposal for a different economy of power with respect to our sexual being: an economy different from that of the ancient Greek men, for whom self-mastery and moderation in the use of pleasures was both conditioned by and predicated upon relations of domination over others, notably women and slaves; but also different from the modern regulation of sexual conduct by means of legal and other institutional obligations, and by means of discourses of truth about sexuality. It is a proposal for a non-universalizable ethics whose importance in the present context lies in the possibility that it might provide a 'practice of freedom' which enhances the feeling of power in a way which other liberated lifestyles do not. Foucault's problem is not that of formulating the moral norms that accord with our present moral constitution, but rather the Nietzschean problem of suggesting ways in which we might become other than what we are.

Notes

An earlier version of this paper was published in French in *Sociologie et Sociétés*, XXIV, 1 (April 1992), and in English in *Political Theory Newsletter*, 6, 1 (May 1994), pp. 62–73. For their helpful comments on earlier drafts, I am grateful to Moira Gatens, Barry Hindess and the anonymous readers for *Sociologie et Sociétés*.

1 Gilles Deleuze, *Foucault*, trans. Sean Hand (University of Minnesota Press, Minneapolis, 1988), p. 90.

2 Nancy Fraser, 'Foucault on modern power: empirical insights and normative confusions', in *Unruly Practices* (University of Minnesota Press, Minneapolis, 1989), pp. 32–3.

3 Jürgen Habermas, *The Philosophical Discourse of Modernity*, trans. Frederick G. Lawrence (MIT Press, Cambridge MA, 1987), p. 276.

4 Ian Hacking, 'The archaeology of Foucault', in David C. Hoy (ed.), *Foucault: A Critical Reader* (Blackwell, Oxford and New York, 1986), p. 40. Similar criticisms of Foucault are made by a number of the contributors to this volume, including Hoy, Walzer, Dreyfus and Rabinow and of course Habermas.

5 Michel Foucault, 'The subject and power', Afterword in H.L. Dreyfus and P. Rabinow *Michel Foucault: Beyond Structuralism and Hermeneutics*, 2nd edn (University of Chicago Press, Chicago, 1983), pp. 208–16.

6 Fraser, *Unruly Practices*, p. 29; cited approvingly by Habermas, *Philosophical Discourse of Modernity*, p. 284.

7 See Peter Dews, *Logics of Disintegration* (Verso, London, 1987), p. 156, where Foucault is represented as proposing 'that subjects are entirely constituted by the operation of power'; also Scott Lash, 'Genealogy and the body: Foucault/Deleuze/Nietzsche', *Theory, Culture & Society*, 2, 2 (1984); and Nancy Fraser, 'Foucault's body language: a posthumanist political rhetoric?', in *Unruly Practices*, pp. 55–66.

8 Foucault, *The History of Sexuality Vol. 1*, trans. Robert Hurley (Allen Lane, London, 1979), p. 93.

9 Foucault, 'Subject and power', p. 221.

10 Ibid., p. 222.

11 I have argued for the necessity of distinguishing between 'power to' and 'power over', in order to rescue Foucault's remarks on power from the charge of incoherence, in Paul Patton, 'Taylor and Foucault on power and freedom', *Political Studies*, XXXVII, 2 (June 1989).

12 Foucault, *History of Sexuality Vol. 1*, p. 95.

13 Foucault, 'Subject and power', p. 225.

14 Foucault, 'The ethic of care for the self as a practice of freedom', *Philosophy and Social Criticism*, 12, 2–3 (Summer 1987), p. 114.

15 Ibid., p. 123.

16 C.B. Macpherson, *Democratic Theory: Essays in Retrieval* (Clarendon Press, Oxford, 1973), essay III, 'Problems of a non-market theory of democracy'.

17 T. Hobbes, *Leviathan*, C.B. Macpherson (ed.) (Penguin, Harmondsworth, 1985), p. 227.

18 Barry Hindess points out the ambiguity of this transfer of power. In Hobbes's account, it is the authority to act which is transferred to the sovereign rather than effective power to govern. See *Discourses of Power: From Hobbes to Foucault* (Blackwell, Oxford, 1996), pp. 28–9.

19 Foucault, 'Ethic of care for the self', p. 129.

20 Foucault, 'Subject and power', p. 210.

21 Macpherson, *Democratic Theory*, p. 62.

22 Deleuze, *Foucault*, p. 93.

23 Macpherson, *Democratic Theory*, p. 56.

24 Ibid., p. 66.

25 Foucault, 'What is Enlightenment?', in P. Rabinow (ed.), *The Foucault Reader* (Penguin, Harmondsworth, 1986), p. 43.

26 Ibid., p. 47.

27 Foucault, 'Truth, power, self: an interview with Michel Foucault', in Luther H. Martin, Huck Gutman and Patrick H. Hutton (eds), *Technologies of the Self* (University of Massachusetts Press, Amherst MA, 1988), p. 15.

28 Foucault, *The Use of Pleasure*, trans. Robert Hurley (Pantheon Books, New York, 1985), p. 80.

29 Foucault, 'Preface to The History of Sexuality, Volume II', in Rabinow (ed.), *The Foucault Reader*, pp. 334–5.

30 Nietzsche, *Beyond Good and Evil*, trans. R.J. Hollingdale (Penguin, Harmondsworth, 1973), paragraph 19.

31 Nietzsche, *Daybreak*, trans. R.J. Hollingdale (Cambridge University Press, Cambridge, 1982), paragraph 23.

32 Mark Warren, *Nietzsche and Political Thought* (MIT Press, Cambridge MA, 1988), p. 138.

33 Foucault, 'Subject and power', p. 211.

34 Foucault, 'On the genealogy of ethics: an overview of work in progress', in Dreyfus and Rabinow (eds), *Beyond Structuralism and Hermeneutics*, pp. 229–37.

5

Foucault, Levinas and the Subject of Responsibility

Barry Smart

A rhetoric of responsibility, including pronouncements on the responsibility of agents of various kinds, in particular the responsibility of *human* agents or subjects for their actions or conduct, has become a prominent and controversial feature of the contemporary political agenda. But if the question of responsibility has become prominent in contemporary social and political discourse, associated ethical implications have rarely been given the consideration they warrant. The (ir)responsibilities of corporate and governmental agents for the production of risks with local and/or global implications have been identified as increasingly problematic features of a late or reflexive modernity, but the ethical dimension has, for the most part, remained implicit.[1] The erosion or dismantling of public and communal provision of health, education and welfare services associated with economic restructuring and the turn towards post-Fordist, flexible forms of capital accumulation is one of the contexts, if not, for some, *the* context, in which the idea, and the necessity, of individuals looking after themselves, making choices and thereby supposedly assuming more responsibility for their care and their fate has been increasingly advanced. Moreover, the implied distinction between 'public' and 'private' and the associated reality of a shift, or off-loading of responsibility from 'state' to 'private individual', is one of the themes currently preoccupying the modern polity. This transformation has led, as Bauman observes, to 'a hard time for moral responsibility; not only in its immediate effects on the poor and unfortunate who need a society of responsible people most, but also (and perhaps, in the long run primarily) in its lasting effects on the (potentially) moral selves. It recasts "being for Others", that cornerstone of all morality, as a matter of accounts and calculation'.[2] In circumstances where being has increasingly become identified with obtaining value for money, the self has effectively become a consumer and the prospect for exercising moral responsibility has diminished.

I intend to respond to the question of responsibility implied in the above by focusing on the ethical dimension, a dimension which a number of analysts contributing to the debate over the transformation of modernity have sought to retrieve;[3] but I want to do so through a reconsideration of Foucault's reflections on power, freedom and subjectivity. In a sense I will be trying to determine what, if anything, Foucault has to say on the subject of responsibility. Let me try to clarify the issues involved.

One of the key issues which has surfaced in discussions of the transformation of modernity is that of a relative shift of emphasis from a subsumption of the 'moral regulation of conduct . . . under the legislative and law-enforcing activity of global societal institutions' to a situation in which, rather than a singular authoritative source to which one can turn or appeal for guidance, agents increasingly encounter a 'pluralism of authorities' and in turn are required to take responsibility and make choices for their 'self-constitution'.[4] The undermining of the prospect of outlining universally binding rules of conduct for agents and the concomitant necessary 'resumption by agents of moral responsibility', identified as a corollary of the increasing pluralism of authority, has lead Bauman to conclude that ethical questions and problems can no longer be marginalized in the analysis of modern society.

It is precisely the identification of the human subject as a moral subject, as an active and creative subject, which has been identified as a significant and distinctive feature of Foucault's later writings and it is to a number of questions which arise in this context that I will be attempting to address my remarks. There are four main themes to which I will attempt to respond in the course of my discussion, namely:

1 Foucault's conception of the subject.
2 The distinction between 'political technology of individuals' and 'technologies of the self' introduced in discussion of the government of conduct.
3 The notion of 'care of the self' and the related conception of an 'aesthetics of existence'.
4 The question of the responsibility of the (moral) subject.

On the Question of the Subject

The late appearance in Foucault's work of an explicit address of the question of the subject has already been well documented.[5] Prior to Foucault's turn to the question of the subject, the focus of his work fell almost entirely upon the exercise of power through 'sovereignty-discipline-government'.[6] In a subsequent reconstitution of the project, Foucault acknowledges that, in the examination of the specific technologies related to 'truth games' employed by human beings to understand themselves, too much attention may have been devoted to technologies of domination and power, that is technologies which 'determine the conduct of individuals and submit them to certain ends'.[7] Foucault then adds that he is 'more and more interested in *the interaction between oneself and others* and in the technologies of individual domination, the history of how an individual acts upon himself, in the technology of self'.[8] The turn to the subject, and in particular the way in which 'a human being turns him or herself into a subject',[9] represents a belated compensation for the earlier neglect of the active subject, the ethical subject, in Foucault's work.

What does Foucault's later work, that is the texts, essays and interviews which emerge with his 'theoretical shift', tell us about his understanding of the subject? As I have implied above, in his work up to and including the first volume on *The History of Sexuality* the subject appears primarily as an effect of social practices of subjection. A constituting (and therefore potentially moral) subject is absent from Foucault's discourse at this stage. In the first volume on sexuality the issue of the constitution of forms of subjectivity is addressed, but it is through a consideration of objectifying confessional technologies in which the truth and meaning of the subject is communicated by an interpreter/therapist who is an 'other', albeit a significant one. If there is any consideration of the subject's self-constitution, it is in terms of the articulation of accounts, dreams and fictions which constitute discursive material for investigation and interpretation by others who reveal the 'truth' of the tales and thereby the 'truth' of the subject. And it is the silence over the question of the self-constituting practices of the subject which lead critics to equate a bleak politics of resignation with Foucault's work – no escape from domination and relations of power, resistance inevitably undermined, etc. And, as I have implied above, it is difficult not to regard Foucault's late re-direction of his project towards technologies of the self as a direct response to his critics.

Although Foucault says in the Vermont interview that he is more and more interested in 'the interaction between oneself and others', there are in practice few signs in his work of a serious consideration of social interaction, of the interactional contexts in which selves are constituted. In consequence, it is understandable that critics should have concluded that 'his ethics privileges a notion of the self establishing a relation with the self, rather than understanding the self as embedded in and formed through types of social interaction'.[10] The impression which emerges from Foucault's work is of self-constitution or self-stylization as a relatively solitary or isolated process. Where, we might ask, is the interactional context? Where is the interest in social interaction between oneself and others made manifest? And does an approach to the question of self-formation or self-stylization, which appears to neglect social interaction, provide a sound basis for the cultivation of a modern ethics of existence?

I am not implying here that the practices of the ancient Greeks constituted an attractive alternative for Foucault. Indeed, he comments that 'it is not anything to get back to',[11] yet there is a sense in which he appears to be arguing, as McNay comments, that 'they provide important insights for a modern ethics'.[12] In particular it is through reflection on the moral world of ancient Greece that Foucault reaches the conclusion that there is no necessary link between ethics and other social structures and that we can therefore 'create ourselves'.

Governing Conduct: From Political Technology of Individuals to Technologies of the Self

Notwithstanding the several attempts which have been made to read into Foucault's earlier works the concerns which receive an explicit address in the later writings, there is evidence of a significant change of analytic emphasis from a focus upon the government of individualization, achieved through political technology of individuals, to a consideration of technologies of the self 'which permit individuals to effect *by their own means or with the help of others* a certain number of operations on their own bodies and souls, thoughts, conduct, and way of being, so as to transform themselves in order to attain a certain state of happiness, purity, wisdom, perfection, or immortality'.[13]

Foucault's turn to questions concerning self-constitution follows a series of observations on struggles against the government of individualization – 'against forms of subjectivity and submission' – and constitutes an overdue attempt to offer clarification of the ambiguous notion of power. The clarification is significant because it introduces the notion of a 'free' subject – 'individual or collective subjects who are faced with a field of possibilities in which several ways of behaving, several reactions and diverse comportments may be realized'[14] – over whom power is exercised. But the clarification of power, specified as a 'set of actions upon other [possible] actions', or again as 'guiding the possibility of conduct and putting in order the possible outcome',[15] does not lead, at this point at least, to an equivalent consideration of the subject, enigmatically identified as possessing a recalcitrant will and as being intransigent about freedom. Indeed, Foucault admits to finding it necessary to undertake a theoretical shift 'to analyze what is termed "the subject" . . . the forms and modalities of the relation to self by which the individual constitutes and recognizes himself *qua* subject'.[16] And it is a shift through which the question of relations of power is reformulated as a question about government, a question about the leading, guidance or direction of conduct or action; a structuring of 'the possible field of action of others'.

But rather than resolve matters, Foucault's clarification of relations of power raises a series of further questions. Relations of power for Foucault are synonymous with sociality. Power is held to be always present in human relations, 'whether it be a question of communicating verbally . . . or a question of a love relationship, an institutional or economic relationship'.[17] Power relations are relations in which influence is exercised over the conduct of free subjects, and as Foucault puts it, 'only in so far as they are free'.[18] Subjects have the potential to block, change, overturn or reverse the relation of guidance, direction, influence, etc. Is there an implication here that the subject is, in part at least, responsible for his or her own fate, in so far as there is always the potential to transform a relation of power into an adversarial confrontation? And what of the responsibilities intrinsic to the exercise of power and relations of guidance and direction, the responsibilities which might be argued to be a corollary of actions which structure the field of other possible actions? It is not clear where Foucault stands on the question of the responsibility of the subject in this, or for that matter in any other sense. Indeed, it might be argued that there remains a significant silence in his work over the question of the extent to which the subject is or can be active and responsible, although his own practice as a politically active philosopher, as an engaged intellectual, and his brief reflections on intellectual practice, seem to tell a different tale. For example, in 'Truth and Power' and 'Questions of Method: An Interview' Foucault appears to be quite categorical about the responsibility of the contemporary intellectual subject. (Perhaps the more voyeuristic biographical details of his pursuit of pleasures tell another tale of a less responsible subject, a subject seemingly oblivious to the *ethos* of care of self and others.)[19]

Where the issue of the self-constitution of the subject through technologies of the self is addressed directly, Foucault is categorical – 'these practices are . . . not something that the individual invents by himself. They are patterns that he finds in his culture and which are *proposed, suggested, imposed on him by his culture, his society and his social group.*'[20] While such an observation may seem relatively uncontentious, it does leave open and unanswered the respect(s) in which subjects are, or can be, recognized as active and responsible, as opposed to being simply relays for the discharge of culturally given technologies of (self-)government. To be more precise, and to address directly one of Foucault's late preoccupations, is it really appropriate to talk of creating oneself, and if so, on what basis does it become possible 'to create oneself'? Foucault takes the view that 'the self is not given to us . . . [and] that there is only one practical consequence: we have to create ourselves as a work of art'.[21] It is through a process of reflection on similarities and differences between the Greek world and the modern West that the conclusion that the self is not given to us is reached. Foucault argues that some of our main ethical principles 'have been related at a certain moment to an aesthetics of existence' and that one important implication is that our assumption that 'an analytical or necessary link [exists] between ethics and other social or economic or political structures' is unfounded.[22] There are two points to be made here. First, Foucault's view is asserted rather than demonstrated. Secondly, the idea that there is no 'necessary link' does not mean that the constitution of the self as a moral subject of action can be considered free of social, economic or political structures. Foucault's own references to cultural practices which are proposed, suggested and imposed draw attention to, but neglect to analyse, the social context(s) in which forms of subjectivity are constituted and subjects participate, along with others, in processes of mutual self-development. An awareness of the formation of the self through social interaction is not entirely absent from Foucault's work. Brief reference, for example, is made to individuals transforming themselves through the help of others and attention is drawn to the importance in the development of care for self of the role of a counsellor, guide, friend, master, 'who will tell you the truth,'[23] but no attempt is made to elaborate on such references, to explore the non-reciprocal relationship with the Other which is at the very heart of social life, the ethical significance of which is anterior to relation with the self.[24]

A further qualification needs to be introduced at this point concerning Foucault's notion of the subject. The discussion of the subject offered by Foucault for the most part appears to be confined to considerations of the constitution of particular forms of subjectivity – mad, sick, delinquent, sexual – and does not entertain any notion of the subject in general.[25] When questioned about the subject Foucault acknowledges that a rejection of an '*a priori* theory of the subject' was necessary to allow analysis of the relations which can exist between 'different forms of the subject and games of truth, practices of power and so forth'.[26] Questioned further on the implications of his position, Foucault attempts to offer clarification. It is argued that the subject

> is a form and this form is not above all or always identical to itself. You do not have towards yourself the same kind of relationships when you constitute yourself as a political subject who goes and votes or speaks up in a meeting, and when you try to fulfil your desires in a sexual relationship. There are no doubt some relationships and some interferences between these different kinds of subject but we are not in the presence of the same kind of subject. In each case, we play, we establish with one's self some different form of relationship.[27]

The existence, under modern conditions, of different forms of subjectivity is not contentious. But do references to 'some relationships and some interferences' between different kinds of subject and the discussion of the 'free subject' in particular suggest something more, perhaps the presence of an unclarified sense of an auto-biographicalizing, albeit de-centred, subject? Do we have here a modern self able to engage in constitutive practices, able to fashion the self, to be creative and reflexive, that is aware of the socially and culturally given character of practices of the self, as well as the latitude they allow and the possibilities they provide for. It is precisely this (Goffmanesque) sense of the subject which informs Foucault's promotion of the virtues of an ethical stylization of the self as necessary for an era in which 'the idea of morality as obedience to a code of rules is now disappearing, has already disappeared'.[28] Is there a trace, a suspicion, of a universalist normativity in Foucault's work as he espouses an ethical stylization of the self? Certainly critics such as Rochlitz believe that Foucault's discussion of the aesthetics of existence contains 'a normative content, even a virtually universalist normativity: referring to a requirement for the autonomy of the person and opposition to unjust suffering'.[29] But perhaps there is another more significant problem associated with Foucault's discussion of the subject, namely the absence of any consideration of the question of the moral responsibility of the subject.

The idea of a progressive governmentalization of power relations 'under the auspices of the state' draws attention to the ways in which the exercise of action upon other possible actions has become increasingly 'elaborated, rationalized and centralized'[30] – in effect, routinized. And it is through this process that moral responsibility for action has been undermined and usurped by legislation of 'universal rule-dictated *duties*'[31] associated with the formation of the modern state practising a pastoral form of power, that is, exercising a 'government of individuals by their own verity'.[32] Signs of increasing discontent with legal-rational intervention 'in our moral, personal, private life' led Foucault to identify a parallel between the present and classical Antiquity, namely the existence of a comparable concern with ethics, with relations to self and others – in effect, although Foucault does not use these terms, a concern with the responsibilities of the subject in the absence of any secure foundations.[33]

There are a number of questions which might be posed at this juncture. Is the parallel drawn by Foucault between the present and classical Antiquity one that extends no further than similarities in respect of problems, or is there, notwithstanding denials to the contrary, a sense in which a way of approaching contemporary predicaments is being sought in classical Antiquity? Foucault certainly implies that something may be learnt from the Greeks about the self, specifically that it has no truth, that there is no true self which analysis can decipher; rather, that the self has to be created. Hence the emphasis placed upon an 'aesthetics of existence' and the articulation of what has been described as 'an ethic for which freedom lies . . . in a constant attempt at self-disengagement and self-invention'.[34] And when reference is made to the need to be aware that 'everything is dangerous' and that, as a corollary, it becomes necessary to make ethico-political choices concerning 'the main danger',[35] is Foucault not assuming the presence of that very form of subjectivity which he neglects to analyse and which may be argued to be in jeopardy, namely the morally responsible self, responsibly identifying and determining how to respond to the main danger?

An Ethic of Responsibility

Ethics constitutes a practice for Foucault, a mode of being, a way of relating to self and thereby others. Drawing on his analyses of the Greco-Roman world, Foucault argues that caring for the self, to know and improve one's self and to exercise mastery over passions and appetites, was fundamental to 'ethics, as a deliberate practice of liberty'.[36] In short, care for the self takes moral precedence over care for others. In contrast, for us a preoccupation with the self has generally been viewed with suspicion and emphasis has instead been placed upon sacrifice of the self and care of others. Care for self, for the Greeks, involved the establishment of self-mastery, the embodiment of a mode of being in which self-control rather than passions and appetites was paramount. For Foucault such a care for self necessarily implies relations with others:

> Care for self is ethical in itself, but implies complex relations with others, in the measure where this *ethos* of freedom is also a way of caring for others. . . . *Ethos* implies also a relation with others to the extent that care for self renders one competent to occupy a place in the city, in the community or in interindividual relationships . . . And the care for self implies also a relationship to the other to the extent that, in order to really care for self, one must listen to the teachings of a master . . . [T]he problem of relationship with others is present all along this development of care for self.[37]

What are we to make of Foucault's understanding? The precedence accorded to care for self is controversial, particularly if the relation to the Other, responsibility for the Other, is to be placed, as Heller suggests, at the centrepoint in ethics. One implication here is that Foucault's interpretation of the Greeks is problematic.[38] McNay suggests that it is highly selective, that although the Ancient Greeks 'may have exercised a degree of liberty in the control of their daily lives, this liberty was nonetheless embedded in a network of social and political obligations. In other words, the ancient Greek sense of the self was always informed by those "analytical and necessary" links that Foucault wishes individuals in contemporary society to divest themselves of.'[39] Is an ethical relationship to the other implied in the contemporary search for styles of existence affirmed by Foucault? Can such an ethical relation be assumed in a context where the interests of the 'modern individual' have diminished, if not largely paralysed, any sense of responsibility for the other? It is all very well talking about creating ourselves as a work of art, but is such a preoccupation with the self necessarily synonymous with caring or showing responsibility for others? The comparison Foucault makes between the Ancient Greek culture of the self and the modern, hedonistic culture of the self suggests not. While the former, emphasizing aesthetics and the importance of exercising a perfect mastery over oneself through imposition of austere practices, is a government of the self which allegedly exemplifies a responsibility towards others, the latter, revealing 'the truth of the self' through the practices of science, no longer has any need for an ascetic relation to the self. The modern subject is constituted through the human sciences and associated normative disciplines largely independently of ethical concerns. And yet, as Levinas, and subsequently Bauman and Heller remind us,[40] the ethical 'face' has not been entirely effaced, the moral gesture has not been completely erased or lost. The significant difference between the moderns and pre-moderns is that we 'rationalize ethics'; we 'query and test the contents of most traditional moral customs and virtues'.[41] The seemingly endless processes of questioning, interpretation, rejection and innovation which have become an intrinsic feature of modern life risk 'discrediting moral gestures fully' and lead Heller to the conclusion that '[m]oderns need to remind themselves constantly of the transcendent, absolute character of the first gesture [of taking responsibility for the other] to protect morals from being colonized by sheer immanent/cognitive claims'.[42] Is there any recognition of, or place for, such a 'gesture' in Foucault's work?

Foucault's late preoccupation was to dwell on the question of how it might be possible to free ethical concerns from dependence upon knowledge – 'My idea is that it's not at all necessary to relate ethical problems to scientific knowledge.'[43] We might go further, indeed we should perhaps go much further, for subjecting ethical matters to scientific interrogation has tended to 'decentre the real moral questions'[44] and diminish the moral self. It has led to the present situation in which the (potential) moral self

has been dissembled into traits; the totality of the moral subject has been reduced to the collection of parts or attributes of which no one can conceivably be ascribed moral subjectivity. Actions are then targeted on specific traits of persons rather than persons themselves, by-passing or avoiding altogether the moment of encounter with morally significant effects.[45]

The question then becomes how might it be possible to regenerate an ethic of responsibility which has been undermined by the prevalence of a modern legislative coding of rules of conduct? While Foucault identifies and explores some of the influences which have contributed to the formation of particular modern forms of subjectivity (for example, Christian asceticism and the renunciation of the self and subsequently the human sciences' disclosure of the truth of the self and constitution, positively, of 'a new self'[46]), he neglects to consider the implications for moral responsibility, for the moral self.

Foucault does not engage directly with the question of the responsibility of the subject, but is it perhaps implied in his critical reflections on the neglect of 'the question of an ethical subject . . . in contemporary political thought'?[47] If so, it needs to be addressed more directly, particularly in the light of enigmatic remarks on the need to 'search for styles of existence as different as possible from each other'.[48] Although questions of ethics only receive an explicit address with Foucault's later writings on classical Antiquity, it has been argued that a concern with the moral implications of modernity is present throughout his work.[49] For example, it is suggested that in an early work on mental pathology Foucault depicts the modern relationship to the self as becoming possible from the moment 'reason ceased to be for man an ethic and became a nature'.[50] And in a subsequent analysis of the human sciences Foucault is credited with making a series of observations on the inability of modern thought to be able 'to propose a morality', an inability that is bound up with the fact that modern thought is 'both knowledge and a modification of what it knows, reflection and a transformation of the mode of being of that on which it reflects. Whatever it touches it immediately causes to move.'[51]

Notwithstanding the fact that it is only with a theoretical shift towards an analysis of the subject that the issue of self-formation as an ethical subject receives a sustained consideration, it has been suggested, as I have noted above, that a subterranean ethical concern runs through all of Foucault's writings. The ethic identified is for thought and it is described as 'a practice which educates . . . readers into an ethical responsibility for intellectual inquiry'.[52] It is an 'ethic for the intellectual',[53] 'an ethic of responsibility for the truth one speaks, for the political strategies into which these truths enter, and for those ways of relating to ourselves that make us either conformists or resisters to those relations. It is a timely ethic *which assists in reclaiming thought's moral responsibilities*';[54] a critical practice which attempts to open up new ways of thinking.

But does an ethic of responsibility for intellectual inquiry exhaust the ethical implications of Foucault's later works on the subject and technologies of the self? Is there, and/or ought there to be, more? What bearing, if any, does such an ethic of the intellectual, an ethic of responsibility for the truth one speaks, have on the elementary, or perhaps a more appropriate term would be the primary moral, matter of care and responsibility for others? Are there ethical implications beyond those identified with intellectual inquiry and the sphere of pleasure? In short, are there wider implications concerning the responsibility of the subject in relation to others, in relation to the question of how we might (should) live?

Reflecting on the Greek cultivation of the self, Foucault notes that while it was articulated by philosophers, knowing 'how "to perfect one's own soul with the help of reason" is a rule "equally necessary for all"'.[55] And on the question of care of the self, Foucault notes that it constituted a 'true social practice', not an exercise in solitude, for the activity of taking care of the self involved communications with others, with guides, advisers and confidants – 'the care of the self and the help of the other blends into pre-existing relations . . . The care of the self – *or the attention one devotes to the care that others should take of themselves* – appears then as an intensification of social relations.'[56] And again – 'The care of the self appears therefore as intrinsically linked to a "soul service", which includes the possibility of a round of exchanges with the other and a system of reciprocal obligations.'[57] If such references do suggest wider implications, and I believe they do, they also suggest that the idea of an ethical relation between care of the self and care for others is more contentious than Foucault seems to allow, as is the implied ethical linking of responsibility with reciprocity.[58] It is only possible for care for self to encompass care for others if there is from the beginning, if there is *already*, a responsibility for the other, an unmeasured and unmeasurable non-reciprocal responsibility which is 'anterior to all the logical deliberation summoned by reasoned decision'.[59] A relationship of responsibility with the other characterizes our social life and it is a relationship in which, as Levinas argues, 'I have to respond to and for the Other without occupying myself with the Other's responsibility in my regard'.[60] It is from the initial moral bearing of being, taking or assuming responsibility for the other that a particular ethical practice of caring for the self follows.

Responsibility for Others: Foucault and Levinas

In discussing the Greeks Foucault makes reference to the close relationship between care of the self and care for others. Exercise of self-mastery or self-government is regarded as a necessary precondition for the government of others. Indeed, 'rationality of the government of oneself' is held to be the same as the 'rationality of the government of others'.[61] Being concerned with oneself, taking care of oneself, is an activity, an activity which is accorded significance because caring correctly for the self is considered to promote correct behaviour 'in relationship to others and for others'.[62] Throughout there is an implication that potential parallels might be drawn between classical Antiquity and our present in respect of the intensity of the relations to self, but there are also, as I have indicated, important differences. For example, whereas in Greco-Roman culture it was taking care of the self which led to knowledge of oneself, in modern Western society emphasis is placed upon the necessity of coming to 'know' in order to be able to 'take care of' the self.

Our morality has been formed through the combined influence of

Christianity with its notions of asceticism and self-renunciation and a 'secular tradition which respects external law as the basis for morality'.[63] In consequence, the idea that a rigorous morality might be based upon giving priority to caring for ourselves is difficult for us to accept. In so far as we have inherited a social morality which, as Foucault remarks, 'seeks the rules of acceptable behaviour in relations with others',[64] the very idea of care of the self appears morally problematic, if not immoral. And it is precisely the absence of any consideration of relations with and responsibility for others which makes Foucault's references to creating ourselves and the autonomy of personal ethics morally problematic.

For the Greeks, caring for the self is said to take moral precedence over care for others 'in the measure that the relationship to self takes ontological precedence'.[65] But is it sufficient to re-present uncritically this particular notion of ontological precedence? In contrast, it might be argued that ontology, 'the intelligibility of being – only becomes possible when ethics, the origin of all meaning, is taken as the starting point'.[66] Furthermore, given the significance already accorded to the thought of classical Antiquity within the tradition of Western philosophy, and Foucault's concern 'to try to think something other than what one thought before',[67] is it appropriate to confine a genealogy of ethics to Greco-Roman culture? Do Foucault's earlier undeveloped observations on the thematic presence of an individualizing political technology of pastorship in Hebraic texts suggest scope for a possible parallel ethical exploration around the question of responsibility for others? Foucault presents pastorship as 'the individualizing power' and in his brief discussion of the ways in which the pastoral theme is developed in Hebrew literature and subsequently taken up and transformed in Christian thought and institutions, there are traces of another possible approach to ethics. Through a series of references to the metaphor of the shepherd Foucault draws attention to the prominence in Hebrew thought of notions of duty towards, caring for, guiding, leading, and ensuring the well-being of others, and in addition offers a passing reference to the theme of (moral) responsibility. However, these references are ultimately left undeveloped and their critical potential for rethinking the ethical relationship between self and other is not explored. In contrast, a critical concern with the question of moral responsibility for others constitutes the heart of the 'post-rational' ethics developed by Levinas.

A cautionary note before proceeding. Levinas, like Foucault, argues against conceptions of the universality of reason, the unity of truth, and human beings as self-conscious subjects, and places emphasis on 'disjunctions, differences, gaps, dispersions in time and knowledge which are refractory to unification or totalization'.[68] But if there are interesting similarities between the two philosophers on some issues, there appear to be important differences in their respective responses to ethical questions and relations.[69]

For Levinas, the ethical relation is an asymmetrical face-to-face relation. It is a relation governed by proximity, the fundamental relation. The ethical relation has primacy; it is prior to both logic and reason. The face-to-face relation is irreducible – 'the face before me summons me. . . . The Other becomes my neighbour precisely through the way the face summons me, calls for me, begs for me, and in so doing recalls my responsibility, and calls me into question.'[70] Note that by the face Levinas does not mean a phenomenon whose mode of being is appearance, but the demand of 'the one who needs you, who is counting on you'. The face in the ethical sense invoked by Levinas is a 'notion through which man comes to me via a human act different from knowing'.[71] An act which is fundamentally and originally ethical; that, for Levinas, is the relation to the other.

Responsibility towards the Other 'demands an infinite subjection of subjectivity', it constitutes a relation of proximity which is 'prior to any commitment . . . "older" than the a priori'.[72] Responsibility for another, for the Other, is, according to Levinas, 'human fraternity itself' and it 'commits me . . . before any truth and any certainty'.[73] The unlimited responsibility for the other comes, Levinas argues, 'from the hither side of my freedom, from a "prior to every memory", an "ulterior to every accomplishment". . . . The responsibility for the other is the locus in which is situated the null-site of subjectivity.'[74] Or as Levinas expresses the relationship elsewhere, 'this attention to the Other . . . can be affirmed as the very bond of human subjectivity, even to the point of being raised to a supreme ethical principle'.[75] And as it is presented in yet another formulation, the alterity of the face constitutes an 'obligation that cannot be effaced'.[76]

In his discussion of the ethical relation, Levinas places the emphasis firmly and deliberately on care for others, rather than care for the self. In contrast, Foucault continues to prioritize the self, to ask whether we can have an 'ethics of acts . . . able to take into account the pleasure of the other? Is the pleasure of the other something which can be integrated in our pleasure. . . ?'[77] Foucault certainly appears to acknowledge the other as a potential focus of our responsibility, but it is always secondary to his preoccupation with the self. In consequence, his contribution to a regeneration of ethics as a 'manner of being' does not ultimately constitute an effective challenge to the modern cult of the self. For care of the self to begin to embrace care of other(s), at the very least an ethics of self-limitation is necessary, and while that might have been a feature of the 'ethical work of the self on the self'[78] in classical Antiquity, it seems to be largely absent from contemporary society, a society 'in which an orderly conduct of life is possible without recourse to the innate human capacity of moral regulation'.[79] While the Greek notion of 'taking care of one's self' constituted an ethical and aesthetic practice of self-mastery, a practice signifying the presence of 'ascetic themes', the modern context in which Foucault ruminates on the virtues of everyone's life becoming a work of art is quite different, one in which self-discovery and self-expression prevail and hedonistic themes predominate. Is the problem, as Foucault argues, that we have lost virtually all trace 'of the idea in our society, that the principal work of art which one has to take care of, the main area to which one must apply aesthetic values, is oneself, one's life, one's existence',[80] or is it that our modern preoccupation with oneself and an associated increasing rationality of human conduct has virtually neutralized the moral impulse, such that taking care of the self now seems to preclude any possibility of taking care of the other? Has the subject of responsibility for the other become a subject of indifference?

Notes

An earlier version of this essay appeared in *Philosophy and Social Criticism*, 21, 4 (1995), pp. 93–109.

1 U. Beck, *Risk Society – Towards a New Modernity* (Sage, London, 1992).

2 Z. Bauman, *Postmodern Ethics* (Blackwell, Oxford, 1993), p. 244.

3 See Bauman, *Postmodern Ethics*; H. Jonas, *The Imperative of Responsibility: In Search of an Ethics for the Technological Age* (University of Chicago Press, Chicago, 1984); and K. Tester, *The Life and Times of Post-Modernity* (Routledge, London, 1993).

4 Z. Bauman, *Intimations of Postmodernity* (Routledge, London, 1992), pp. 201–4.

5 P. Dews, 'The return of the subject in late Foucault', *Radical Philosophy*, 51 (Spring, 1989), pp. 72–95; B. Smart, 'On the subjects of sexuality, ethics and politics in the work of Foucault', *boundary 2*, 18, 1 (1991), pp. 201–25.

6 Michel Foucault, 'Governmentality', *I & C*, 6 (1979).

7 Michel Foucault, 'Truth, power, self: an interview with Michel Foucault', in Luther H. Martin, Huck Gutman and Patrick H. Hutton (eds), *Technologies of the Self* (University of Massachusetts Press, Amherst MA, 1988), p. 18.

8 Ibid., p. 19 (emphasis added).

9 Michel Foucault, 'The subject and power', Afterword in H.L. Dreyfus and P. Rabinow (eds), *Michel Foucault: Beyond Structuralism and Hermeneutics* (Harvester Press, Brighton, 1982), p. 208.

10 L. McNay, *Foucault and Feminism* (Polity Press, Cambridge, 1992), pp. 163–4.

11 Michel Foucault, 'On the genealogy of ethics: an overview of work in progress', in P. Rabinow (ed.), *The Foucault Reader* (Penguin, Harmondsworth, 1986), p. 347.

12 McNay, *Foucault and Feminism*, p. 164.

13 Foucault, 'Truth, power, self', p. 18 (emphasis added).

14 Foucault, 'Subject and power', p. 221.

15 Ibid.

16 Michel Foucault, 'The ethic of care for the self as a practice of freedom', *Philosophy and Social Criticism*, 12 (1987), p. 6.

17 Ibid., p. 122.

18 Foucault, 'Subject and power', p. 221.

19 J. Miller, *The Passion of Michel Foucault* (Harper Collins, London, 1993).

20 Foucault, 'Ethic of care', p. 122 (emphasis added).

21 Foucault, 'Genealogy of ethics', p. 351.

22 Ibid., p. 350.

23 Foucault, 'Ethic of care', p. 118.

24 Bauman, *Postmodern Ethics*; A. Heller, 'The elementary ethics of everyday life', in G. Robinson and J. Rundell (eds), *Rethinking Imagination – Culture and Creativity* (Routledge, London, 1994); and E. Levinas, *The Levinas Reader*, Sean Hand (ed.) (Blackwell, Oxford, 1989).

25 Michel Foucault, *Foucault Live*, S. Lotringer (ed.) (Semiotext(e), New York, 1989), pp. 313, 329–30.

26 Foucault, 'Ethic of care', p. 121.

27 Ibid.

28 Foucault, *Foucault Live*, p. 311.

29 R. Rochlitz, 'The aesthetics of existence: post-conventional morality and the theory of power in Michel Foucault', in T.J. Armstrong (ed.), *Michel Foucault: Philosopher* (Harvester Wheatsheaf, Brighton, 1992), p. 250.

30 Foucault, 'Subject and power', p. 224.

31 Bauman, *Postmodern Ethics*, p. 54.

32 Michel Foucault, 'Omnes et singulatim', *The Tanner Lectures on Human Values*, Vol. II, S.M. McMurrin (ed.) (Cambridge University Press, London, 1981), p. 240.

33 Foucault, 'Genealogy of ethics', p. 343.

34 J. Rajchman, *Michel Foucault – The Freedom of Philosophy* (Columbia University Press, New York, 1985), p. 38.

35 Foucault, 'Genealogy of ethics', p. 343.

36 Foucault, 'Ethic of care', p. 116.

37 Ibid., p. 118.

38 Heller, 'Elementary ethics of everyday life'.

39 McNay, *Foucault and Feminism*, p. 164.

40 Levinas, *Levinas Reader*; Z. Bauman, 'Effacing the face', *Theory, Culture & Society*, 7, 1 (1990), pp. 5–38; Heller, 'Elementary ethics of everyday life'.

41 Heller, 'Elementary ethics of everyday life', p. 52.

42 Ibid.

43 Foucault, 'Genealogy of ethics', p. 349.

44 Heller, 'Elementary ethics of everyday life', p. 50.

45 Bauman, *Postmodern Ethics*, p. 127.

46 Foucault, 'Truth, power, self', p. 49.

47 Foucault, 'Ethic of care', p. 125.

48 Foucault, *Foucault Live*, p. 330.

49 J. Bernauer, 'Beyond life and death: on Foucault's post-Auschwitz ethic', in Armstrong (ed.), *Michel Foucault: Philosopher*; Rajchman, *Michel Foucault – The Freedom of Philosophy*.

50 Michel Foucault, *Mental Illness and Psychology* (Harper and Row, New York, 1976), p. 87.

51 Michel Foucault, *The Order of Things – An Archaeology of the Human Sciences* (Vintage Books, New York, 1973), p. 327.

52 Bernauer, 'Beyond life and death', p. 269.

53 Rajchman, *Michel Foucault – The Freedom of Philosophy*, p. 124.

54 Bernauer, 'Beyond life and death', p. 271 (emphasis added).

55 Michel Foucault, *The Care of the Self, Volume 3: The History of Sexuality* (Allen Lane/ Penguin, London, 1988), p. 48.

56 Ibid., p. 53 (emphasis added).

57 Ibid., p. 54 (emphasis added).

58 Bauman, *Postmodern Ethics*, p. 220.

59 E. Levinas, *Time and the Other* (Dusquesne University Press, Pittsburgh, 1987), p. 111.

60 Ibid., p. 137.

61 Foucault, *Care of the Self*, p. 89.

62 Foucault, 'Ethic of care', p. 118.

63 Foucault, 'Truth, power, self', p. 22.

64 Ibid.

65 Foucault, 'Ethic of care', p. 118.

66 Levinas, *Levinas Reader*, p. 231. See also Bauman, 'Effacing the face', pp. 16–18.

67 Foucault, *Foucault Live*, p. 256.

68 N. O'Connor, 'The personal is political: discursive practice of the face-to-face', in R. Bernasconi and D. Wood (eds), *The Provocation of Levinas: Rethinking the Other* (Routledge, London, 1988), p. 58.

69 G. Salemohamed, 'Of an ethics that cannot be used', *Economy and Society*, 20, 1 (1991), pp. 120–30.

70 Levinas, *Levinas Reader*, p. 231. See also Bauman, 'Effacing the face', p. 83.

71 Foucault, 'Truth, power, self', p. 171.

72 Levinas, *Levinas Reader*, p. 90.

73 Ibid., pp. 106–10.

74 E. Levinas, *Otherwise than Being or Beyond Essence* (Martin Nijhoff, London, 1981), p. 10.

75 E. Levinas, 'Useless suffering', in Bernasconi and Wood (eds), *Provocation of Levinas*, p. 159.

76 E. Levinas, 'The paradox of morality: an interview', in Bernasconi and Wood (eds), *Provocation of Levinas*, p. 179.

77 Rainbow, *Foucault Reader*, p. 346.

78 Foucault, *Care of the Self*, p. 91.

79 Bauman, *Postmodern Ethics*, p. 29.

80 Foucault, 'Genealogy of ethics', p. 362.

6

Feminism, Foucault and 'Subjects' of Power and Freedom

Jana Sawicki

Since the early 1980s Foucault's work has been especially influential among North American feminists. Why? Among the many influential French critical theorists Foucault was distinct in so far as his aim was to intervene in specific struggles of disenfranchised and socially suspect groups such as prisoners, mental patients and homosexuals. In so far as Foucault's discourse appeared to be more activist and less narrowly academic than those of some of his post-structuralist counterparts, it compelled activist feminist theorists to take a serious look at his work, even if they were predisposed to dismiss other intellectual trends emanating from Paris. Moreover, during the early 1980s a particularly impassioned and embittered set of feminist debates, known as the 'sex wars', took place. Promising as it did to radically alter the terrain of sexual theory, Foucault's *History of Sexuality* emerged as one of several key texts proffered by pro-sex feminists who were challenging feminist orthodoxies concerning gender and its relationship to issues of sexual freedom. Finally, during the 1980s US women of colour openly criticized 'Second Wave' feminists' exclusionary practices. Some anti-racist feminists argued that Foucault's analysis of power and his genealogical critiques of the exclusionary functions of universalism and essentialism could be used to understand such tendencies within white, middle-class feminism.

In addition, the following convergences of feminism and Foucault were especially striking: Foucault's provocative analyses of the productive dimensions of disciplinary powers exercised outside the confines of the narrowly defined political realm of the modern liberal state overlapped with those of feminists already engaged in the project of exploring the micropolitics of 'private' life. His analytic of power/knowledge could be used to further feminist explorations into the dynamics of patriarchal power at the most intimate levels of experience in the institutions of marriage, motherhood and compulsory heterosexuality, and in the everyday rituals and regimens that govern women's relationships to themselves and their bodies. In particular, his emphasis on the sexual body as a target and vehicle of 'biopower' promised to open up new possibilities for understanding the 'controlled insertion of bodies into the machinery' not only of production, but also of reproduction and sexuality. The history of modern feminist struggles for reproductive freedom might be understood as central to the history of biopower.

In addition to his analysis of micropower and his emphasis on the body as a site of power, Foucault's critique of Enlightenment humanism and its appeals to a universal a priori subject of knowledge and history also echoed radical challenges that feminists posed to fundamental epistemological and political assumptions in modern Western philosophical thought. His critical genealogies of 'subjectification' and his scepticism regarding universalism and essentialism in modern emancipatory theories coincided with feminists' ambivalence about core concepts of liberalism and Marxism (that is, the pre-social individual, the subject of history, authenticity, autonomy, false consciousness, and so forth) for feminist politics. Finally, both feminists and Foucault identified the 'crucial role of discourse in its capacity to produce and sustain hegemonic power and emphasized the challenges contained within marginalized and/or unrecognized discourses'.[1]

It would be surprising if the emergence of Foucaultian feminist discourses had not produced a counter-discourse. Indeed, the relationship between Foucault and feminism has not been an entirely happy one. Criticisms have been launched from both sympathetic and more hostile camps. Most feminists point to Foucault's androcentric gender blindness: some do not regard it as a fatal flaw, others believe it contaminates the entire enterprise.

In what follows, I address a central issue in debates among feminists about the value of Foucault (and other poststructuralists) for feminism, namely, the question of the subject and the possibility of resistance. I begin by presenting the most trenchant feminist criticisms of Foucault. Then, I briefly outline two basic trends in feminist appropriations of Foucault – namely, those that use his analyses of disciplinary power to isolate disciplinary technologies that subjugate women as both objects and subjects, and those that acknowledge domination, but centre on cultures and strategies of resistance to hegemonic regimes of power. The former face the problem of agency. The latter attempt to develop the possibilities of a post-humanist politics opened up by genealogical critique. Finally, I construct my own response to feminist critics, drawn from the later volumes on *The History of Sexuality* and selected interviews from the early 1980s.[2]

Feminism and Foucault: Critique, Convergence and Possibility

It is by now commonplace to point to a fundamental tension in Foucault's work on disciplinary power. In *Discipline and Punish* and *The History of Sexuality, Vol. 1* whenever Foucault spoke of the subject he referred principally to the subject as 'subjected' – as the product of dominating mechanisms of disciplinary power. Foucault sometimes seemed to be describing forms of power that insinuate themselves so deeply within the subject that it is difficult to imagine how change might be possible. At the same time he claimed that wherever there is power, there is resistance. Presumably, what makes disciplinary power so effective is its ability to grasp the individual at the level of its

self-understanding – of its very identity and the norms that govern its practices of self-constitution. As 'subjected', the individual is either bound to
others by dependency or control, or to categories, practices and possibilities
of self-understanding which emerge from medico-scientific discourses associated with the 'normalizing' panoptic disciplines (for example, medicine,
criminology, psychoanalysis, sexology, etc.) that Foucault describes in his
genealogical writings. Thus, in his portraits of disciplinary society even modes
of self-governance seem to emerge as perniciously disciplinary.

In one of the most impressive critical analyses of Foucault's middle writings
to date, Nancy Fraser characterizes the scenario of the perfected Panopticon
as one in which 'disciplinary norms have become so thoroughly internalized
that they . . . [are] not experienced as coming from without'.[3] In other words,
the difference between autonomy and internalized domination is erased.
Fraser argues that Foucault's lack of explicit normative foundations makes it
impossible for him to make such a distinction at all. If this is the case, then his
assertions that resistance to power is everywhere appear at best gratuitous,
and at worst incoherent. In short, his notion of resistance would appear to
require some grounding in a theory of an autonomous subject.

Despite her significant reservations about feminist appropriations of
Foucault, Fraser has consistently made use of genealogical critique and discourse analysis in her own compelling critiques of the welfare state.[4] This has
not been true of Nancy Hartsock, a leading feminist critic of post-
structuralism, who argues that Foucault's 'wholesale' rejection of modernity
and its emancipatory theories, his refusal to envision alternative orders, and
his emphasis on resistance and destabilization over transformation rob feminism of elements (in particular, the effort to establish epistemological and
moral foundations for its enterprise) that are indispensable to its emancipators' goals. Hartsock claims: '[S]ystematically unequal power relations
ultimately vanish from [Foucault's] work.'[5] Moreover, like feminist literary
critic Barbara Christian, Hartsock is suspicious of Foucault's alleged moves
to reject a constitutive subject and universal theories of history at a time
when many marginal groups are finally breaking silence, rejecting their object
status within dominant discourses, and constructing oppositional political
subjectivities, theories and progressive visions of their own.[6]

Ultimately, Hartsock claims that Foucault's analytic of power fails feminism because it is not a theory developed *for* women. It is the theory of a
colonizer who rejects and resists the colonizers, but who, because he does not
think from the perspective of the colonized, 'fails to provide an epistemology
which is useable for the task of revolutionizing, creating and constructing'.[7]
She regards his vision of struggle as a 'war of all against all', as dystopian and
unacceptable.

In a more sympathetic reading of Foucault's contributions to critical
theory, Joan Cocks echoes Hartsock when she comments upon Foucault's
'anarchistic' tendencies:

> [W]e must be clear on his two great weaknesses, both constitutional weaknesses of
> anarchism. These are the inability to support any movement that through its

massiveness and disciplined unity would be popular and yet powerful enough to undermine an entrenched legal-political regime; and the inability to stand on the side of any positive new cultural-political order at all, such an order's always being at once a new system of imposed prohibitions and permissions, with respect to which opposition properly can respond only negatively. Both inabilities are symptoms of a basic failure of nerve before the whole question of order – which, after all, every tolerable as well as intolerable mode of social life must and will have, and which any serious countermovement at some juncture will have to develop as well.[8]

What does Hartsock propose instead? It is noteworthy that Hartsock links the inadequacy of Foucault's account of power and knowledge to his social location as a privileged white male; for the logic of her standpoint epistemology commits her to the view that certain situations are more likely to produce distortions and partial visions than others. Employing a feminist revision of Marxian standpoint epistemology, she argues for the epistemic privilege of the feminist standpoint. Among the features that she identifies as essential to this revised theory are the following:

> First, rather than getting rid of subjectivity or notions of the subject, as Foucault does, and substituting his notion of the individual as an effect of power relations, we need to engage in the historical, political, and theoretical process of constituting ourselves as subjects as well as objects of history. . . . Second . . . if we are to construct a new society, we need to be assured that some systematic knowledge about our world and ourselves is possible . . . Third . . . we need a theory of power that recognizes that our practical daily activity contains an understanding of the world . . . a 'standpoint' epistemology . . . [based upon] the claim that material life . . . not only structures but sets limits on the understanding of social relations, and that, in systems of dominations the vision available to the rulers will be both partial *and will reverse the real order of things.*[9]

Hartsock finds Foucault's analysis of power deficient in so far as it presumably rejects subjectivity (and the possibility of transformative agency), systematic knowledge and epistemological foundationalism.

Hence the most trenchant criticisms of Foucault by feminists identify two major defects in his work: his rejection of modern foundationalist epistemologies (and their humanistic philosophies of the subject), and the related question of the adequacy of his politics of resistance. (Who resists power? Towards what ends should resistance aim? Can Foucault envision possibilities of collective resistance?) These feminist critiques of Foucault overlap significantly with those from the non-feminist quarters of social and political theory.[10] Thus, they point to the dangers of relativism, nihilism and pessimism often associated with his work.

To be sure, despite such criticisms, many feminists have used Foucault's analysis of disciplinary power effectively to address the micropolitics of gender. For example, in her analyses of the fashion/beauty complex in contemporary America, Sandra Bartky gives compelling descriptions of disciplinary technologies that produce specifically feminine forms of embodiment. Bartky suggests that many women have resisted or ignored feminist critiques of prevailing standards of fashion and beauty because abandoning them threatens women with deskilling and challenges their very sense of identity. Thus, this form of patriarchal power operates by attaching women to certain norms of feminine identity.

Bartky's use of Foucault corrects a deficiency that most feminists find in his writings, namely, its androcentrism. Yet, she also reproduces a problematic dimension of the Foucaultian account of modern disciplinary practices to which I have already alluded. She, too, portrays forms of power that insinuate themselves within subjects so profoundly that it is difficult to imagine how we might alter them.

Despite his rejection of totalizing theory and teleological narratives of closure, Foucault's holistic rhetoric and sometimes shrill condemnations of the carceral society in *Discipline and Punish* lent credence to those who claimed that in this book Foucault was describing a wholly disciplined society. As we have seen, critics claimed that he provided no convincing account of how resistance to power is possible.

Elsewhere, I have argued that despite its occasional holistic rhetoric, *Discipline and Punish* was not intended as a portrait of the whole of modern society, but rather, a genealogy of the emergence of the ideal of a perfectly administered one. Bentham's Panopticon is not a symbol of modern society, but a theoretical model that should be analysed in terms of its impact. Foucault's view of power is neither deterministic, nor systemic in any closed sense. He is not describing modern society *tout court*, but particular practices – that is, practices of subjection – found within it.

In her own defence – one that might also be enlisted in support of Foucault, who, after all, referred to himself as a 'hyper- and pessimistic activist' – Bartky writes: 'Theoretical work done in the service of political ends may exhibit a "pessimism of the intellect", but the point of doing such work at all is the "optimism of the will" without which any serious political work is impossible.'[11] Moreover, as Deborah Cook has suggested, Foucault and Bartky are not alone. Much of left-wing political theory in the twentieth century (Horkheimer, Adorno, Sartre, Merleau-Ponty) has expressed despair about the efficacy of traditional emancipatory theory. Even Habermas has suggested that our chances for emancipation today 'are not very good'.[12] Cook claims that Foucault opens a space for the resistance of 'those who have yet to be defined within the traditional political spectrum' – namely, women, homosexuals, lesbians, queers, mental patients, the imprisoned, post-colonial subjects, etc.[13] Indeed, as I will suggest below, despite his scepticism about our capacity to control history (a ruse of certain versions of universal humanism) and his belief that total emancipation – 'the realization of a society where the individual is entirely free to define him or herself' – is not possible, he did identify areas he believed were vulnerable to criticism, forms of subjection which might be effectively resisted.[14] While he was sceptical about the prospects of total emancipation, he believed it was possible to alter particular normalizing practices and thereby make particular lives more tolerable.

Furthermore, Bartky and Foucault maintain that there is a value in negative criticism, criticism that does not point to specific remedies or alternatives.

John Rajchman's fitting description of Foucault's critical task provides another defence for this view:

> One task for 'critical thought' is thus to expose [the costs of our self-constitution] . . . , to analyze what we did not realize we had to say and do to ourselves in order to be who we are. . . . The experience of critical thought would start in the experience of such costs. Thus, before asking, or at least when asking, what we must do to behave rationally, this kind of thinking would ask: What are 'the forms of rationality' that secure our identity and delimit our possibilities? It would ask what is 'intolerable' about such forms of reason . . .[15]

Through genealogical analysis, description and criticism of existing power/knowledge regimes, Foucault (and Bartky) hoped to open the space necessary for resistance by freeing us from uncritical adherence to particular disciplines and identities, or, using his later terminology, particular 'technologies of the self'.

Other feminist engagements with Foucault (as well as Lacan and Derrida) have produced exciting and provocative efforts to open up new possibilities for political agency. In a brilliant and imaginative, if problematic, effort to revise modern conceptions of emancipatory politics and identity, Judith Butler argues that feminist politics without a feminist subject is possible and desirable. In Butler's framework 'feminist subject' refers to a fixed, stable and essentialist identity (whether natural or socially constructed) constituting the ground and reference point of feminist theory and practice. What Butler objects to about identity politics is their tendency to appeal to a pre-discursive 'I' as their ground and support – their tendency 'to assume that an identity must first be in place in order for political interests to be elaborated and, subsequently, political action to be taken'.[16]

Butler contends that critics of Foucault and other poststructuralists are wrong to conclude that discursive constructionist entails historical determinism. To the contrary, she states: 'Construction is not opposed to agency; it is the necessary scene of agency.'[17] Butler describes identities as self-representations – that is, 'fictions' that are neither fixed nor stable. Hence the subject is not a thing, a substantive entity, but rather a process of signification within an open system of discursive possibilities. The gendered self is a regulated, but not determined, set of practices. Butler states: '[An ontology of gender] is, thus, not a foundation, but a normative injunction that operates insidiously by installing itself into political discourse as its necessary ground.'[18]

Of course, to claim that the subject and its identifications are merely effects of practices of signification is not to deny that these effects are real or that identity is artificial and arbitrary. Discursive practices are rule-governed structures of intelligibility that both constrain and enable identity formation. Neither wholly determined nor wholly arbitrary, the view of identity promulgated here is one which attempts to move beyond the dichotomy of free will versus determinism and to recognize the possibilities for critical and transformative agency that do not require us to establish an absolute and incontestable ground of knowledge and experience beyond relations of power. Drawing on Lacanian psychoanalytic theory, Butler locates agency within domains of cultural possibility and intelligibility produced by the very failures of dominant gender norms to contain the multiplicity of gender expressions that exceed and defy the norm by which they are generated.

In effect, Butler endorses Foucaultian critical genealogies of the mechanisms that have produced dominant understandings and possibilities of gender identity as a strategy for bringing liminal identities into play – that is, such liminal types as the 'assertive female', the 'effeminate man', the 'macho gay', the 'lipstick lesbian', and so forth. She concludes:

> If identities were no longer fixed as the premises of a political syllogism, and politics no longer understood as a set of practices derived from the alleged interests that belong to a set of ready-made subjects, a new configuration of politics would surely emerge from the ruins of the old.[19]

What I find particularly illuminating in Butler's position is its articulation of the poststructuralist argument against the subject. It is the foundationalist subject that is challenged, not the practices of assuming subject positions and representing oneself. Indeed, the latter are inevitable. Nor is agency denied; it is simply reformulated as enactments of variation within regulated, normative and habitual processes of signification. Poststructuralists like Foucault do not deny that we can or should 'constitute ourselves as subjects' as Hartsock alleges, for this is unavoidable. It is the epistemological move to ground our politics in foundational subject that is challenged and bypassed.

Foucault and Butler shift the focus of political analysis from the epistemological project of grounding political and social theories to analysing the production of certain forms of subjectivity in terms of their costs. Both conclude that the costs associated with modernist practices of identity formation have been too high. Finally, both seem to be suggesting that we develop a form of politics that is relatively independent of modernist foundational epistemological projects.

Another alternative to identity politics based on some naturalized or essentialized subject may be found in the writings of Donna Haraway. Haraway has introduced the notion of a politics based on 'affinities' or political kinship. She recommends that we draw upon the writings of women of colour to learn how to construct political unities 'without relying on a logic of appropriation, incorporation, and taxonomic classification'.[20] What distinguishes these modes of identity formation is their self-consciously political character. What they attempt to avoid is the reduction of politics to projects of self-discovery and personal transformation, or to the formation of narrowly defined counter-cultural communities.[21]

The new political identity offered by Haraway is crystallized in the image of the 'cyborg'. Created by the very forces that we oppose in post-industrial capitalist patriarchal societies, the cyborg is neither wholly human, machine nor animal. It defies categorization and takes pleasure in the fusion of boundaries (human–animal, human–machine, nature–culture), but also takes responsibility for their construction. It is an identity stripped of innocent origins and yet opposed to domination. Although many may find her optimism ungrounded, Haraway describes the cyborg's perspective as one of hopeful possibility:

Feminisms and Marxisms have run aground on Western epistemological imperatives to construct a revolutionary subject from the perspective of a hierarchy of
oppressions and/or a latent position of moral superiority, innocence, and greater
closeness to nature. With no available original dream of a common language or
original symbiosis promising protection . . . to recognize 'oneself' as fully implicated in the world, frees us of the need to root politics in identification, vanguard
parties, purity, and mothering.[22]

In effect, Haraway's cyborg politics retrieves and subversively repeats elements of identity politics. It is, in Butler's terms, an identity politics with a
difference. It involves a continuation of the practice of writing narratives of
marginalized subjects. Partially rooted as it is in the experiences of women of
colour, Haraway's cyborg politics emphasizes the significance of personal
storytelling as a strategy of resistance. The power to signify, to enter the
struggle over meanings, is crucial to any feminist politics. However, these stories do not rely on the origin myths of essentialist feminisms and humanism;
instead they explore the theme of identity on the margins of hegemonic
groups and thereby attempt to deconstruct the authority and legitimacy of
dominant humanist narratives by exposing their partiality. Nor do the sto-
rytellers appeal to a seamless identity. As partial and mixed, such identities
remain open to establishing connections with others despite many
differences.

Thus, narratives of oppressed groups are important in so far as they
empower these groups by giving them a voice in the struggle over interpretations without claiming to be epistemically privileged or incontestable. They
are not denied the 'authority' of experience if, by 'authority', one means the
power to introduce that experience as a basis for analysis, and thereby to
create new self-understandings. What is denied is the authority of unanalysed
experience. Rather than 'construct defences of . . . experience', to use Edward
Said's phrase, they promote knowledge of it.[23] Here 'knowledge' is understood as potentially linked to relations of power and not as a completely
autonomous domain of inquiry.

Thus far, I have suggested that it is not evident that under Foucault's influence feminism is deprived of elements absolutely indispensable to its
liberatory aims as long as one is willing to jettison the utopian humanist
notion of *total* emancipation. Foucault was in fact pessimistic about this
hope. Nonetheless, he had no monopoly on this characteristic, and he
believed that particular intolerable relations of power could be resisted.

In addition, to assume, as Hartsock does, that emancipatory politics
requires a foundationalist subject of history is to beg the questions that
Foucault and others have raised about the degree to which Enlightenment
humanisms have either masked forms of disciplinary power that operate by
producing forms of modern individuality or participated in extending domination. Moreover, Foucault does not deprive feminists of developing a
systematic knowledge of society; instead he warns us of the normalizing
impact of certain forms of such knowledge. Finally, while Foucault and feminists who appeal to him do repudiate Cartesian or transcendental
subjectivities, this does not leave us without relatively autonomous subjects

capable of resisting the particular forms of subjection that Foucault has identified in modern society.

In what follows, I turn to Foucault's last writings to develop the outlines of a more complete response to those critics troubled by Foucault's positions on the humanist subject and the possibilities of social transformation.

The Late Foucault on Subjectivity, Power and Freedom[24]

Foucault himself offered another set of possibilities for thinking about subjectivity, freedom and resistance in his last writings on the Enlightenment and Ancient Greek ethics. His return to Kant and to ancient ethics was partly inspired by his desire to develop the outlines of a more positive account of freedom and a clarification of his relationship to Enlightenment humanism.

In the early 1980s Foucault entered into dialogue with critics who demanded criteria for distinguishing malevolent and benign or beneficial forms of power. Moreover, as I have suggested, this coincided with a softening of his critique of the Enlightenment. Whereas in his middle writings he sometimes implied that traditional emancipators' theories were inherently totalizing, hence dominating, in his later works he suggested that theory, along with everything else, is simply 'dangerous'. 'My point is not that everything is bad, but that everything is dangerous.'[25] As if in response to the progressive and liberal critics (for example, Habermas, Rorty, Fraser), who challenged his model of power and resistance for its lack of normative guidance, Foucault clarified the distinction between domination and power. Whereas 'domination' refers to a situation in which the subject is unable to overturn or reverse the domination relation – a situation where resistance is impossible – 'power' refers to relations which are flexible, mutable, fluid and even reversible. Foucault remarks:

> . . . the important question . . . is not whether a culture without restraints is possible or even desirable but whether the system of constraints in which a society functions leaves individuals the liberty to transform the system. Obviously constraints of any kind are going to be intolerable to certain segments of society. But a system of constraint becomes truly intolerable when the individuals who are affected by it don't have the means of modifying it.[26]

In so far as Foucault distinguishes domination from power, he denies that all forms of power or order are pernicious. Hence, he distances himself from anarchism.

Furthermore, Foucault also distinguishes among forms of power such as exploitation, racial or ethnic hegemony, and 'subjection'. He endorses efforts by colonized peoples to liberate themselves from totalitarian domination. Thus, Hartsock is mistaken when she claims that Foucault does not acknowledge systematically unequal power relations. Yet, in his own work, rather than focus on top-down forms of totalitarian domination, he attempted to provide tools for those struggling against the latter form of power, namely, subjection. Thus, he states: '[N]owadays, the struggle against the forms of subjection – against the submission of subjectivity – is becoming more and more important, even though the struggles against forms of domination and exploitation have not disappeared.'[27] Indeed, what Foucault found problematic about the theme of 'liberation' is the fact that not only can it sometimes be a ruse of power, as in the case of those versions of sexual liberation that rely on the repressive hypothesis, but it often does not go far enough. Reversing power positions without altering relations of power is rarely liberating. Neither is it a sufficient condition of liberation to throw off the yoke of domination; for a liberated people is still left with the problem of deciding upon acceptable forms of political society for themselves. Ultimately, for Foucault, liberty or freedom is not a state of being or an institutional structure but a practice:

> [Liberty] is never assured by the institutions and laws that are intended to guarantee them. This is why almost all of these laws and institutions are quite capable of being turned around. Not because they are ambiguous, but simply because 'liberty' is what must be exercised.[28]

For example, although Foucault supported homosexual rights, he more often cautioned rights activists about the limits of liberal reform and stressed the importance of establishing 'practices of freedom' – that is, new attitudes and patterns of behaviour, new cultural forms that give such legal reforms their force.

Unlike Kant, Foucault preferred to emphasize the importance of expanding our sense of possibility in the present rather than imagining alternative social orders. Yet he did not jettison appeals to Enlightenment values such as reason, autonomy and human dignity. In a lecture on Kant's essay 'What is Enlightenment?' published the year of his death, Foucault situates his own work within a philosophical tradition devoted to philosophical and historical reflection on the significance of the present for self-understanding. He identifies with a version of Kantian critical reflection and thus locates himself squarely within the Enlightenment tradition of critical theory. Foucault comments:

> one [does not have] to be 'for' or 'against' the Enlightenment . . . one has to refuse everything that might present itself in the form of a simplistic and authoritarian alternative: you either accept the Enlightenment and remain within the tradition of its rationalism . . . or else you criticize the Enlightenment and then try to escape from its principles of rationality.[29]

In another essay he elaborates:

> . . . there is the problem raised by Habermas: if one abandons the work of Kant . . . one runs the risk of lapsing into irrationality. I am completely in agreement with this, but at the same time our question is quite different. . . . What is this Reason that we use? What are its historical effects? What are its limits and its dangers? How can we exist as rational beings, fortunately committed to practising a rationality that is unfortunately crisscrossed by intrinsic danger? . . . If it is extremely dangerous to say that Reason is the enemy that should be eliminated, it is just as dangerous to say that any critical questioning of this rationality risks sending us into irrationality.[30]

In other words, while Foucault believed that a constant critique of the historical instantiations of political rationality is necessary, he refused to capitulate to what he referred to as the 'blackmail of the Enlightenment'. He continued to operate with (Kantian) liberal humanist values such as liberty, dignity and autonomy – even rights and obligations. He also refused to choose between rationality and its critique; he used reason to critique itself. What he wanted to preserve of our Enlightenment heritage was not 'faithfulness to doctrinal elements', but rather the attitude of critique and inquiry into the limits of possibility in the present.[31]

Foucault regarded Enlightenment as a complex historical process. In contrast, 'humanism' is a theme, a set of characterizations of the human, that represents a variety of points of view. Consider his following remarks about humanism:

> What we call humanism has been used by Marxists, liberals, Nazis, Catholics. This does not mean that we have to get rid of what we call human rights, but that we can't say that freedom or human rights has to be limited to certain frontiers. . . . What I am afraid of about humanism is that it presents a certain form of our ethics as a universal model for any kind of freedom. I think that there are more secrets, more possible freedoms, and more inventions in our future than we can imagine in humanism as it is dogmatically represented on every side of the political rainbow.[32]

In effect, Foucault finds humanism unreliable because as a theme in history it has meant so many different things, has been enlisted in so many different causes. But this is not its only problem. It also 'presents a certain form of ethics as a universal model for any kind of freedom'. In particular, he objected to forms of humanism that begin with an a priori theory of the subject and proceed to define the universal and necessary conditions for the possibility of ethical action and thought. Thus, even Kantian humanism with its relatively abstract noumenal subject delineates necessary criteria of autonomous moral action for any subject such as intention and duty. What Foucault objects to is the tendency to supply innate structures of autonomous subjectivity – the tendency to reify and render necessary contingent structures of being. As one commentator aptly characterizes the situation:

> Foucault resists the subject of Kantian humanism for fear of the mistaken claims of necessity, the optional and 'loaded' metaphors and concerns that Kant transcendentalizes in his depiction of the free subject. Although Foucault is committed to freedom, he is reluctant to theorize that freedom in terms of the subject. Instead, Foucault seems to opt for a minimalist theory of freedom: a theory which says only as much as it needs to make an ethical commitment to freedom intelligible without hypostatizing innate structures of the autonomous subject.[33]

Foucault's turn to Ancient Greek ethics can be understood as his effort to establish a normative basis for practices of self-formation and invention (that is, 'practices of liberty') which avoid the universalism of the Kantian 'science of morals' and its inquiry into the necessary structures of morality, and which, in so far as they operate at the practical and not the theoretical level, might provide us with a practice aimed at the concrete realization of our ideals.

What did Foucault admire about Greek ethics? Why did he spend the last years of his life writing about them? Foucault denied that his studies of the Ancients represented a radical shift in direction: 'My objective [over the past twenty years] . . . has been to create a history of the different modes by which, in our culture, human beings are made subjects.'[34] Whereas his earlier genealogies focused on anonymous processes through which individuals are constituted heteronomously, in his later genealogies of the self he focused on modes of self-constitution, historical processes through which individuals develop particular relationships to themselves. Foucault's preoccupation with the Greeks was also inspired by his desire to develop the outlines of a more positive account of freedom. Rather than define freedom principally in terms of resistance to normalization, a strategy which is more reactive than affirmative, Foucault turned to art as a way of facing the question of order that he so often avoided in his earlier writings. His aim was to suggest the outlines of criteria for distinguishing between better and worse expressions of freedom without capitulating to a traditional liberal micropolitics of subjection. He was fascinated by the fact that the Greeks had developed a plurality of ethical schools devoted to providing disciplinary models (technologies of self) for self-mastery and self-formation, that is, for an art of life. In effect, they enacted a *rapport à soi* (a relation to self) in which ethical comportment was dissociated from both ethico–religious imperatives and scientific determination.

Foucault identifies an important similarity between modernity and antiquity. He remarks:

> I wonder if our problem nowadays is not, in a way, similar to [the Greeks], since most of us no longer believe that ethics is founded in religion, nor do we want a legal system to intervene in our moral, personal, private life. Recent liberation movements suffer from the fact that they cannot find any principle on which to base the elaboration of a new ethics. They need an ethics, but cannot find any other ethics than an ethics founded on so-called scientific knowledge of what the self is, what desire is, what the unconscious is, and so on.[35]

The Greek art of existence interested Foucault because it offered a 'strong structure of existence without any relation to the juridical per se, [yet] with an authoritarian system, [and] . . . a disciplinary structure'.[36] Greek ethics offered a more autonomous, more pluralistic, less pernicious mode of limiting freedom and forming the self than 'modern morals'. To be sure, these practices of self-creations were only relatively autonomous. The possibilities for self-constitution are not created *ex nihilo*. They are instead 'patterns that [the individual] finds in his culture and which are proposed, suggested and imposed on him by his culture, his society, and his social group'.[37] Niko Kolodny captures the essence of Foucault's position when he writes:

> [T]his does not make ethical self-constitution a tragic resignation to determination by culture or history. Such resignation would follow only if Foucault conceptualized freedom in the form of absolute self-determination: if he held that the only freedom worth the name were freedom from every conceivable social constraint . . . the freedom Foucault has in mind is instead the relative freedom – marked by the fluidity, reversibility and mutability of relations of power – that individuals in one society enjoy relative to another.[38]

Of course, Foucault realized that a simple return to Greek ethics was neither possible nor desirable. He recognized that ancient 'practices of freedom' were exercised in the context of sexual domination and slavery, that they were embedded in a cult of aristocratic virility. Nonetheless, he believed it was possible to retrieve the Greek notion of the self's work on itself in the present, to retrieve an art of existence to supplant the moralization and normalization operating in pernicious modern technologies of the self.

Foucault also admired the Greek's recognition of the social importance of art, of its applicability to life itself. 'Why should the lamp or the house be an art object, but not our life?', he asks.[39] In a similar vein, Alasdair MacIntyre has suggested:

> [T]he cultural place of narrative has been diminished and the modes of interpreta-
> tion of narrative have been transformed until it has become possible for modern
> theorists . . . to understand the form of narrative, not as that which connects story-
> telling with the form of human life, but precisely as that which segregates narrative
> from life, which confines it to what is taken to be a separate and distinctive realm
> of art . . . [T]he relegation of art by modernity to the status of an essentially minor-
> ity activity and interest further helps protect us from any narrative understanding
> of ourselves.[40]

Like MacIntyre's, Foucault's aestheticism need not be read as either elitist or escapist. Indeed, it is echoed in Haraway's call for a cyborg politics, a politics that partly involves attention to forms of self-constitution and narrativization of marginal subjects that resist the normalizing tendencies of hegemonic medico-scientific discourses.

I have argued that feminists who have developed Foucault's radical insights are not obviously left without useful tools for struggle. Indeed, as I have suggested, Foucault's principal objective was not to provide an alternative emancipatory theory at all, but rather to provide tools that subjugated individuals might enlist in a particular set of struggles, namely, 'struggles which question the status of the individual . . . struggles against the "government of individualization"'.[41] If the practices of freedom that he identifies appear excessively individualistic, this is not because he is an individualist, but rather because this is the level of struggle on which he focused. To be sure, as we have seen, he recognized other forms of oppression as well. As Michael Kelly has pointed out, Foucault addresses 'normative questions about resistance as practical not theoretical issues . . . [as] justified in the context of a prac-tice. . . . The demands of critique arise from and are met by practice.'[42] Criticisms of Foucault that fail to recognize the rather limited and specific nature of his project miss the point.

At the same time, Foucault's rhetoric is masculine, his perspective is andro-centric, and his vision rather pessimistic. Nonetheless, his methods and cautionary tales have been useful and productive for feminist intellectuals struggling to combat dangerous trends within feminist theory, and for practice-feminist intellectuals who share neither his androcentrism nor his exclusive focus on subjection. Finally, Foucault asks us to reconsider the value of the emancipatory practices and theories that have been handed down to us through Western capitalist patriarchal traditions. Thus, his work fuels self-critical impulses within feminism that are indispensable.

Notes

Portions of this paper appeared in J. Sawicki, 'Foucault, feminism and questions of identity', in G. Gutting (ed.), *The Cambridge Companion to Foucault* (Cambridge University Press, Cambridge, 1994).

1 Irene Diamond and Lee Quinby (eds), 'Introduction', in *Feminism and Foucault: Reflections on Resistance* (Northeastern University Press, Boston MA, 1988), p. x.

2 Deborah Cook has written a compelling defence of the importance of Foucault's interviews for understanding the political dimensions of his work in *The Subject Finds a Voice: Foucault's Turn Toward Subjectivity* (Peter Lang Publishing, New York, 1993), pp. 97–107.

3 Nancy Fraser, *Unruly Practices: Power, Discourse, and Gender in Contemporary Social Theory* (University of Minnesota Press, Minneapolis, 1989), p. 49.

4 See Chapters 7 and 8 of *Unruly Practices*, and 'A genealogy of dependency: tracing a keyword of the U.S. welfare state', *Signs* (Winter 1994), pp. 303–36.

5 Nancy Hartsock, 'Foucault on power: a theory for women?', in Linda Nicholson (ed.), *Feminism/Postmodernism* (Routledge, New York, 1990), p. 168.

6 Hartsock asks: 'Why is it that just at the moment when so many of us who have been silenced begin to demand the right to name ourselves, to act as subjects rather than objects of history, that just then the concept of subjecthood becomes problematic? Just when we are forming our own theories about the world, uncertainty emerges about whether the world can be theorized. Just when we are talking about the changes we want, ideas of progress and the possibility of systematically and rationally organizing human society become dubious and suspect. Why is it only now that critiques are made of the will to power inherent in the effort to create theory?' See Hartsock, 'Foucault on power', pp. 163–4. See also Barbara Christian, 'The race for theory', *Cultural Critique*, 6 (Spring 1987), pp. 51–63.

7 Hartsock, 'Foucault on power,' p. 164.

8 Joan Cocks, *The Oppositional Imagination: Feminism Critique and Political Theory* (Routledge, New York, 1989), p. 74. See also Ann Ferguson, *Blood at the Root: Motherhood Sexuality, and Male Domination* (Pandora Press, London, 1989), for a similar criticism.

9 Nancy Hartsock, 'Foucault on power', pp. 171–2 (emphasis added).

10 For examples of this non-feminist criticism, see the articles by Taylor, Walzer and Habermas in David Couzens Hoy (ed.), *Foucault: A Critical Reader* (Basil Blackwell, New York, 1986).

11 Sandra Bartky, 'Introduction', *Femininity and Domination: Studies in the Phenomenology of Oppression* (Routledge, New York, 1990), p. 7.

12 Jürgen Habermas, 'Modernity – an incomplete project', trans. Seyla Benhabib, in Hal Foster (ed.), *The Anti-Aesthetic* (Bay Press, Port Townsend WA, 1983), p. 13. Quoted in Deborah Cook, *The Subject Finds a Voice*, p. 109.

13 Cook, *The Subject Finds a Voice*, p. 110.

14 Ibid., p. 116.

15 John Rajchman, *Truth and Eros: Foucault, Lacan, and the Question of Ethics* (Routledge, New York, 1991), p. 11.

16 Judith Butler, *Gender Trouble: Feminism and the Subversion of Identity* (Routledge, New York, 1990), p. 142.

17 Ibid., p. 147.

18 Ibid., p. 148.

19 Ibid., p. 149.

20 Donna Haraway, 'A cyborg manifesto: science, technology, and socialist feminism in the late twentieth century', in *Simians, Cyborgs, and Women: The Reinvention of Nature* (Routledge, New York, 1991), p. 157.

21 Cf. Diana Fuss, *Essentially Speaking: Feminism, Nature, and Difference* (Routledge, New York, 1989), p. 101.

22 Haraway, 'Cyborg manifesto', p. 176.

23 See Fuss, *Essentially Speaking*, p. 115, for Said quote.

24 Ideas developed in this section are largely indebted to my work with an honours student

at Williams College, Niko Kolodny, whose outstanding thesis, 'The Late Foucault', has significantly influenced my reading of Foucault's later work.

25   Michel Foucault, 'The subject and power', Afterword in H.L. Dreyfus and P. Rabinow (eds), *Michel Foucault: Beyond Structuralism and Hermeneutics*, 2nd edn (University of Chicago Press, Chicago, 1983), p. 232.

26   Michel Foucault, 'Sexual choice, sexual act: Foucault and homosexuality', in L. Kritzman (ed.), *Michel Foucault: Politics, Philosophy, Culture*, trans. Alan Sheridan (Routledge, New York, 1988), p. 294.

27   Foucault, 'Subject and power', p. 213.

28   Michel Foucault, 'Space, knowledge and power', an interview by Paul Rabinow in P. Rabinow (ed.), *The Foucault Reader* (Pantheon, New York, 1984), p. 246.

29   Michel Foucault, 'What is Enlightenment?' in Rabinow (ed.), *Foucault Reader*, p. 43.

30   Foucault, 'Space, knowledge and power', pp. 248–9.

31   Foucault, *'What is Enlightenment?'*, p. 44.

32   Michel Foucault, 'Truth, power, self: an interview with Michel Foucault', in Luther H. Martin, Huck Gutman and Patrick H. Hutton (eds), *Technologies of the Self* (University of Massachusetts Press, Amherst MA, 1988), p. 15.

33   Niko Kolodny, 'Late Foucault', p. 43 .

34   Foucault, 'Subject and power', p. 208

35   Michel Foucault, 'On the genealogy of ethics: an overview of work in progress', in Rabinow (ed.), *Foucault Reader*, p. 343.

36   Ibid., p. 348

37   Michel Foucault, 'The ethic of care for the self as a practice of freedom', in James Bernauer and David Rasmussen (eds), *The Final Foucault* (MIT Press, Cambridge MA, 1987), p. 11.

38   Kolodny, 'Late Foucault', p. 52.

39   Foucault, 'Genealogy of ethics', p. 350.

40   Alasdair MacIntyre, *After Virtue* (University of Notre Dame Press, Notre Dame, Indiana, 1981), pp. 210–11. This passage was quoted in Kolodny's 'Late Foucault', p. 55.

41   Foucault, 'Subject and power', pp. 211–12.

42   Michael Kelly, 'Foucault, Habermas and the self-referentiality of critique', in Michael Kelly (ed.), *Critique and Power: Recasting the Foucault/Habermas Debate* (MIT Press, Cambridge MA, 1994), p. 382.

7

Beyond Good and Evil: The Ethical Sensibility of Michel Foucault

William Connolly

> To be ashamed of one's immorality – that is a step on the staircase at whose
> end one is also ashamed of one's morality.
>
> —Friedrich Nietzsche[1]

The Evil of Goodness

Is Foucault, who continues to live among us, a creative carrier of a generous
sensibility? Or a dangerous thinker who threatens political restraint by scram-
bling fundamental parameters of morality? He is both. He challenges
established morality in pursuit of a higher ethical sensibility, but danger is
inscribed in the effort to shift the terms and bases of these doctrines. For to
challenge fixed conceptions of will, identity, responsibility, normality and
punishment is to be cruel to people (and aspects of oneself) attached to established moral codes; it is to open up new uncertainties within established terms
of judgement; and sometimes it is to incite punitive reactions among those
whose sense of moral self-assurance has been jeopardized. The Foucaultian
sensibility shares these characteristics with every experiment in morality,
including those enacted today in courts, families, schools, churches, hospitals,
armies, welfare offices, prisons and workplaces.

Foucault's ethical sensibility of 'care' amidst social conflict and coordination operates, then, within a series of paradoxes that threaten to derail it. But,
as I receive his political spirituality, the most promising route is to struggle to
overcome resentment against the paradoxical circumstances in which we are
set (for no god guarantees life without paradox; indeed, most of the ones I
have encountered embody it), and to negotiate this slippery terrain with intellectual daring and political care.

Let me consider a recent essay by James Miller to introduce the
Foucaultian sensibility I admire. Miller seeks to protect a liberal politics of
limits against Foucaultian assaults on the morality of good and evil. He
thinks that liberalism, with its commitment to rule of law, rights and individual responsibility provides the conditions for a politics of limits. Foucault
blurs these limits and threatens those moral stabilizations. In Foucault's 1971

interview with *Actuel*, 'the most freewheeling magazine of the French counter-culture', Miller finds Foucault running roughshod over the limits that freedom and order require.[2] Miller informs us that the interview is entitled 'Beyond Good and Evil', that Foucault attacks humanism because it 'restricts the drive for power' (a fragment from Foucault), and that Foucault wages 'total war against society' (Miller's phrase). This sounds like a refusal of self-limitation, all right – one, as Miller puts it, that Foucault reconsidered in his later work when he moved closer to liberalism.

But I find this same 1971 interview to embody an admirable ethical sensibility, one in which ingredients crucial to a future perspective are outlined with insufficient introduction of reservations and cautions that become installed later. Foucault finds a covert problem of evil to be lodged within the conventional politics of good and evil. Evil not as actions by immoral agents who freely transgress the moral law but evil as arbitrary cruelty installed in regular institutional arrangements taken to embody the Law, the Good or the Normal. Foucault contends, along with Nietzsche, Arendt and Todorov, that systemic cruelty flows regularly from the thoughtlessness of aggressive conventionality, the transcendentalization of contingent identities, and the treatment of good/evil as a duality wired into the intrinsic order of things. A modern problem of evil resides, paradoxically, within the good/evil duality and numerous dualities linked to it. Evil, again, not as gratuitous action by free agents operating in an innocent institutional matrix, but as undeserved suffering imposed by practices protecting the reassurance (the goodness, purity, autonomy, normality) of hegemonic identities. To reach 'beyond' the politics of good and evil is not to liquidate ethics but to become ashamed of the transcendentalization of conventional morality. It is to subject morality to strip searches.

There is cruelty involved in such strip searches. But they also take a precarious step towards a social ethic of generosity in relations among alternative, problematic and (often) rival identities. They promote a politics of limits through genealogies of ambiguity and arbitrariness in cultural norms that have become naturalized. This agenda can be heard in lines from the essay in question:

> The campaign against drugs is a pretext for the reinforcement of social repression; not only through police raids, but also through the indirect exaltation of the normal, rational, conscientious, and well-adjusted individual.[3]

> We emphasize the fear of criminals; we brandish the threat of the monstrous so as to reinforce the ideology of good and evil, of the things that are permitted and prohibited – precisely those notions which teachers are now somewhat embarrassed to communicate.[4]

And then, in response to a suggestion that the distinction between the normal and the pathological is today more fundamental than that between good and evil, Foucault says:

> They reinforce each other. When a judgement cannot be framed in terms of good and evil, it is stated in terms of normal and abnormal. And when it is necessary to justify this last distinction, it is done in terms of what is good or bad for the

individual. These are expressions that signal the fundamental duality of Western consciousness.[5]

What, then, is the ethical point of genealogies of good/evil and normal/abnormal? Foucault, at a later stage, suggests it:

> We have to dig deeply to show how things have been historically contingent, for such and such a reason intelligible but not necessary. We must make the intelligible appear against a background of emptiness, and deny its necessity. We must think that what exists is far from filling all possible spaces.[6]

Several elements in the Foucaultian ethical sensibility are discernible here:

1   Genealogical analyses that disturb the sense of ontological necessity, historical inevitability and purity of discrimination in established dualities of identity/difference, normality/abnormality, innocence/guilt, crime/accident and responsible agency/delinquent offender.
2   Active cultivation of the capacity to subdue resentment against the absence of necessity in what you are and to affirm the ambiguity of life without transcendental guarantees.
3   Development of a generous sensibility that informs interpretations of what you are and are not and infuses the relations you establish with those differences through which your identity is defined.
4   Explorations of new possibilities in social relations opened up by genealogy, particularly those that enable a larger variety of identities to coexist in relations of 'studied' indifference on some occasions, alliance on others, and agonistic respect during periods of rivalry and contestation.

Together these elements suggest the 'political spirituality' of Foucaultianism, or if you think I project too much into these texts, Fou-connoism. Indeed, in what follows I use Nietzsche to fill out Foucault and Foucault to fill out Nietzsche until we reach a perspective I am willing to endorse.

From Morality to Politics

If you think that a stubborn source of evil resides in the paradoxical relation of identity to the differences through which it is constituted, you might deploy genealogy to expose the constructed, contingent and relational character of established identities. Doing so to contest the conversion of difference into otherness by individuals and collectivities striving to erase evidence of dependency on the differences they contest. Doing so to open up other relational possibilities between interdependent, contending identities by subtracting the sense of necessity from every identity.

But many moralists find such a strategy to be self-defeating. Every neo-Kantian and teleocommunitarian in North America, for instance, has issued this charge against Foucault (and those lumped with him as 'postmodernists') at some point during the decade of the 1980s. Those who pursue genealogy for ethical reasons, it seems, are caught in a pragmatic contradiction or trapped in a (unique) pit of incoherencies; as a result, they emerge either as nihilists who refuse ethical restraint or as parasites who are killing the moral host from which they suck sustenance. How can you have a morality without grounding it in the Law or the Good, or, at the very least, in the Contract, the Rational Consensus, the Normal or the Useful?

From my (Foucaultian) perspective, these responses too often reflect a transcendental egoism that requires contestation. Each is egoistic because it silently takes its own fundamental identity to be the source that must guide moral life in general; it is transcendental because it insists that its identity is anchored in an intrinsic Purpose or Law or potential consensus that can be known to be true. In Nietzsche's language, such transcendental egoists insist 'I am morality itself and nothing besides is morality'. They veil egoism in the demand to universalize what they are by presenting it as what they are commanded to be by the Law or elevated to by experience of the Good. They present themselves as disinterested *servants* of the Law or the Good, and they respond to each challenge to their ego-idealism through a ritual of reiteration, restating the external, necessary, intrinsic character of the fundament they serve.[7]

But so what? How does this rejoinder speak to the fundamental question posed to the genealogist? That is, 'How can a *genealogist* cultivate an ethical sensibility? And what makes such a sensibility *ethical*?' A Foucaultian line of reply might be to challenge theories of intrinsic moral order with a competing ethical sensibility: to create a little space between morality and ethics – with appropriate apologies to Hegel.

A moralist often (but not always) thinks that a moral code can be separated from other elements in social and political practice and presented more or less systematically, whereas a post-Nietzschean thinks that, at best, an ethical sensibility can be cultivated that informs the quality of future interpretations, actions and relationships. More definitively, a moralist explicitly or implicitly gives priority to the idea of a fundamental order of identity, gender, sexuality, and so on governing cultural formations. One type accentuates the verb form 'to order', construing morality to be obedience to a god or nature or the dictates of reason or a transcendental argument or a categorical imperative. Another accentuates the noun form 'order', construing 'moral order' now as an inherent, harmonious design of being. Both types often anchor moral order in a god, either as a commander of last resort, a postulate required to give virtue its just reward in the last instance, or an ultimate source of the harmonious design discernible in being. Those who eschew a theological story present narratives in which the fundamental nature of things is supposed to be highly compatible with strong conceptions of identity, agency, rationality, autonomy, responsibility and punishment. The moralist, to put it briefly, finds some way or other to smooth out Nietzschean conceptions of 'life', 'will to power', '*différance*', and so on in the name of a smooth moral economy of equivalences, by projecting an intrinsic purpose, a law, or the plasticity of nature/bodies into the order of things.[8]

Moral order as inherent command or harmonious purpose or as (inter)subjective imposition by humans whose subjectivity acts upon plastic bodies and nature – often these are united in some unstable combination. Sometimes, such perspectives are explicitly articulated, but more often today they are implicitly installed in narratives of nature, identity, gender, sexuality, agency, normality, responsibility, freedom and goodness.

A post-Nietzschean ethical sensibility might, first, claim that most contemporary moralists are implicated in one or several of these moral economies, and, secondly, contest the sense that they exhaust the range of admirable alternatives. As the contestation proceeds, instructive points of convergence unfold between one traditional type of moral order delineated above – the design/teleological conception – and a post-Nietzschean sensibility.

Consider a few intersections between a teleological morality and an anti-teleological ethic. First, both challenge authoritarian temptations residing within the command tradition. Secondly, both construe the self to be a complex microsocial structure, replete with foreign relations, rather than a 'disengaged' unit solid or universal enough to anchor morality in itself. Thirdly, both oppose, though differently, plastic conceptions of nature and bodies often presupposed by command theories, paying attention to how human powers of agency and mastery are inflated by these presumptions of plasticity and 'disembodiment'. Fourthly, both pursue a morality/ethics of cultivation in place of one of command or rational demonstration: neither attempts to isolate a systematic 'moral theory'; each cultivates a *sensibility* that enters into the interpretations and actions it endorses.[9]

It is this last intersection I will pursue. Both the genealogist and the teleologist, then, advance an ethics of cultivation. What is cultivated? Not a Law or a categorical imperative but possibilities of being imperfectly installed in established institutional practices. Where are these possibilities located? How are they cultivated? These are the difficult questions for both perspectives.[10] Charles Taylor, to my mind the most thoughtful and flexible among contemporary defenders of a teleocommunitarian morality, speaks of 'moral sources' ambiguously lodged between established practices and a higher, fugitive experience of intrinsic purpose floating above them. Taylor's 'moral sources' are neither simple objects to be represented nor transcendental laws to be deduced. A 'source' changes as it is drawn into discursive practice, but it also provides indispensable sustenance from which moral articulation draws:

> Moral sources empower. To come closer to them, to have a clearer view of them, to come to grasp what they involve, is for those who recognize them to be moved to love or respect them, and through this love/respect to be better enabled to live up to them. And articulation can bring them closer. That is why words can empower; why words can at times have tremendous moral force.[11]

If you substitute genealogy for articulation, affirm for recognize, ethical sensibility for moral force, and (reading between the lines) 'the abundance of life' for 'a purposive god', you have at once marked momentary points of convergence and fundamental lines of divergence between a teleocommunitarian morality and an agonopluralistic ethic. These two orientations produce each other as competitors; they manufacture a competition in which neither is in a good position to write its adversary off as inconceivable, incoherent or unthinkable because the elements of strength and weakness in each are too close for comfort to those in the other. These two sensibilities are well-suited – to use terms to be redeemed later – to enter into competitive relations of agonistic respect.

Taylor almost recognizes this moment of affinity within difference with respect to Nietzsche, but he fails to do so with respect to Foucault and Derrida. Nonetheless, the line of demarcation he draws between a viable moral sensibility and the amoralism of 'postmodernism' cannot be sustained once Nietzsche has been admitted into the charmed circle of ethics. Taylor anchors his highest morality in an ambiguous relation between two dimensions: an identity deepening itself through progressive attunement to a higher purpose in being. A post-Nietzschean might draw corollary sustenance from a contingent identity affirming the rich abundance of 'life' exceeding every particular organization of it. In the Nietzschean tradition, such fugitive sources as 'life', 'bodies', 'earth', 'will to power', 'the oblivion of difference', '*différance*', 'resistances', an 'untamed exteriority' and 'untruth' play a structural role remarkably close to the roles that 'a god', 'intrinsic purpose', 'a higher direction' and 'the essentially embodied self' play in the teleological tradition that Taylor invokes. Several of the anarchistic sources on the first list serve, in Nietzsche's texts, as contestable 'conjectures' or projections informing the ethical sensibility he cultivates. Genealogy takes you to the edge of the abyss of difference, even though it cannot bring this surplus within and around the organization of things to presence.[12] Taylor's sources also embody this ambiguous, fugitive character because the higher direction cultivated is never fully articulable by finite beings and because human articulation always changes the inchoate source it draws into the (revised) linguistic web. Nietzsche, Foucault and Taylor (almost) converge in grasping the productive role of excess in ethico-political interpretation, separating themselves from a host of realists and rationalists who either have yet to plumb this dimension of their own practices or (as Taylor may do) are driven to treat the experience of excess as a 'lack' or 'fault' in a divided self always yet to be remedied.

In Nietzsche's work, as I read it, 'life', and other terms of its type, functions as an indispensable, non-fixable marker, challenging every attempt to treat a concept, settlement or principle as complete, without surplus or resistance. This projection challenges alternatives that project a commanding god, a designing god, an intrinsic identity, or the sufficiency of reason. The case for it is closely linked to recurrent demonstrations of the operational failure of the other contenders to achieve the presence their representatives (sometimes) promise.[13] The excess of life over identity provides the fugitive source from which one comes to appreciate, and perhaps to love, the an-archy of being amidst the organ-ization of identity\difference.

Genealogy by itself can lead either to repression of the experience of contingency it enables or to passive nihilism. Unless genealogy is combined with tactics applied by the self to itself it may well fuel the very resentment against the an-archy of being its advocates are trying to curtail. That is why Nietzsche and Foucault alike are involved serially with the genealogy of fixed experience and the application of tactics by the self to itself. Both are crucial to the generous or 'noble' sensibility endorsed by each. Neither alone nor both in conjunction can *guarantee* the effects sought. This latter acknowledgment is a defining mark of a post-Nietzschean sensibility because the demand for guarantees in this area is precisely what fosters the most authoritarian versions of the moralities of Law and Purpose.

A post-Nietzschean ethical sensibility, then, strives, first, to expose artifice in hegemonic identities and the definitions of otherness (evil) through which they propel their self-certainty; secondly, to destabilize codes of moral order within which prevailing identities are set, when doing so crystallizes the element of resentment in these constructions of difference; thirdly, to cultivate generosity – that is, a 'pathos of distance' – in those indispensable rivalries between alternative moral/ethical perspectives by emphasizing the contestable character of each perspective, including one's own, and the inevitability of these contestations in life; and fourthly – as Foucault eventually endorsed – to contest moral visions that suppress the constructed, contingent, relational character of identity with a positive alternative that goes some distance in specifying the ideal of political life inspiring it.[14] I draw these themes from Foucault and Nietzsche, respectively: the ethical importance of the struggle against existential resentment is emphasized by Nietzsche, and the politicization of an ethical sensibility is emphasized by Foucault. Before pursuing Foucault on the second register, let me quote from the madman himself concerning the basis of an admirable ethical sensibility:

> Thus I deny morality as I deny alchemy, that is, I deny their premises: but I do *not* deny that there have been alchemists who believed in these premises and acted in accordance with them. – I also deny immorality: *not* that countless people *feel* themselves to be immoral, but that there is any *true* reason to so feel. It goes without saying that I do not deny – unless I am a fool – that many actions called immoral ought to be avoided and resisted, or that many called moral ought to be done and encouraged – but I think that one should be encouraged and the other avoided for *other reasons than hitherto*. We have to *learn to think differently* – in order at last, perhaps very late on, to attain even more: *to feel differently*.[15]

The 'we' is a solicitation rather than a command. A new sensibility is *rendered possible* through genealogies. Then a set of experiments is enacted by the self upon its self to revise vengeful sensibilities that have become fixed. Nietzsche, like Foucault after him, commends a set of artful techniques to modify these contingent installations, these 'feelings'. The sensibility that these techniques install functions as a corollary to the cultivation of 'virtues' in teleological theories. Thus, to cite one example of such a practice, Nietzsche in *Daybreak* marks the importance of 'little deviant acts' in a life where accumulated conventions are always becoming naturalized and moralized. 'For nothing *matters more*', Nietzsche asserts, 'than that an already mighty, anciently established and irrationally recognized custom should be once more confirmed by a person recognized as rational. . . . All respect to your opinions! But *little deviant acts are worth more.*'[16] Ethical generosity becomes effective when it is installed in the feelings, and this involves a series of tactics patiently applied by a self to itself: 'All the virtues and efficiency of body and soul are acquired laboriously and little by little, through much industry, self-constraint, limitation, through much obstinate, faithful repetition of the same labours, the same renunciations.'[17] Echoes from the Christian tradition can be heard here as elsewhere in Nietzsche, but these techniques of the self are designed to foster affirmation of a contingent, incomplete, relational identity interdependent with differences it contests rather than to discover a transcendental identity waiting to be released or to acknowledge obedience to a commanding/designing god.

When Nietzsche, and later Foucault, commend the self as a work of art acting modestly and artfully upon its own entrenched contingencies, the aim is not self-narcissism, as neo-Kantians love to insist. *The point is to ward off the violence of transcendental narcissism*: to modify sensibilities of the self through delicate techniques, to do so to reach 'beyond good and evil', so that you no longer require the constitution of difference as evil to protect a precarious faith in an intrinsic identity or order. The goal is to modify an already contingent self – working within the narrow terms of craftsmanship available to an adult – so that you are better able to ward off the demand to confirm transcendentally what you are contingently.[18] In Foucault's terms, 'care of the self' is the operative practice. In Nietzsche's terms,

> one thing is needful: that a human being should *attain* satisfaction with himself, whether it be by means of this or that poetry and art; only then is a human being at all tolerable to behold. Whoever is dissatisfied with himself is continually ready for revenge; and we others will be his victims, if only by having to endure his ugly sight.[19]

The 'ugliness' that Nietzsche opposes, then, reflects the demand to ratify a contingent identity by transcendental means. Look around at the next faculty meeting if you need empirical verification of this ratification process.

But so far I have merely outlined some of the aspirations within this ethical sensibility. We have so far only glimpsed the dangers, paradoxes and limits within which it operates.

The Ontological Problematic

Foucault resists the language of 'life' that Nietzsche invokes.[20] He does so, I think, to fend off the suggestion such a term conveys to some (though not to the mature Nietzsche) either of an elemental energy directly accessible to experience by non-linguistic means or of a vital, purposive force that must be allowed expression regardless of the implications it carries for anyone or anything else. But if Foucault denies a law or purpose in being while also resisting the language of life (and 'will to power'), does this mean that the ethical sensibility he endorses is free of ontological (or 'essentialist') dimensions?[21] Does this sensibility liquidate every semblance of 'the universal'?

In a recent essay on Foucault's 'cultivation of the self' Pierre Hadot asserts that Foucault misreads the Stoics and the Epicureans in a way that vitiates his own ethic. To these Greeks, 'the point was not to forge a spiritual identity by writing but to free oneself from one's individuality, to raise oneself to universality'.[22] Foucault's reduction of the universal back into the individual, Hadot fears, results in a solipsistic self: 'by defining his ethical model as an ethic of existence, Foucault might have been advancing a cultivation of the self which was too purely aesthetic – that is to say, I fear a new form of dandyism, a late-twentieth century version'.[23] I fear that Hadot, in the company of others, collapses the space in which the distinctive Foucaultian sensibility is formed, doing so by the way he deploys 'the universal' in relation to 'the self', the 'aesthetic' and 'dandyism'.

Foucault, I want to say, affirms a hypothetical universal that does not conform to any possibility that Hadot recognizes. He affirms a hypothetical, ontalogical universal, one designed to disturb the closure and narcissism of dogmatic identities, one affirmed to be a contestable projection, and one treated as an alternative to ontologies of Law and Purpose. Foucault struggles, against the grain of the language he uses and is used by, not to project a 'logic' or order into the fundamental character of being. He invokes what might be called an ontalogy, a 'reading' of the fundamental character of being that resists imputing a logic to it and affirms its alogical character. It is this fugitive, deniable and contestable experience, always resistant to articulation, that is approached through the arts of genealogy and affirmed through techniques of the self. And it is this critical task that must be renewed perpetually because of pressures installed in language and other elements of communal life to reinstate the fundamental 'logic' of good and evil into the experience of being.

Consider again a quotation presented earlier. Foucault says 'we have to dig *deeply* to show how things have been historically *contingent*, . . . intelligible but not *necessary*', making 'the intelligible appear against a *background of emptiness*'. A deep contingency, a lack of necessity in things, a background of emptiness – these themes, inserted into the agenda of genealogy, gesture towards the ont-alogical universal Foucault would endorse. The 'emptiness' of things suggests the absence of a Law or Purpose governing existence. In a similar way, numerous expressions of 'plenitude', 'doubles' and an 'untamed exterior' gesture towards an abundance that exceeds any particular set of conventions without assuming the form of a Law, Identity or Purpose governing things – an emptiness with respect to an intrinsic order, an abundance with respect to any fixed organ-ization of actuality. These are fugitive experiences to cultivate through genealogy, doing so to enhance generosity in rivalries between identity and alter-identity that provide each with its ambiguous conditions of existence.[24]

In one essay, Foucault strives to express this ontalogical problematic most actively. Here he makes it clear that the ont-alogy installed in his researches is not one that is or is likely to become known to be true. It takes the form of a 'happy posit-ivism' (hyphen added) or 'critical principle' through which questions are posed and critical comparisons with other positions are explored. It shares this paradoxical character with all other fundaments presumed or posited to date in ethico-political interpretation, even though many of the latter strive so hard to conceal this status of their own faith. Allow me to condense a few pages in 'The Order of Discourse' into a few lines, doing so to underline how Foucault both elaborates his stance and exposes tactics by which alternative stances of its type conceal their posit-ivistic and comparative character.

'*It seems to me,*' Foucault says, 'that beneath this apparent veneration of discourse, under this apparent logophilia, a certain fear is hidden. It *is just* as *if* prohibitions, thresholds and limits have been set up in order to master, at least partly, the great proliferation of discourse in order to remove from its richness its most dangerous part.' Next, marching orders are presented to those who endorse such semblances: 'And *if* we want to' . . . analyse the terms of this fear, *then* 'we must call into question our will to truth'; 'we must not imagine there is a great unsaid or a great unthought . . . which we would have to articulate or think at last'; 'we must not imagine that the world turns towards us a legible face which we would have only to decipher'. This stack of negative imperatives, stretched in front of a small 'if', finally culminates in an affirmative whose standing at the end of a long chain of hypotheticals has (almost) been forgotten: 'We must conceive discourse as a violence which we do to things, or in any case as a practice which we impose on them; and it is in this practice that the events of discourse find the principle of their regularity.'[25]

Two things. First, Foucault's conception of discourse, containing its own uncertainties and proliferations, is initially presented as a critical principle 'we' pursue in our researches. But as the imperatives that operationalize this practice pile up, it shortly begins to be heard as an imperative of being as such. The posit-ivism on which it is founded is all too easy to forget. This contrived forgetfulness, condensed into the space of a couple of pages, mimics and exposes the ontological forgetfulness of moralist-political discourse. The hypothetical character of the fundamental presumptions becomes buried beneath the weight of discursive practice, and because it is impossible to proceed without implicitly invoking some set of fundaments, this set, too, all too readily becomes received as a set of absolute imperatives installed in the order of things. Genealogy breaks up this inertia of presumption that constantly reinstates itself as Nature, God, Law, or Purpose; it scrambles the sense of ontological necessity implicit in contingent consolidations.[26]

Secondly, Foucault contests implicit and explicit ontologies of intrinsic order and plasticity not simply by showing how each conceals the hypothetical character and multiple sites of undecidability in its own imperatives but also by projecting in competition with them an (always underdeveloped) ontalogy of that which is 'violent, pugnacious, disorderly . . . , perilous, incessant . . . , and buzzing' within discursive practice.

If this anti-logical logos is hypothetical, comparative and problematical, why struggle to operationalize it through critical comparison to other familiar alternatives? There is unlikely to be a final answer to this question, just as there is none forthcoming with respect to the alternatives against which it contends. But one response resides in the fact that every interpretation presupposes or invokes some such problematical stance with respect to the fundamental character of being; to try to eliminate such a stance altogether from interpretation is either to repress crucial dimensions of one's own perspective or to lapse into a passive nihilism of resolute silence. Passive nihilism cedes the activity of interpretation to dogmatic perspectives; it secretly concedes too much to fundamentalists by treating the problematical standing of its own projections as a sufficient reason to withdraw from the field of interpretation. It still presumes that this condition of discourse is a 'fault' or 'lack' that 'ought not to be' rather than a productive source of creativity that makes life possible and keeps things moving.

The Foucaultian problematic elicits fugitive, subterranean elements in contemporary experience, where old verities have fallen on to hard times and where the sense of violence in them may be more palpable to more people. Foucault's ontalogical projection speaks to a problematical experience increasingly available, while contending against insistencies and resentments that press us to deny, evade, avoid or defer its fugitive power. Its thematization alters the terms of contestation in political discourse. Familiar debates between the advocates of Law, Purpose and Normality no longer seem to exhaust the available terms of debate. The sense of necessity governing the old debate is broken, and a set of complementary assumptions not subjected to debate by these debating partners now become open to interrogation. Each alternative, including the one Foucault advances, is now more likely to be received as a 'problematic' rather than as a 'position' or 'theory': it is construed as a particular, tension-ridden gathering of impulses, insistences, presumptions and questions through which interpretation proceeds rather than as a coherent set of imperatives on which it 'rests'.[27] Such a modification in the terms of self-presentation can have salutary effects on the character of ethical discourse.

Foucault identifies, though more lightly and obliquely than the mentor who inspires him, *ressentiment* as a source from which the problematics of moral order are constructed. Some of us now begin to hear each of these orientations as point and counterpoint in the same melody of deniable revenge; more of us refuse to treat them as The Set that exhaust the possible terms of ethical debate. Foucault says:

> Nothing is fundamental. That is what is interesting in the analysis of society. That is why nothing irritates me as much as these inquiries – which are by definition metaphysical – on the foundations of power in a society or the self-institution of a society, etc. These are not fundamental phenomena. There are only reciprocal relations, and the perpetual gaps between intentions in relation to one another.[28]

It will assist my reading if you read the first sentence along two registers: 'Nothing is *fundamental*' in the sense that no fundamental Law or Purpose or Contract governs things; '*Nothing* is fundamental' in the sense that energies and forces exceeding the social construction of subjects and things circulate through 'gaps' in these institutionalizations.

So there is a politics of forgetfulness built into the character of language, the imperatives of social coordination, the drives to revenge against the contingency of things, and the insecurities of identity. Genealogy disturbs this forgetfulness, in the interests of drawing us closer to the experience that nothing is fundamental. The results of genealogy are then to be translated into noble effects, as you reach towards a sensibility beyond good and evil. But how can this combination of genealogical disturbance and noble sensibility ever establish itself securely in a self or a culture at any particular time? It cannot. The Nietzsche/Foucault sensibility (taking various forms such as passing by, generosity, agonistic respect, a pathos of distance, the spiritualization of enmity) consists of a set of elements that cannot be combined together perfectly at any single time. They lack 'compossibility' not because of 'weakness of will' or 'the crooked timber of humanity', where the primordial 'fault' resides within the self, but because the accentuation of one element in this combination at any moment necessarily impedes the other at that time. The (post-)Nietzschean ideals of nobility, a pathos of distance, agonistic care, and passing by never arrive; they are at best always coming to be. One element is always incompletely articulated with the other to which it must be united. Here we encounter a 'rift' or dissonance not within but between human capacity and the temporality in which it is set:

> More and more it seems to me that the philosopher, being of necessity a man of tomorrow and the day after tomorrow, has always found himself, and had to find himself in contradiction to his today.[29]

This means, I take it, not only that the cultivator of such a sensibility regularly encounters conflict with a culture inscribed by the logic of good and evil, but that the pursuer, given the continuing power of forgetfulness amidst the quest to incorporate generosity into one's corporeal sensibilities, always has more to do to arrive beyond the logic of good and evil. To celebrate such a philosophy is always to offer 'A Prelude to a Philosophy of the Future', and that paradoxical condition too must be affirmed by those who struggle against *ressentiment*. Foucault places this Nietzschean theme on a political register when he says, perhaps in response to a question posed by Charles Taylor during a collective interview, 'the farthest I would go is to say that perhaps one must not be for consensuality, but one must be against nonconsensuality'.[30] In a Nietzschean–Foucaultian world, something is always out of joint ethically because it is impossible to combine all the elements of nobility perfectly in one site at one time. The struggle to reach beyond good and evil is salutary, but the claim to have arrived there is always a falsification that reiterates the dogmatism of the duality you oppose. That is why, I think, Foucault celebrates the ambiguity of politics and finds politics, in one of its registers or another, always to be appropriate.

An Ethico-politico Spirituality

An ethical sensibility, *anchored* in an ontological problematic, *rendered* through genealogies of the possible, *cultivated* through tactics applied by the self to itself, *embodied* as care for an enlarged diversity of life in which plural constituencies coexist in more creative ways than sustained by a communitarian idea of harmony or a liberal idea of tolerance, *politicized* through a series of critical engagements with established social apparatuses of good/evil, normal/abnormal, guilt/innocence, rationality/irrationality, autonomy/dependence, security/insecurity. Several of these dimensions can be heard in the following celebration of 'curiosity':

> I like the word [curiosity]. It evokes 'care'; it evokes the care of what exists and might exist; a sharpened sense of reality, but one that is never immobilized before it; a readiness to find what surrounds us strange and odd; a certain determination to throw off familiar ways of thought and to look at the same things in a different way . . . ; a lack of respect for the traditional hierarchies of what is important and fundamental.[31]

Let me locate this sensibility more actively on a political register. I do so, first, by modifying the received democratic imaginary to correspond more closely to a timely politics of care for the strife and interdependence of contingent identity\difference relations; secondly, by considering what relationships such a sensibility might strive to establish with the fundamentalisms circulating through contemporary life; and, thirdly, by engaging tensions that persist between an ethic of cultivation and persistent circumstances of political engagement.

Foucault does not articulate a vision of democracy. His early objections against political ideals as prisons militates against it; and his later, cautious affirmation of a positive political imagination never takes this form. But numerous comments in the context of his participation in public protests and demonstrations are suggestive on this score. It seems to me that a series of correspondences can be delineated between the ethical sensibility cultivated by Foucault and an ethos of democracy they invoke. Consider three dimensions of democratic practice in this light.[32]

1 *Democracy within the Territorial State*   A viable democratic ethos embodies a productive ambiguity at its very core. Its role as an instrument of rule and governance is balanced and countered by its logic as a medium for the periodic disturbance and denaturalization of settled identities and sedimented conventions. Both dimensions are crucial. But the second functions politically to extend the cultural effects of genealogy, to open up the play of possibility by subtracting the sense of necessity, completeness and smugness from established organ-izations of life. If the democratic task of governance ever buries the democratic ethos of disturbance and politicization under the weight of national consensus, historical necessity and state security, state mechanisms of electoral accountability will be reduced to conduits for the production of internal/external others against whom to wage moral wars of all too familiar sorts.

2 *The Limits of the State*   We live during a time when an asymmetry between the globalization of relations and the confinement of electoral

institutions to the territorial state functions too often to intensify state chauvinism and violence. The nostalgia in political theory (and many other sites,
too) for a 'politics of place', in which territoriality, sovereignty, electoral
accountability, nationality and public belonging must all map the same space,
depoliticizes global issues and fosters democratic state chauvinism. During
the late-modern time, productive possibilities of thought and practice might
be opened up by a creative disaggregation of elements in the modern democratic imagination, paying attention, for instance, to how a democratic ethos
might exceed the boundaries of the state, even when electoral institutions of
democratic accountability are confined to the state. During a time when corporate structures, financial institutions, intelligence networks, communication
media and criminal rings are increasingly global in character, democratic
energies, active below and through the state, might also reach beyond these
parameters to cross-national, extrastatist social movements. A new and timely
pluralization of attachments, identifications and spaces of political action,
already unfolding before us in the late-modern era, might eventually compromise the state's ability to colonize the terms of collective identity at key
historical moments. Foucault's 1981 declaration at a press conference on
behalf of the boat people is suggestive on this score in its protest against
treatment of the stateless by states, in its insistence on extending political
identifications beyond the state, and in its identification of that which diverse
constituencies within states share that might serve as a contingent basis for
extrastatist, cross-national mobilization:

> There exists an international citizenry that has its rights, that has its duties, and that
> is committed to rise up against every abuse of power, no matter who the author, no
> matter who the victims. After all, we are all ruled, and as such, we are in solidar-
> ity. . . . The will of individuals must be inscribed in a reality that the governments
> wanted to monopolize. This monopoly must be wrested from them bit by bit, each
> and every day.[33]

3   *The Politicization of Non-statist Global Movements*   Boundary-crossing
political movements, with respect to, say, gay/lesbian rights, disturbance of
international patterns of state secrecy and surveillance, contestation of the
state's monopoly over potent symbols of danger and practices of security, and
the renegotiation of first-world patterns of consumption that impinge on the
future of the earth can both contribute to the democratic drive to participate
in the events that define our lives and ventilate dead pockets of air within contemporary states. As a variety of cross-national, extrastatist movements
already in motion accelerate, they might extend the democratic ethos beyond
the state through a pluralization of democratic spaces of action. They might
compromise the state as the ultimate source of collective identity whenever a
crisis arises and contest its monopoly over the rules of boundary-crossing.

These, then, are some of the elements in the ethico-political sensibility of
Michel Foucault: genealogies that dissolve apparent necessities into contingent formations; cultivation of care for possibilities of life that challenge

claims to an intrinsic moral order; democratic disturbances of sedimented identities that conceal violence in their terms of closure; practices that enable multifarious styles of life to coexist on the same territory; and a plurality of political identifications extending beyond the state to break up the monopolies of state-centred politics.

But surely, politicization of the Foucaultian sensibility will continue to meet with opposition and outrage from the various fundamentalisms circulating through contemporary life. Nietzsche and Foucault both teach us how the more optimistic hopes of the Enlightenment on this score are unlikely to succeed. Theistic and secular priests persist as voices in and around us: the inertia of shared practices, forces of *ressentiment*, the pressures of guilt arising from ambivalent identifications, the effects of social coordination on the reification of selves and institutions – all these forces press upon the effective generalization of generous sensibilities. They make genealogies and politicizations of dogmatic identities into perpetual tasks. They render the move 'beyond good and evil' always a movement and never a secure achievement. What, then, can be the terms of engagement between an ethical sensibility affirming care for the contingency of things and those moral fundamentalisms that oppose it as nihilistic, relativistic or parasitic? (As if everyone, everything, and every institution were not parasitical in some way!)

One salutary possibility Foucault cultivates, I think, is to convert some relations of antagonism between fundamentalists and genealogists into those (as I call them) of agonistic respect. The effective possibilities here are limited, but they are nonetheless real. Agonistic respect constitutes an element in an impossible utopia, worth pursuit even amidst the impossibility of its final realization.

Agonistic respect, as I construe it, is a social relation of respect for the opponent against whom you define yourself even while you resist its imperatives and strive to delimit its spaces of hegemony. Care for the strife and interdependence of contingent identities, in which each identity depends upon a set of differences to be, means that 'we' (the 'we' is an invitation) cannot pursue the ethic that inspires us without contesting claims to the universality and sufficiency of the moral fundamentalisms we disturb – hence genealogy and deconstruction. But this antagonism can be translated into something closer to agonistic respect in some cases, as each party comes to appreciate the extent to which its self-definition is bound up with the other and the degree to which the comparative projections of both are contestable. We opponents can become bonded together, partially and contingently, through an enhanced experience of the contestability of the problematic each pursues most fervently. This is what Nietzsche meant by the 'spiritualization of enmity',[34] although he thought the capacity to operationalize such a relationship was limited.

Agonistic respect differs from its sibling, liberal tolerance, in affirming a more ambiguous relation of interdependence and strife between identities over a passive letting the other be. The latter may be desirable on occasion, but it is less available in late-modern life than some liberals presume. It is not sufficient to shed 'prejudice' because our identities are bound up with each other in a world where pressures to enact general policies are always active. It 'cuts' deeper than tolerance because it folds contestation into the foundations of the putative identity from which liberal tolerance is often derived and delimited. But, still, it remains close enough to liberal tolerance to invite comparison and critical negotiation, pressing its debating partner to fold the spirit of genealogy more actively into its characterization of 'the individual' and arguing against the spirit of complacency so often lodged in bifurcations between the private and the public.

There is considerable irony and foolishness in a call to agonistic reciprocity because it invites the fundamentalist to incorporate an element we endorse into its own identity. The invitation may be refused. But the call is made in the context of showing him through genealogy some of the ways in which his fundamentals too are questionable and contestable. And we do not demand that the fundamentalist incorporate the entire sensibility of the opponent as a condition of respect; we merely call on the fundamentalist to acknowledge the contestability of its claim to intrinsic moral order and to affirm self-restrictions in the way it advances its agenda in the light of this admission. In this way, space for politics can be opened through a degree of reciprocity amid contestation; new possibilities for the negotiation of difference are created by identifying traces in the other of the sensibility one identifies in oneself and locating in the self elements of the sensibility attributed to the other. An element of care is built into contestation and of contestation into care. But, as I have already said once, such invitations are often rejected.

So the difficulties continue. There are, additionally, numerous times and places where the terms of opposition are likely to remain implacable even after the initial positions have been softened by reciprocal acknowledgement of the contestability of each stance. Debates over the di(per)versity of sexuality, over abortion, and, perhaps, over the right to take one's own life when one decides the time is right, might have this character to varying degrees. Some fundamentalists who treat homosexuality as per-verse, for instance, might be moved to cultivate either a studied indifference or agonistic respect in relation to those who celebrate sexual di-versity. But they will be less likely to do so with respect to the issue of gay parents. Those who celebrate diversity here will have to try to disrupt their operational presumptions concerning what is 'natural', maintaining confidence in the possible efficacy of genealogy and struggle in exposing the social constitution of the perversity they fear.[35] So, introduction of a Foucaultian sensibility more actively into the terms of political contestation, first, is likely to be refused by many constituencies and, secondly, to encounter obdurate instances of non-negotiability even between constituencies willing to engage it.

The Foucaultian faith, if I may put it this way, is that more extensive cultivation of a political ethos of agonistic care makes a real difference in private and public life, even if it remains a minority stance within that life, for it is a political problematic of interrogation, engagement and negotiation, not a political doctrine of intrinsic identity, consensus and resolution. Its impossible utopia is agonistic respect among differences irreducible to a rational consensus in settings where it is often necessary to establish general policies. It locates freedom in the gaps and spaces fostered by these collisions and negotiations rather than in a pattern of harmonious unity or private sanctuary it hopes to realize. It counsels recurrent disturbance and negotiation of the numerous paradoxes of political life over attempts to conceal, resolve or repress them.

These last reflections, linking an ethical sensibility to an ethos of politics, reveal another tension between these two registers amidst the durable connection between them. An *ethic of cultivation* requires attention to the nuances of life; it applies tactics patiently and experimentally to the self; it affirms ambiguity and uncertainty in the categories through which ethical judgement is made. But *a politics of engagement and insurgency* often generalizes conflicts so that one set of concerns becomes overwhelmed by others; it opens up the probability of more totalistic definitions of one side by its opponents; it sometimes foments rapid transformations exceeding the temporal and spatial rhythms of ethical cultivation. Cultivation of care for the contingency of things and engagement in political contestation, then, are locked into a relation of strife amidst their mutual implication.[36]

There is no way to eliminate these tensions, unless you endorse some fictive model of political agency that has never been instantiated anywhere. The tension already identified between genealogy and sensibility now catapults into the medium of politics. The struggle against resentment of a world in which 'nothing is fundamental' involves a willingness to act in such ambiguous circumstances,[37] because although these two registers are in tension with each other; they are also interdependent – the ethical sensibility requires the ethos as one of its conditions of existence and vice versa. The aspiration is to draw agonistic respect from the effects of politics and to fold agonistic respect into the art of politics. The danger flows from suppression of such tensions and ambiguities in the name of private tranquillity, rational harmony or consummate political agency.

Perhaps I can allow Foucault to have the last word (for the moment):

> There's an optimism that consists in saying that things couldn't be better. My optimism would consist rather in saying that so many things can be changed, fragile as they are, bound up more with circumstances than necessities, more arbitrary than self-evident, more a matter of complex, but temporary, historical circumstances than of inevitable anthropological constants. . . . You know, to say that we are much more recent than we think, is to place at the disposal of the work that we do on ourselves the greatest possible share of what is presented to us as inaccessible.[38]

Notes

I would like to express my appreciation to Jane Bennett, David Campbell, Tom Dumm, Dick Flathman, Bonnie Honig and Tracy Strong for criticisms of the first draft of this chapter.

This chapter first appeared in *Political Theory*, 21, 3 (1993), pp. 365–89. Sage Publications Inc.

1 Friedrich Nietzsche, *Beyond Good and Evil: Prelude to a Philosophy of the Future*, trans. Walter Kaufmann (Vintage, New York, 1966), p. 83.

2 James Miller, 'The politics of limits' (paper delivered at the 1991 convention of the American Political Science Association, 1–4 September, Washington, DC), paragraph 13.

3 Michel Foucault, 'Revolutionary action: "Until Now"', in Donald Bouchard (ed.), *Michel Foucault: Language, Counter-Memory, Practice* (Blackwell, Oxford, 1977), p. 226.

4 Ibid.

5 Ibid., p. 230. I bypass here Miller's crude charge that, in calling in the same essay for an attack on the 'whole of society', Foucault legitimizes attempts to eradicate all social institutions. It becomes clear what Foucault has in mind when he says, 'I believe, on the contrary, that this particular idea of the "whole of society" derives from a utopian context.' Foucault attacks 'the dream' of 'the whole of society' because the dream of wholeness and harmony it pursues requires the destruction, elimination, or repression of everything that does not fit in with it.

6 Michel Foucault, 'Friendship as a way of life', in *Foucault Live*, Sylvere Lotringer (ed.) and trans. John Johnston (Semiotext(e), New York, 1989), p. 208.

7 I hope it becomes clear as we proceed that not all those who anchor their morality in the Law or the Good are locked into transcendental egoism. Only those who insist that the 'other' cannot devise a morality unless he or she accepts these fundamentals are so locked in. Thinkers like Foucault, Derrida and Nietzsche are excellent at bringing out the subterranean fundamentalism of many who otherwise deny it.

8 A world with no commanding or designing god is likely to be marked by discordances, accidents and chance. This is exactly the world in which Nietzsche and Foucault cultivate an ethical sensibility. Such a world, in turn, is not a likely source of a teleological ethic. A world with an omnipotent god, as the nominalists tried to show the Thomists, is unlikely to be one limited by any prior design of the world, for an omnipotent god flourishes in a highly contingent world it can vary in any way at any time; its omnipotence is threatened by any design that restricts it. A teleological morality without a god is problematic, then, but it is also difficult to construct one with an omnipotent god. It is not that a god filling the bill is impossible to construct, but such a delicate construction raises the question as to whether it is discovered or invented to fill the exact purpose it is supposed to reveal. On the other hand, an omnipotent god seems most compatible with a morality grounded in a transcendental imperative, and neo-Kantians have had a hell of a time demonstrating this imperative without recourse to such a deeply contestable faith. Hans Blumenberg pursues these issues, in his history of onto-theological aporias and debates that have marked the West since the inception of Augustinianism: Blumenberg, *The Legitimacy of the Modern Age* (MIT Press, Cambridge MA, 1983). A last 'theological' point: although there are powerful pressures binding the command and design traditions to the authority of a god, a 'post-Nietzschean' ethic need not resist every conception of divinity. A god as 'absence', for instance, might be compatible with a post-Nietzschean sensibility. So might some versions of polytheism. I prefer 'nontheistic reverence for the ambiguity of being'.

9 In these comparisons I take Charles Taylor to represent the 'teleological' model. His version of it, I think, brings out effectively assumptions implicit in the other formulations. He might resist the title I have bestowed on him, but the language through which his morality is couched is very teleological by comparison to the Nietzschean/Foucaultian sensibility defended here. Those are the only terms of comparison that interest me at the moment. See Charles Taylor, *Philosophical Papers*, Vols 1–2 (Cambridge University Press, New York, 1985).

10 Notice how the favourite critique that neo-Kantians pose against teleocommunitarians loses its bite against post-Nietzscheans. They contend that it is impossible to reach universal agreement on the nature of the good, commending instead the same quest with respect to rights or the procedures of justice. I concur that a grounded consensus on the good is unlikely, even though I emphasize much more than neo-Kantians do how much established conventions are treated implicitly by neo-Kantians and teleocommunitarians as if they were so grounded, for both parties tend to eschew genealogy, limiting their ability to identify limits to pluralism in established regimes.

11 Charles Taylor, *Sources of the Self: The Making of Modern Identity* (Harvard University Press, Cambridge MA, 1989), p. 96. A powerful argument in Taylor's study is that advocates of

'disengaged' morality are unable to account for the sources of their own moral inspirations. Bernard Williams, in an insightful review of this study, points to the strength of this argument, while claiming that Taylor's framework of analysis is not well suited to come to terms with Nietzschean thought: 'I think that Taylor, in his search for the sources of value, seems not to have taken seriously enough Nietzsche's thought that if there is, not only no God, but no metaphysical order of any kind, then this imposes quite new demands on ourself-understanding.' *New York Review of Books*, 4 November 1990, p. 48. I concur with this judgement.

12 In *Identity and Difference*, trans. Joan Stambaugh (Harper and Row, New York, 1969), Martin Heidegger speaks of 'the oblivion of difference'. 'We speak of the difference between Being and beings. . . . That is the oblivion of difference. The oblivion here to be thought is the veiling of the difference as such' (p. 50). The thought is similar to Nietzsche's elusive presentations of life. You never lift the veil of difference as such, for difference is that which differs from the organ-ized, conceptualized, fixed and determinate. But you might encounter the oblivion of difference through artful techniques; you might experience the way in which the organ-ization of experience draws on that which is itself not yet organ-ized.

13 Hence the indispensability of deconstruction and genealogy to the sensibility in question.

14 'But, in the end, I've become rather irritated by an attitude, which for a long time was mine, too, and which I no longer subscribe to, which consists in saying: our problem is to denounce and to criticize; let them get on with their legislation and their reforms. That doesn't seem to me the right attitude.' Lawrence D. Kritzman (ed.), *Michel Foucault: Politics, Philosophy, Culture*, trans. Alan Sheridan (Routledge, New York, 1988), p. 209.

15 Friedrich Nietzsche, *Daybreak*, trans. R.J. Hollingdale (Cambridge University Press, Cambridge, 1982), #103, p. 104 (original emphasis). Alan White gives an excellent reading of this formulation in *Within Nietzsche's Labyrinth* (Routledge, New York, 1990).

16 Nietzsche, *Daybreak*, #149, p. 97 (original emphasis). In *Will to Power*, trans. Walter Kaufmann and R.J. Hollingdale (Random House, New York, 1967), #1019, Nietzsche lists six practices that have been wrecked by the church's monopoly and misuses of them. They are asceticism, fasting, the monastery, feasts, the courage to endure one's nature, and death. In each of these cases, Nietzsche would refigure the practice in question into one that fends off existential resentment and fosters a 'nobility' that reaches beyond the ugly narcissism of good and evil. The notes in *Will to Power* that focus on the body also focus on the priority of techniques of the self over rational argumentation or direct reform of 'the will' in fostering a generous ethical sensibility.

17 Nietzsche, *Will to Power*, trans. Walter Kaufmann (Vintage, New York, 1968), #995.

18 Narcissus loved not himself but his image in the pond. The transcendental narcissist loves the image of itself that it projects into a transcendental command or direction.

19 Friedrich Nietzsche, *The Gay Science*, trans. Walter Kaufmann (Vintage, New York, 1974), #290, p. 233.

20 Nietzsche himself invokes the vocabulary of life in one way in his early work and in a modified way in his later work. I will not pursue that issue here, but it is the later uses to which I am drawn.

21 I generally try to avoid the language of 'essentialism'. It means, variously, a philosophy that pretends that a highest law, nature or principle can be brought into full presence; the confidence that there is a fundamental law or purpose governing existence that can be more closely approximated in life through hermeneutic piety; and the claim that every actor and every interpreter invokes a set of fundamental assumptions about the character of being in every act and interpretation. Thus anyone can successfully accuse anyone else of 'being an essentialist' in some way or another. Foucault, as I read him, is not an 'essentialist' on the first two scores but is one on the third. He comes close to what one might call the 'vague essentialism' advanced by Gilles Deleuze and Felix Guattari in *A Thousand Plateaus* (University of Minnesota Press, Minneapolis, 1970). 'So how are we to define this matter-movement, this matter-energy, this matter-flow, this matter in variation that enters assemblages and leaves them? It is a destratified, deterritorialized matter. It seems to us that Husserl brought thought a decisive step forward when he discovered a region of vague and material essences (in other words, essences that are vagabond, inexact and yet rigorous), distinguishing them from fixed, metric and formal essences' (p. 407). Husserl did

not pursue this insight far enough. Deleuze and Guattari do in Plateau 6, 'How do you make yourself a body without organs?'. The strategies they endorse there are initially more extreme and dangerous than Foucault or Nietzsche would endorse. For American conceptions that cultivate a lawless essentialism more cautiously, see Jane Bennett, *Unthinking Faith and Enlightenment* (New York University Press, New York, 1986) and Donna Haraway, *Primate Visions* (Routledge, New York, 1989).

22   Pierre Hadot, 'Reflections on the notion of "the cultivation of the self"', in Timothy J. Armstrong (ed. and trans.), *Michel Foucault: Philosopher* (Routledge, New York, 1992), p. 229.

23   Ibid., p. 230. Hadot goes on to say, 'For my part, I believe firmly . . . in the opportunity for modern man . . . to become aware of our situation as belonging to the universe. . . . This exercise in wisdom will therefore be an attempt to open ourselves up to the universal'.

24   This ontalogical level is the one that Habermasians, to date, have been hesitant to engage in Foucault. While they do not postulate a Law or Design in being, the terms through which 'communicative ethics' is delineated seems to presuppose a plasticity of bodies and things that is challenged by Foucault. These two competing 'communicative ethics' will enter into more reflective engagement with one another when both parties actively consider how differences in their most fundamental projections into nature and bodies enter into their divergent readings of 'discourse'. Habermas evinces awareness of this dimension when he engages communitarians. In one note, he indicates how Sandel would have to explicate the normative content of 'community, embodied and shared self-understanding' more carefully to sustain his theory: 'If he did, he would realize just how onerous the burden of proof is that neo-Aristotelian approaches must bear, as in the case of A. MacIntyre in *After Virtue*. . . . They must demonstrate how an objective moral order can be grounded without recourse to metaphysical premises.' *Moral Consciousness and Communicative Action* (MIT Press, Cambridge MA, 1990). Habermas, in turn, would have to show how the conception of nature he presupposes in his discourse ethics is superior to the projection that Foucault endorses in 'The order of discourse' and elsewhere. It only defers the engagement to reduce Foucault's options to a choice between a morally obnoxious 'vitalism' or the model of communication Habermas himself invokes. I pursue this issue between Habermas, Foucault and Taylor in 'The irony of interpretation', in Daniel Conway and John Seery (eds), *Politics and Irony* (St. Martin's Press, New York, 1992).

25   Foucault, 'The order of discourse', in Michael Shapiro (ed.), *Language and Politics* (Blackwell, Oxford, 1984), pp. 125–7 (emphases added). I find the second half of the last sentence to be more credible than the first. The first might suggest that the level of violence is the same in all instances and hence that it is always impossible to curtail violence.

26   The forgetfulness pursued here runs deeper than I have so far intimated. It is built into the very character of shared vocabularies, where the conditions of existence of a common language require an imposition of equivalency within the concepts deployed that 'forget' those excesses that do not fit into these configurations. Nietzsche discusses this level of forgetting in *On the Genealogy of Morals*, trans. Walter Kaufmann (Random Books, New York, 1967). In the texts in which this logic of equivalences is discussed, he also develops linguistic strategies that cut against it.

27   See 'Polemics, politics, and problematizations: an interview with Michel Foucault', in P. Rabinow (ed.), *The Foucault Reader* (Pantheon, New York, 1984), pp. 381–9.

28   Foucault, 'An ethics of pleasure', in *Foucault Live*, p. 267.

29   Nietzsche, *Beyond Good and Evil*, #212, p. 137.

30   Foucault, 'Politics and ethics: an interview', in Rabinow (ed.), *Foucault Reader*, p. 379. Foucault refuses the language of 'regulative ideal' in pointing out his own double relation to consensus.

31   Foucault, 'The masked philosopher', in Kritzman (ed.), *Politics, Philosophy, Culture*, p. 328.

32   These dimensions are developed more fully in W. Connolly, *Identity\Difference: Democratic Negotiations of Political Paradox* (Cornell University Press, Ithaca NY, 1991) especially the last two chapters, and 'Democracy and territoriality, millennium', December 1991, pp. 463–84.

33   Quoted in Didier Eribon, *Michel Foucault*, trans. Betsy Wing (Harvard University Press, Cambridge MA, 1991), p. 279. Thomas Keenan, in 'The "paradox" of knowledge and power', *Political Theory* (February 1987), discusses this statement thoughtfully and extensively.

34 'The Church has at all times desired the destruction of its enemies: we, we immoralists and anti-Christians, see that is to our advantage that the church exists. . . . In politics, too, enmity has become much more spiritual – much more prudent, much more thoughtful, much more for-bearing. . . . We adopt the same attitude toward the 'enemy within': there too we have spiritualized enmity, there too we have grasped its value.' F.W. Nietzsche, *Twilight of the Idols*, trans. R.J. Hollingdale (Penguin, New York, 1968), under 'Morality as anti-nature', pp. 43–4.

35 When presenting these thoughts, I have found that about this juncture someone will interrupt, charging: 'Murder is perverse! Torture is perverse! Your ethics of "generosity" sanc-tions these perversities. Certainly it lacks the ability to oppose them.' But, of course, it does not carry such implications. Its governing sensibility of care for the interdependence and strife of identity\difference obviously opposes such acts. Indeed, very often, murder and torture express the very dogmatism of identity and abstract revenge against life that this sensibility seeks to cur-tail. So why is the charge so predictable at this juncture? I suspect that some who wrap themselves in a fictive law they cannot demonstrate would like to punish those who keep pounding away, first, at the paradox of identity and, secondly, at the cruelties installed in transcendental narcis-sism. The next time this charge is issued, examine the demeanour of the one who issues it. Does he look like he could kill you? Fortunately, there are still laws to restrain dogmatists from acting on these impulses.

36 These comments on tensions between an ethic of cultivation and a politics of critical engagement are inspired from one side by a critique delivered to me every other day by Dick Flathman and from another by a critique offered by Stephen White of a paper of mine at the 1991 meeting of the Southern Political Science Association, Tampa, Florida entitled 'Territoriality and democracy'. Flathman is tempted by an anti-politics that expects little of politics because of its ugly character. This sensibility is brought out effectively in *Toward a Liberalism* (Cornell University Press, Ithaca NY, 1990) and in a study of Hobbes soon to be pub-lished by Sage in its 'Dialogue with modernity' series. White finds my 'ethic of cultivation' to be in conflict with a 'politics of radical hope'. I find the terms in which he recognizes the tension to be too stark for my position. I do not have 'radical hopes' for a political transformation; rather, I support radical critiques that might open up new spaces for life to be while supporting new pos-sibilities of democratic change. Together, these two put considerable pressure on the position I seek to inhabit. It is only after I compare the tensions in my stance with those in their's, respec-tively, that my confidence begins to reassert itself.

37 How can resentment find expression against a world lacking the kind of agency capable of receiving this animus? It cannot. That is what makes existential resentment so dangerous, for it preserves itself by manufacturing viable substitutes on which to displace itself. It (re)invents the logic of good and evil to locate evil agents to hold responsible for an apparent contingency of things that should not be this way. But where, asks Nietzsche, comes this last 'should not'? From the same pool of existential resentment that keeps refilling itself. The logic of good and evil keeps returning – hence the continuing need for genealogy. Not even an 'overman' can simply surpass this logic. It is timely to laugh at the overman, too.

38 Foucault, 'Practicing criticisms', in Kritzman (ed.), *Politics, Philosophy, Culture*, p. 256. Does Foucault underplay the tendency of 'God', 'the Law', 'Nature' and 'Intrinsic Purpose' to reinstate themselves offstage even as the contingencies within them are addressed on stage? Probably. But I prefer to say that he acts as if these enactments can be challenged through counter-enactments. Girard, Freud, Lacan, and others show how final markers reinstate them-selves even though they lack the transcendental basis that their most earnest supporters yearn for. In Freud, guilt flows from the ambivalent identification with a model that one has just (perhaps in the imagination) killed; it precedes the God and the Law invented retroactively to explain it. Freud and others challenge moralisms that translate the experience of guilt into a transcenden-tal source. But the next step is to develop strategies through which to politicize violences accompanying the conversion process. This is where the genius of Foucault shines.

Part III

POLITICAL TRADITIONS

8

The Disciplinary Moment: Foucault, Law and the Reinscription of Rights

Duncan Ivison

> When today one wants to object in some way to the disciplines and all of
> the effects of power and knowledge that are linked to them, what is it that
> one does, concretely, in real life . . . if not precisely appeal to this canon of
> right, this famous formal right . . . ? But I believe we find ourselves in a kind
> of blind alley here.[1]

The rule of law is a norm at the centre of liberal political order. Because of the
indeterminacy and contentiousness of judgements about proper conduct, an
umpire is needed to provide a definitive resolution to conflicts as a necessary
condition for the existence of civil society. But this umpire must both provide
for the law of a community and yet act through a law, where these secondary
(or tertiary) umpiring procedures are justifiable in terms which do not simply
replay the disputes which led to the need for an umpire in the first place. That
is, there are rules about the ways of going about changing the rules which
define the structure of the political game (separation of powers, definition of
offices) in the first place.[2] Even more importantly, the rule of law is connected to thicker visions of the body politic in so far as it prefigures, in its
procedures and constraints, the main features of a particular ideal of political community. In this sense it almost always functions constitutively, and
never simply as a restraining or negative value.

Now law can be constitutive in any number of different ways, most of
which I cannot go into here. But building on what I have said so far, and looking forward to our discussion of Foucault, I want to note a distinction
commonly made in liberal discussions of the rule of law: the differentiation
between domains in which law is said to be created and those within which it
is then applied. This is a porous and probably unconvincing distinction.
However, there are institutions designated as being the primary site of one or
the other, though with overlaps, and any understanding of the rule of law in
late-modern democracies must come to grips with the relation between these
institutions and domains. This is the ground of classic separation of powers

doctrine (and to a different extent, balance of power doctrines). To explore this in any depth is not the purpose of this chapter. But I do want to note the open and constrained practices of interpretation (of rules, statutes, codes) which accompany the delineation of these domains, and which are part of the practices of the rule of law.[3] The 'creation' of law then (at least in the legal literature) includes, for example, the interpretation of legislation by courts in light of a set of ideals or substantive doctrines. To change a law in the course of interpreting it might not be (strictly speaking) to create one, but I shall not discuss these complications here.[4] The core idea is that interpretation in some way expands law to meet standards or functions which cannot simply be read off the black letter of the rule, or the original intentions of its 'framers'. Interpretation is *constructive*: it imposes purpose on a law to make it the 'best possible' given a set of relevant conditions (historical context, underlying principle, etc.).[5] Conversely, though the application of a law must always involve interpreting it in some way, the emphasis on application is meant to delimit the role of interpretation (especially by the judiciary). The core idea here is that focusing on application is meant to put less emphasis on the possibilities for interpretation and expansion, and more on applying the law in as straightforward a way as can be deduced as intended by those designated as 'law-makers'.

The rule of law organized around these two domains and interpretive emphases attracts particular kinds of theoretical and political attention. Institutions and decision-makers which are said to have the power to create or change rules are held responsible for outcomes and states of affairs related to those powers. Institutions and decision-makers which are said have the power and responsibility for applying rules laid down by others, attract attention related to those powers.[6] They might be challenged as to whether or not they are simply applying the rules as best they can in accordance with some regulative standard, or they might be accused of misapplying those rules.

Foucault challenges these conventional distinctions, and the purpose of this chapter is to follow and evaluate the way he does this. For Foucault, the rule of law is implicated in the creation and maintenance of specific forms of political order. The power it exercises is always creative and productive and yet not in reference to some supervening moral good, or to characteristics inherent in the notion of law as such. Nor is it best understood according to classical separation of power (or balance of power) doctrines. Foucault tells a story as to how the political function of law – as helping to constitute the regulative norms of the *civitas* – came to be supplanted by something else: discipline. And discipline is, of course, a manifestation of his unique (now almost conventional) account of the circulation of power in civil society.

Foucault is notorious for relating almost all of his discussions of political and social phenomena to questions of power. Particularly central to this perception is his analysis of the emergence and eclipse of what he calls the 'juridico-discursive' conception of power. Changing conceptions of law, and more specifically the rule of law, play a crucial role in this story. However, it is often assumed by commentators that for Foucault, law becomes simply the epiphenomenona of a grid of impersonal relations of power that overlays all social and political practices. This implies that Foucault does not have much to say about law or the rule of law, and hence attention shifts to the emphasis on the ubiquity of power and its manifestation in 'disciplinary practices'. Even among philosophers of law and critical legal theorists who have taken Foucault's work seriously – and there are many – one rarely finds an extended discussion of what precisely Foucault says about law in the many different places in his work where it is discussed. Instead, the disciplinary moment of *Discipline and Punish*, that is, the eclipse of the juridico-discursive conception of power (the rule of law), is seen as wholly supplanting the force of law. The discussion of law then necessarily becomes a discussion of something else – power, discipline, governmentality, practices of self, etc.[7]

I want to stand back from this approach however, or, more precisely, invert it. I want to ask: what is the power of the juridico-discursive model itself? In what way is Foucault's own conception(s) of law prefigured in his critical histories of liberal theories of the rule of law? Perhaps surprisingly, the alternative conception of law therein seems to include a conception of rights. How can Foucault talk of rights given what we are usually told about his conception of the person, and his supposed contempt for liberal humanism?

The answers to these questions cannot be neatly matched to conventional tags in the philosophy of law. Foucault is certainly not a legal positivist; the law is never simply an independent, institutionalized mode of rule application. Nor is he a natural law theorist, for reasons which if not obvious now, will become so below. He might be something of a legal realist, in so far as he sees rules always needing to be supplemented by other forces, but would not accept that it is simply judges who create the law. He is some kind of critical legal theorist, but not of the influential neo-Marxist strand. Nor is he easily slotted into the poststructuralist strand, if that category is based primarily on an indeterminacy thesis to do with legal meaning (and meaning in general). I cannot defend this here, but the indeterminacy of meaning and the proliferation of interpretation so central to Derrida's writings on the law, for example, are at least not central in the same way in Foucault's. He seems more interested in norms – though for distinctive reasons – than most deconstructionists. Thus I will resist the plausible if not fashionable tendency to lump together a seamless poststructuralist or postmodern faction in the philosophy of law. If anything, Foucault seems to be more interested in the history of law, particularly in relation to early-modern political theory and (later in life) in Ancient Greece and Rome, than in the philosophy of law *per se*. But it is an historical interest informed by philosophical preferences. And I want to try to draw those preferences out below.

In section I, then, I turn to two accounts of the person and his or her rights in relation to civil society and the rule of law that inform Foucault's approach: those of Nietzsche and Hobbes. But I shall concentrate less on the Nietzchean legacy than on the Hobbesian, which is unusual for standard interpretations of Foucault but more accurate, I think, in relation to the particular issues at hand. In section II, I turn briefly to some extracts from

and Punish and other writings to show the seemingly contradictory
.aken by Foucault on the emergence of discipline and the relevance
., rights. In section III, I pause to consider the nature of rights from a more
standard liberal perspective. I compare this, in sections IV and V, with the
later Foucault's rights talk and his invocation of 'practices of liberty'.

I The Rule of Law and Civil Society

Nietzsche remarks helpfully that 'willing seems to me to be above all something *complicated*, something that is a unit only as a word'.[8] He does so while
casting some doubts on the idea that the will is linked necessarily to a special
kind of causal imperative, that is, to an 'I' rather than to some event or state
of affairs. The fiction consists of believing 'wholeheartedly that willing *suf-
fices* for action', that the cause of the action (outcome) is understood wholly
in terms of a mode of prescription, as if it is brought about *ex nihilo*.[9]
Nietzsche famously turns this on its head. Not only is there no '"being"
behind doing, effecting [or] becoming', but *'you are being done*, in every
moment. Mankind at all times has mistaken the passive for the active: it is
their constant grammatical mistake.'[10] There could hardly be a more devas-
tating attack on the idea of a pre-given autonomous agent, and more
precisely, on the centrality of a particular way of acting – that is, voluntarily
to that agent.

Nietzsche goes on to develop his own account of what autonomy might
mean, and especially about the need to escape the numbing customs of cooperative (that is, liberal) institutions. It is defiantly 'supra-moral' (*übersittlich*),
the truly autonomous agent alone as 'judge and avenger of one's own law'.[11]
So when Nietzsche talks about rights he means a certain balance of power, a
mutual recognition of power. But the moment an individual's power appears
'shaken and broken, our rights cease to exist': conversely, if we have grown
very much more powerful, the rights of others' cease to exist for us as well.
This is a relation between equals, but the content of equality is given in terms
of a recognition of power, and a 'pride' in maintaining it.[12]

But what else might follow from a sceptical attitude towards the idea of a
pre-given autonomous agent, or to a model of action that is always deliber-
ated or voluntary action? A key aspect of the moral and political psychology
of early modern political theorists such as Hobbes and Locke was the recognition of the heteronomous nature of (an all too) human agency. They saw the
problem of government not simply as the impersonal coordination of similar
subject/citizens by a formal–rational law, but also the administration and
regulation of the social sphere that often meant going beyond the black letter
of Law. As Locke put it: 'Allegiance is neither due nor paid to Right or
Government which are abstract notions but only to persons having right or
government.'[13] Government was not a set of practices resting on a frame of
abstraction, but on men. I shall say a few words about Hobbes here.[14]

For Hobbes, an individual's autonomy was not a metaphysical or political presupposition. It was a problem. Not because it was true, but because people acted as if it were so. Though human behaviour was in part driven by self-interest, it was more often than not constituted by a concatenation of imaginary phantasms, customs, opinions, habits, teachings, norms and passions. As he put it in the *Leviathan*, 'the actions of men proceed from their opinions'.[15] These opinions were not filtered through private rational deliberations, but imbibed (unreflectively for the most part) from the swirling mass of competing representations and doctrine championed by nasty priests, lawyers, parliamentarians, political opportunists and university professors. Worse, people were only too willing to go to war and die for these beliefs, cheered on by factional elites. The clergy were a particularly odious caste for Hobbes, since they had convinced people that damnation was a fate worse than death, and thus encouraged civil war.

The Hobbesian solution is familiar but often overstated. The absolute sovereignty of the Leviathan stems in part from his (much neglected) observation that the 'power of the mighty hath no foundation but in the opinion and belief of the people'.[16] The Hobbesian theory of power, then, is complex. Absolute force often backfires: 'Suppression of doctrine does but unite and exasperate, that is, increase both the malice and power of them that have already believed them.'[17] So there are times when cooperation is more important than mere compliance, and the impersonality of the office of sovereign – reinforcing its role as *arbitrator* – is meant to point towards this. It also points towards the valorization of a different kind of politics, at least different from the apparent chaos of mid-seventeenth-century England.

The problem is a coordination problem, a coordination (not harmonization) of heteronomous – but fundamentally equal – individual wills. This last qualification is very unNietzschean. Nietzsche had little to say about human equality, save to lament its levelling and corrosive effects on the unique and incomparable, or as existing only between such persons. But equality was central to the problem of political order in early-modern political thought since the fundamental form of conflict at the heart of political order and disorder is one between equals, and this cannot be solved by some pre-existing order of difference. The weak are never so weak to accept (without chaotic consequences) subordination to a supposedly natural superior, and the strong are never so strong as to be *sure* of their total supremacy. Note this is only the barest (but still significant) sense of equality; that all men stand in the same relation to nature, which is not to say, of course, that all men come to possess equal power. This is why Hobbes is so sensitive to the more ethereal qualities of power, that it is often based on nothing more substantial than a 'reputation for power', and is a self-fulfilling prophecy of sorts, something elites had learnt only too well.[18]

Now Foucault claimed that Hobbes was 'the one who has circumvented this discourse of permanent struggle and civil war . . . thereby saving the theory of the state'[19] (the second part of this claim has interesting implications for understanding the relation between Foucault's idea of the state and his conception of politics which I touch on below). What is circumvented is the confrontation of forces marked by actual 'blood, battles, and corpses', and what remains after the roar of battle has subsided is a certain 'state of representations . . . which are played off against each other' not quite as in war but always potentially so.[20] Compare this with another rendering of the establishment of civil society by Foucault: 'the rule of law [does not] finally replace warfare: humanity installs each of its violences in a system of rules and thus proceeds from domination to domination'.[21] He sets up his own play of representations here, between the 'violences' done to subjects in war and in society, and the points at which these two states of affairs (war and society) become either relentlessly indistinguishable or importantly different.[22] It is not clear that he settles on one or the other, and this ambivalence is even more apparent in his rather odd discussion of rights. What is at stake is a particular representation of law. Might it be that one way the 'growth of capabilities and autonomy' can be 'disconnected' from the 'intensification of power relations' is to provide a new representation of Right?[23]

II   The Disciplinary Moment

Reading *Discipline and Punish*, it is difficult at times to know whether Foucault intends the Panopticon, that embodiment of 'disciplinary power', as a metaphor for the development of modern power relations *tout court* – that we are living in some kind of 'carceral society' – or that it is meant strictly as an example of the specific local research he insisted was the grounds for his idea of 'critique'. The ambiguity is heightened by the example, since although Bentham did not intend Panopticism to be considered a utopian or totalized theory of society, he did think it appropriate for a wide range of different practical and institutional settings. It provided Foucault, of course, with an exquisite example of 'disciplinary technology', an 'anatomo-politics' of the human body seeking out the 'optimization of its capabilities', the increase of its usefulness and 'docility', and its integration into systems of economic (that is, discreetly effective) regulation.[24] This technique for making useful individuals is then transposed into the most central and productive sectors of society – factories, schools, universities, the 'war-machine' – into the means through which the development of the capacities of men and women are carried out. As Dreyfus and Rabinow put it, disciplinary technology 'gradually overflowed its institutional bounds'.[25]

But just how far does this overflow run? It appears to flood the whole of the social body. Thus, for Foucault, the contractarian moment of early-modern political thought is also the disciplinary moment, where 'individuals' (used without qualification here; that is, not only certain kinds of individuals – prisoners, patients, etc.) are constituted as 'correlative elements of power and knowledge'.[26] Foucault's claim appears to be that the theories of sovereignty and rights which emerged from the natural law tradition of the seventeenth and eighteenth centuries were superimposed on disciplinary technologies in such a way as to conceal their '*actual* procedures, [and] the element of domination inherent in [their] techniques'.[27] And this process appears to have been relentless, penetrating to the core of liberal democratic societies' most important legitimating theories and values – including the concept of rights:

> The general juridical form that guaranteed a system of rights that were egalitarian in principle was supported by these tiny, everyday, physical mechanisms, by all those systems of micro-power that are essentially non-egalitarian and asymmetrical that we call the disciplines. . . . [T]he disciplines provide, at the base, a guarantee of the submission of forces and bodies. *The real corporeal disciplines constituted the foundation of the formal juridical liberties. The contract may have been regarded as the ideal foundation of law and political power; panopticism constituted the technique, universally widespread, of coercion* . . . The 'Enlightenment', which discovered the liberties, also invented the disciplines.[28]

It is not just that rights discourse misses the actual workings of disciplinary power, but more strongly, it is itself a particularly efficient mask *and* conductor of this power: 'sovereignty and disciplinary mechanisms are two absolutely integral constituents of the general mechanisms of power in our society'.[29] The juridical liberties are not only utterly non-transcendental or universal, but act in concert with this insidious form of power/knowledge:

> We have entered a phase of juridical *regression* in comparison with the pre-seventeenth-century societies we are acquainted with; we should not be deceived by all the Constitutions framed throughout the world since the French Revolution, the Codes written and revised, a whole continual and clamorous legislative activity: these were the forms that made an essentially normalising power acceptable.[30]

And rights can hardly be said to be something belonging exclusively, or at least meaningfully, to individuals.

> The individual is not to be conceived as a sort of elementary nucleus, a primitive atom, a multiple and inert material on which power comes to fasten or against which it happens to strike, and in so doing subdues or crushes individuals. In fact, it is already one of the prime effects of power that certain bodies, certain gestures, certain discourses, certain desires, come to be identified and constituted as individuals. . . . The individual which power has constituted is at the same time its vehicle.[31]

And yet: 'This does not mean we have to get rid of what we call human rights or freedom, but that we can't say that freedom or human rights has to be limited at certain frontiers.'[32] What is Foucault getting at? What did he mean by writing a kind of declaration of rights in the course of defending Vietnamese boat people (and in other places, various dissidents and activists) – 'Face aux gouvernements, les droits de l'homme' – wherein he claimed that there is an 'international citizenry' whose duty is to 'rise up against every abuse of power, whoever the author, whoever the victims', indeed there is an 'an absolute right' (*un droit absolu*) to do so?[33] Why was he interested in the arguments of the Levellers in the English Civil War, and those of the French anti-absolutist Boulainvilliers? And in one of his last interviews, he referred to 'the rights of each person . . . immanent' in the 'serious play' of dialogue, as opposed to polemics. The polemicist proceeds, 'encased in privileges' that he never questions (these might even include rights-claims! See section III below), and his interlocutors are first and always enemies. The 'serious' discussant, on the other hand, seems to recognize her interlocutor as 'a subject having the right to speak'.[34]

What could be the basis for any new form of right, if that was what was necessary? Foucault's rights talk seems incongruous in relation to his work as a whole, as is his apparent interest in the problematics of early-modern political theory and modern liberalism. We're not used to thinking he was interested in liberalism or rights other than to destroy them.[35]

III   Liberal Rights

The rights of a juridical subject can refer to a number of different things, but perhaps most importantly in the liberal tradition (and those parts emerging from the natural law school), to the extent to which an individual can *effectively* claim something: that is, a protected liberty right others have a duty to allow the exercise of. What is added to moral argument by invoking rights? There is considerable controversy on this point, ranging from those who simply assert the sanctity of rights, to those who deny it adds anything altogether, or at least could be easily replaced by something else (like duty). I shall not enter into this here. Rather, I will take it that most liberals want to affirm a sense of rights which is connected to a distinctive kind of respect for the person as a potential maker of claims; that is, as a grounds for self-respect with regard to having at least some areas of non-dependence on others, and a respect for others similarly perceived.[36] Thus H.L.A. Hart has argued influentially that our general rights (rights in absence of special conditions arisen between men and women in certain transactions or relationships) are merely specific instantiations of a fundamentally 'equal right of all men to be free'.[37] In being able to claim, demand or insist on certain actions, perhaps most importantly in the realm of those we might call 'our mandatory rights' (for example, a right to self-preservation, or the preservation of humankind) a degree of discretion is made a part of our moral lives, and in that way helps us to live a life that is worthwhile. Worthwhile, that is, in being free in relation to a range of possible actions, and having the capacity to reflect upon and pursue one's own plans and purposes. Not all rights are by definition mandatory, and thus they can be insisted upon or not depending upon the circumstances or their relation to other moral considerations (think about relations between friends).

Now this composite right to be free is sometimes characterized as a 'natural' right. What work is the word 'natural' doing here? For Hart, all this means is that '[men] have this right *qua* men and not only if they are members of some society or stand in some special relationship to each other, nor is this right conferred by men's voluntary action'.[38] The justification rests on a deep principle of human freedom: rights are distinguished from other moral considerations in that they protect and enhance human freedom. The important point is that 'natural' seems to mean both non-conventional and/or logically pre-political. The defender of natural rights is thus committed, at the least, to the possibility of the existence of 'objective' (that is, non-conventional) moral rules defining rights (though the content of these rights might be determined according to circumstances of time and place). Natural rights are 'fictions', but only in the sense that they address how individuals *ought* to be treated or what should be the case; they are not meant as claims about what is in fact the case.[39] Thus committed, the defender of natural rights also presupposes certain elements of the human condition that hold universally for all persons, no matter what their cultural or communal embeddedness (hence why we are more prone to call them *human* rights); that there exists a minimal moral agency in all persons, a basic rationality and capacity for choice and valuing. The point isn't to deny that people are not constituted by social goods, or that the development of human capacities has nothing to do with one's particular community or society. Rather, the claim is that there are many different kinds of political and non-political arrangements which *can* (although don't necessarily) suffice for the minimal development of these basic capacities or moral agency.[40] This is also to claim that the capacities here are so basic and important that they would even form part of what it would be to have a personal commitment in the first place (think about what is involved in understanding an attachment as a 'commitment'). It does not follow from our being social, the rights theorist might argue, that the development of our human agency is impossible outside a *particular* form of political society, as opposed to within a range of different forms.

How we come to recognize these capacities is not presupposed. Philosophers are increasingly dissatisfied with the idea that the sheer rationality of morality can overcome the variety of ethical perspectives in our world today, or even that it should attempt to. Our recognition of others as creatures 'like us' might depend more on our 'sentimental education' – our ability to sympathize or empathize with lives that at first glance seem very different from ours – than on our ability to grasp the requirements of an essential moral law.[41] In other words, there is a sense of the lightness of touch such a theory of human nature seems to exert; not so much a theory as a working through of what we mean by 'we'.

The rights theorist also need not assert that rights hold an absolute priority with regard to the common good, or any other moral consideration. Some of the most recent and powerful interpretation of rights – whether 'natural', 'human', 'political' or 'social' – have argued that it is the *combination* of private interest and public good that both characterizes many of the fundamental rights we appeal to and explains their centrality in our political culture. A. John Simmons has put this very well:

> In pursuing both the good for humankind and the various goods for particular human beings, communities, and societies, the necessary limitation and coordination of our activities are expressed morally in the natural rights we possess, derivable from certain features of the admittedly more complex self and the enduring aspects of its many possible social embodiments. These natural rights do not destroy the possibility of genuine community among persons; rather, they can facilitate and protect community, not only in hopelessly pluralistic, but in strongly homogeneous societies.[42]

From another perspective, Habermas has recognized both the limiting and coordinating function of rights in relation to the construction of 'communicative conditions'.[43] Claims about the possibility of 'discursive will-formation' are expressed as rights of participation or communication in order to make the communicative conditions 'operational' and realizable. These rights go towards constituting the practices of bargaining and rational discourse, thus 'legally constituted political will-formation' always points beyond itself, that is, it remains open to the 'communicative flows' of 'autonomous public spheres' where certain beliefs, issues and arguments have yet to be institutionalized into decision-making processes.[44] Thus communicative rights, or social rights, can emerge from outside established positive law, from the 'spontaneity' of an antecedent public sphere. Interestingly, the 'negative' civil rights of the liberal tradition are not rejected or deconstructed here, but are seen by Habermas as providing a brake (a form of self-limitation) on the tendency of legally constituted processes of political will formation to 'puff' themselves up into a 'totality . . . the purported centre or society'.[45] They too become part of the realization of the common (communicative) good.

IV   Foucault and Rights

It is tempting to start off any comparison between Foucault's use of rights talk and that of contemporary liberal theory by saying that he simply rejects the entire juridical edifice as a means of effective political agency. This would seem to follow from the standard accounts of his notion of power/knowledge, and his conception of the person. But this would be too quick. The issues discussed above provide an opportunity for us to consider Foucault on power and the self a bit more carefully (though not exhaustively). The important thing here is to see how Foucault argues for a certain way of reading this tradition of political discourse.

As much as it seems that Foucault has simply equated law or Right with the functioning of discipline, this is not quite right. Indeed, 'law, particularly in the eighteenth century, was a weapon of struggle against . . . monarchial power . . . [and] law was the principal mode of representation of power (and representation should not be understood here as a screen or illusion, but as a real mode of action)'.[46] Thus a simple equivalence between law and domination is unhelpful. The point about abandoning the juridical mode of sovereignty has to do with what Foucault calls a 'concrete analysis' of modern relations of power: it is almost a methodological point about developing an understanding that is 'more empirical, more directly related to our present situation, and which implies more relations between theory and practice'.[47]

Briefly, power for Foucault did not exist in a concentrated or distributive form, and was not something that could be fully captured by saying it emanated from the will of a sovereign or the consent of the people. This is not to say that consent was never a condition for the existence or maintenance of

power, but that power was not by *nature* the manifestation of this kind of consensus. A relation of power is a kind of action that does not necessarily act
immediately or directly on others, but acts on their actions, whether now or
in the future. It is always a way of acting upon an acting subject (or subjects).
Its 'real nature' is not reducible to some primal act of violence or locus of
consent (though each might represent instances of specific forms or exercises
of power), but rests on the idea of *conduct* (*conduite*) with all of its multiple
senses in both English and French ('to conduct oneself appropriately', 'to
conduct an orchestra', 'to insist on proper conduct'). If a power relationship
is any set of actions upon other actions, understood on a continuum which
runs from the slightest manipulation to brutal violence, then it would appear
that almost everything involves power. And this is precisely Foucault's point:
'in human relations, whatever they are . . . power is always present: I mean the
relationships in which one wishes to direct the behaviour of another'.[48] But
how can the concept of power, or a power relation, have any analytical value
whatsoever if every human relation is one of power? If power is always present, are we always being dominated or subjugated, can we ever be free? How
can it make sense to appeal to any form of rights?

First, we cannot use 'domination' or 'subjugation' as synonyms for power
relations or exercises of power, since though they are possible instances of
these relations, they do not exhaust the possibilities of the conception.
Foucault insists that a state of domination is a distinctive kind of power relation, namely, one in which the relations of power are fixed in such a way that
they are 'perpetually asymmetrical and the margin of liberty is extremely
limited'.[49] Whether a power relation is also a 'state of domination' is a matter
for specific investigation, and thus it is wrong simply to equate the two.
Investigations of relations of discipline and subjectivation (*mode d'assu-
jetissement*) can 'in no way . . . be equated with a general analytics of every
possible power relation'.[50] Thus Foucault is constantly insisting on the importance of sticking close to the ground in our investigations (in our
archaeologies and genealogies), and to seek out the specific set of circumstances that make up the complex interplay of concepts and practices in
modern social relations. But Foucault himself seems to make sweeping statements about the nature of *all* the juridical liberties and constitutions of the
post-revolutionary age being in concert with discipline, of subverting the liberties they claim to protect (see the quotes in section II). Has he shown us
this? Or is he instead, in certain places, trying to point to ways in which the
manifestation of these liberties – including rights – can be situated among a
different set of questions, and put to different kinds of uses? The answer to
the first question is no, the answer to the second is more interesting.

An incoherence which comes immediately to mind is that Foucault has so
deconstructed the notion of the individual (as an 'effect' of relations of power,
etc.) that it is absurd to say any such person would be able to claim something
like a right. To this common complaint there is a short response: the questioning of Man hardly extinguishes man himself. Foucault links the concept
of Man in very specific ways with 'humanism', by which he means a set of

themes that have appeared throughout human history in all sorts of different contexts, whether 'Christian humanism' or 'Marxist humanism', etc., within which (at least since the seventeenth century) there has been a particular account of the person which draws on different religious, scientific or philosophical foundations. (The Heideggerian tone of these discussions deserves separate treatment.) The point is not to deny the possibility of self, but to promote 'new forms of subjectivity' by refusing the 'individuality' which has been 'imposed' on us for centuries.[51]

So given that Foucault does not completely obliterate the idea of self, what does he offer in place of what we have? Again, the answer is not as straightforward as the question, for in fact what he offers is a (partial) history of how we've come to be, what he calls 'practices of the self', a general theme of much of his later work. The intention seems to have been to follow up on his claim that there was no universal form of the subject found everywhere, but instead one constituted through the 'rules, styles, [and] inventions' of particular cultural and political environments, including practices of subjectivation, or indeed 'practices of liberty'. He saw this as following on from his earlier studies of truth and power, but on a slightly different tack, an 'historical ontology in relation to ethics through which we constitute ourselves as moral agents', that is, the problem of individual conduct.[52]

As many commentators have pointed out, the possibility of such a history means that wherever Foucault discusses the omniscience of power, resistance is not far behind, because as we have seen, his account presupposes that power always works on the basis of an acting subject.[53] The self here, minimally, is an active corporeal being with certain basic bodily capacities and possibilities for action, and one who sees him/herself as such a being, for seeing oneself as a corporeal being has to come from somewhere. Interestingly, this relation to self is already present in some form in the seventeenth century.[54] But Foucault sees this as entirely derivative of an emerging scientific world-picture, and instead goes back to the Greeks in search of an ethics of self where the ethical substance and mode of subjectivation had less to do (he claims) with a general Morality or prohibitive code, and more to do with an 'art of existence' or 'technique of self'.[55] Ethics, then, is simply a *rapport à soi*, whereby an individual constitutes him/herself as a moral subject of his or her own actions, making him/herself a subject of ethical conduct. Foucault implies that this is mainly a critical enterprise, not the propagation of some kind of permanent 'aestheticized existence', but rather the development of capacities to detach (if only temporarily) one's ethics from conventional moralities and norms. Thus liberty is itself a practice, one that will allow these minimal corporeal individuals to 'decide upon receivable and acceptable forms of existence or political society'. The liberty of men

is never assured by the institutions and laws that are intended to guarantee them. This is why almost all of these laws and institutions are quite capable of being turned around. Not because they are ambiguous, but simply because 'liberty' is what must be exercised.[56]

It might be that rights–claims constitute one of these 'practices of liberty'.

Before seeing what direct evidence there is for this potential answer, allow me to pull together some of the strands of Foucault's account of self and liberty presented above. Foucault is undoubtedly making an evaluative judgement here between 'states of domination' and states of minimal domination, or the 'strategic game' of liberties. Indeed, the function of philosophy (of what Foucault sometimes calls 'critique') is to challenge 'all phenomena of domination at whatever level or under whatever form they present themselves'.[57] The valuing seems to lie in the relation between practices of liberty and the relation to self; it is this relation which is valuable and important and must be actualized against those states of domination which seek to subvert it. The point is to question any hypothesis that suggests freedom is to be found in the loosening of certain repressive locks to reveal a hidden or imprisoned nature. In short, Foucault problematizes the claim that in liberating oneself the ethical problem is solved: 'Liberation opens up new relationships of power, which have to be controlled by practices of liberty.'[58] The key question always remains – how can I practice freedom?

Many critics have argued that when Foucault talks about these practices of liberty he has somehow smuggled back in normative notions of liberal humanism, such as autonomy, reciprocity, dignity and human rights. Moreover, it is claimed that he must do so if he is to have any answer to the question 'why resist?'.[59] On one level this claim makes sense if you insist that resistance and liberty are only comprehensible in relation to some kind of foundational claim about their worth, and/or you believe that Foucault generally obliterates the possibility of any form of human agency. I have rejected the latter claim, and will say no more about it here. The point about norms, however, is an important one, and brings out the crux of many of the issues we have been examining up to now. It seems undeniable that Foucault both values the practices of liberty, in the sense that it is a preferred state of affairs to being dominated or subjugated, and at the same time appears to deny the grounds for saying so. Though Foucault sees no need to provide any kind of philosophical foundation for the worth of liberty, he does still ground it in something – the actual experiences of domination. In other words, we distinguish between domination and practices of liberty in our engagement in specific practices and 'apparatuses', whether it be prisons, asylums, hospitals, whatever. No a priori theory can promise us freedom, and we achieve it only in relation to particular practices and struggles. The risk of bad judgements here, of 'unphilosophical' thinking, is one Foucault is only too willing to take, since he thinks wide-ranging normative theories (especially with regard to wholesale political change) have been, on the whole, 'disastrous'. But this is disingenuous of Foucault, for he is positing a norm of sorts, an 'antinorm', a picture of a minimal, active, corporeal agency:

> The problem, you see, is one for the subject who acts – the subject of action through which the real is transformed. If prisons and punitive mechanisms are transformed, it won't be because a plan of reform has found its way into the heads of social workers; it will be when those who have to do with penal reality, all those people, have

come into collision with each other and with themselves, run into dead-ends, problems and impossibilities, been through conflicts and confrontations; when critique
has been played out in the real, not when reformers have realized their ideas.[60]

And so it is with rights. This 'historico-political discourse' (as opposed to
the 'philosophico-juridical discourse'; note the work the word 'political' is
doing here)[61] does not presuppose the universal subject of the jurist or
philosopher, but rather the subject in battle. The subject seeks to make right
hold sway, but it is a *'singular right* marked by a relation of conquest, domination . . . its role is not one . . . above the fray . . . [or] . . . to found a
reconciliatory order; but to posit a right that is marked by asymmetry and
that functions as a privilege to be maintained or re-established'.[62] Thus
recourse to 'human' rights or 'natural' rights is always a tactical recourse,
which, in the context of 'the permanence of war in society', does not seek to
gauge unjust governments or violence by 'the ideal principle of reason or law',
but to 'awaken beneath the form of institutions and legislations the forgotten
past of real struggles . . . the blood that has dried on the codes of law'.[63]
Foucault turned, at different times, to a consideration of the political discourse of the English Civil War, particularly that of the Levellers, to show this,
providing, needless to say, a rather unorthodox reading of these texts and one,
to be fair, not fully developed. And yet Foucault locates here a set of practices
he calls 'the art of not being governed' which emerged alongside and against
the developing arts of government between the fifteenth and seventeenth centuries. These were a 'sort of general cultural form, at once moral and political
[and] a way of thinking', an art of 'not being governed, or of not being governed in this particular way, or at this price'. It was a form of critical
reflection, Foucault claimed, at the centre of 'the natural law problematic'
(and eventually the liberal problematic), which returned to the question of
'how can we not be governed? . . . what are the limits of the rights of government?.'[64] So the play of representations emerges once again, for he allows that
this appeal to 'not being governed' is a 'cultural form' *at once* moral, political and personal. Indeed, it is 'political' in a way that philosophico-juridical
appeals are not, which is to say it invokes a juridical concept in a very
unjuridical way.[65] There is a similar move in *The History of Sexuality* in the
discussion of life versus biopower: 'It was life more than the law that became
the issue of political struggles, *even if the latter were formulated through affir-
mations concerning rights . . . this "right" was the political response to all these
new procedures of power'.*[66]

But if the invocation of a right is to be perceived as a tactic, it must necessarily rest upon a wider background acceptance that a right is an effective
thing to invoke in that situation, as opposed to doing something else (the
rationality of civil society – or the Leviathan – seems to make it so). All
rights talk, whether singular or natural, is to some extent tactical, for it is
always a case of *using* it to pre-empt and/or facilitate a possible action or
range of actions. Why did the Levellers turn to the concept of rights when
they did? It was hardly an unambiguous linguistic and practical legacy on
which to draw in terms of, say, the rights of 'the people' versus the sovereign.[67]

These questions are only partly answered in pointing out that they had a particular tactical (political?) use for rights.

The comparative picture Foucault draws between these 'singular' rights and the natural or human rights of the jurist rests in large part on the account of self presupposed in each case. It also relies heavily upon Foucault's assertion that representations of practical conflict – and ultimately war – pattern social and political relations, and that notions of strategy and tactics are thus the most appropriate instruments for analysing relations of power. Law, then, is itself a player in conflict, rather than a means to its resolution. But the play of representations returns again, since Foucault admits a danger in 'this comedy', in this mimicry of 'war, battles, annihilations, or unconditional surrenders' which informs our repertoire of speaking about politics (especially when we do so 'polemically'). This is that ways of speaking are also ways of acting, that in 'putting forward as much of one's killer instinct as possible', one could validate – if only symbolically – 'the real political practices that could be warranted by it'. A polemical use of rights, then, would be to 'fall back continually on [them]', not to take risks, and thus not to 'advance'.[68] This seems to imply that there is a non-polemical way of talking about rights.

V Conclusion

Thus rights, reset as singular demands made in the midst of an ongoing battle in war and then again among a battle of representations in peace, appear to serve the corporeal subject's practices of liberty. Is this that far from the kind of rights theories examined above in section III? There rights were portrayed as special demands which relate to valued aspects of human nature and social relations. Thus framed, human nature involves certain basic capacities which are assumed to be valuable, or at least central, to leading a life that is human in any number of different social and cultural contexts. It does not follow from this that rights are always prioritized above other moral considerations, nor is it necessary to posit an abstract universal subject beyond saying that there are certain basic capacities all human beings would want to develop, enhance and protect. But Foucault would, no doubt, have trouble with even that, as his notion of an 'acting subject' is limited strictly (and vaguely) to certain capacities for action, where assertions of a basic rationality (above all) are a matter for dispute and blurred distinctions. Rights claims are part of the work of freedom, but appear to be the product of a perpetual battle of representations at the heart of our conceptions and practices of political order.

And yet, outside some rather embarrassing remarks made in the course of a discussion with Maoists about the possibilities of post-revolutionary justice,[69] Foucault never completely ruled out the possibilities of a new form of right.[70] Whatever shape he thought it might take – and I have suggested his notion of 'practices of liberty' and 'non-polemical dialogue' might be embryonic versions – it could not be, as it were, something 'beyond law'. The historically constituted nature of the juridification of civil society is such that any kind of 'anti-legalization' would not be a counter strategy, but only a dream. Any alternative is always and already patterned by law. If, given the rise of the norm, the juridical is meant to be in 'regression' (see section I), this should not lead us to think of the disappearance of law.[71] Indeed, law operates increasingly as a norm rather than as a sword in liberal jurisprudence, but so much so that its own interpretive and self-regulative mechanisms have recognized its becoming a 'social law': a law of preferences, positive discriminations and discretions.[72] It is purposive, instrumental, and interpreted as such. Equality before the law exists along a continuum, it might be for everyone but is applied to (and administered in relation to) a whole range of specific categories: the wage earner, consumer, single mother, Aborigine, or professional. Foucault saw brilliantly how well the material and formal elements of law worked in concert, but it is unclear whether he would recognize – after the exposure of these antinomies – that there could still be a representation of law that was not simply a conduit of violence but a 'political response' to all the new relations of power.

But when Foucault talked of Hobbes as circumventing civil war and 'saving the theory of the state', he pointed to at least one right which is less reducible than many others – one which Foucault himself recognized was beginning to play a larger role in the political discourse of the state in the seventeenth and eighteenth centuries[73] – the right to live. How does this prevail? Only after the actual wars have stopped, or the violent clash of opposing factions has been at least temporarily calmed. Something then has to create the conditions for social order, for the possibility of *some* kind of identity. For Hobbes it was a civil peace backed by the power of a Leviathan. For Locke, an almost self-regulating civil society. For Foucault, perhaps all we can say is that the clamour for Right only ever muffles the sound of war continuing on around us.

Notes

I am grateful to Moira Gatens, Barry Hindess, Jeffrey Minson, Paul Patton, Quentin Skinner and Natalie Stoljar for their generous and constructive comments.

1 Michel Foucault, *Power/Knowledge*, Colin Gordon (ed.) (Harvester Press, Brighton, 1980), pp. 107–8.

2 So there can be rules about rules about rules. Rules define the object of the political game and the primary rules generated therein (which might include secondary rules too of a kind; for example, contract rules), but also the 'game' of changing the object political game. And the way one engages in this 'third-tier' is, in turn, also governed by a set of rules. In Hartian terms, this level of activity is concerned with processes that create, maintain or destroy parts of the 'rule of recognition' – that rule which identifies what counts as a law in the first place. See H.L.A. Hart, *The Concept of Law* (Clarendon Press, Oxford, 1961), and Jean Hampton, 'Democracy and the rule of law', in Ian Shapiro (ed.), *The Rule of Law* (New York University Press, New York, 1994), 13–44, at 35–8.

3 I am grateful to Natalie Stoljar for pressing me on this distinction as it was formulated in an earlier draft of this chapter, and suggesting numerous alternatives.

4 See F. Sejersted, 'Democracy and the rule of law', in Jon Elster and Rune Slugstadm (eds), *Constitutionalism and Democracy* (Cambridge University Press, Cambridge, 1988), pp. 139–40, 147–9. Cf. Ronald Dworkin, *Law's Empire* (Harvard University Press, Cambridge MA, 1986), particularly chapters 2 and 7.

5 Dworkin, *Law's Empire*, p. 52; see pp. 227–8: 'When a judge declares that a particular principle is instinct in law, he reports not a simple-minded claim about the motives of past statesmen, a claim a wise cynic can easily refute, but *an interpretive proposal*: that the principle both fits and justifies some complex part of legal practice, that it provides an attractive way to see, in the structure of that practice, the consistency of principle integrity requires' (emphasis added).

6 I am indebted to the brief but lucid discussion in Leslie Green, 'The nature of law today', *American Journal of Political Science*, 89, 1 (1994), pp. 206–10.

7 A notable exception to this is Tom Keenan, 'The paradox of knowledge and power: reading Foucault on a bias', *Political Theory*, 15, 1 (1987), pp. 5–37, especially at 19–29. See also Alan Hunt and Gary Wickham, *Foucault and the Law: Towards a Sociology of Law as Governance* (Pluto, London/Boulder CO, 1994).

8 Friedrich Nietzsche, *Beyond Good and Evil*, trans. and introduced by R.J. Hollingdale (Penguin, Harmondsworth, 1979), §19 (p. 29) (original emphasis).

9 Ibid., p. 30 (original emphasis). See the excellent discussion by Bernard Williams, 'Nietzsche's minimalist moral psychology', *European Journal of Philosophy*, 1, 1 (1993), pp. 4–14; and Alexander Nehamas, *Nietzsche: Life as Literature* (Harvard University Press, Cambridge MA, 1985), especially chapter 3.

10 Friedrich Nietzsche, *The Genealogy of Morals*, trans. and introduced by Walter Kaufmann (Random Books, New York, 1989), First Essay, sec. 13 (p. 45); *Daybreak*, trans. and ed. R.J. Hollingdale, introduced by Michael Tanner (Cambridge University Press, Cambridge, 1982), p. 120.

11 *Thus Spoke Zarathustra*, trans. R.J. Hollingdale (Penguin, Harmondsworth, 1969), p. 89.

12 *Daybreak*, pp. 66–7. For the development of these arguments in contemporary circumstances, see the essay by Paul Patton in this volume, and Bonnie Honig, *Political Theory and the Displacement of Politics* (Cornell University Press, Ithaca NY, 1993), especially chapter 3.

13 Locke MS (Bodleian) c 28, fo 85v.

14 I have developed the following remarks in greater detail; see *The Self at Liberty: Political Argument and the Arts of Government* (Cornell University Press, Ithaca, New York, 1997).

15 Thomas Hobbes, *Leviathan*, C.B. Macpherson (ed.) (Penguin, Harmondsworth, 1981), chapter 18, p. 233. But see *Behemoth or the Long Parliament*, 2nd edn, Ferdinand Tonnies (ed.) (Frank Cass, London, 1969). Stephen Holmes provides an excellent reading of it in his 'Political psychology in Hobbes's Behemoth', in Mary Deitz (ed.), *Thomas Hobbes and Political Theory* (University Press of Kansas, Kansas, 1990), pp. 120–52.

16 Hobbes, *Behemoth*, p. 16.

17 Hobbes, *Behemoth*, p. 62.

18 Hobbes, *Behemoth*, p. 95. See Holmes on the importance of the phenomena of 'self-fulfilling prophecies' and the channelling the power of religion at pp. 122–3, 142–3.

19 In 'Il faut défendre la société', MS, Centre Michel Foucault, quoted in Pasquale Pasquino, 'Political theory of war and peace: Foucault and the history of modern political theory', *Economy and Society*, 22, 1 (1993), pp. 77–88, at p. 83; and 'Thomas Hobbes: la condition naturelle de l'humanité', *Revue Française de Science Politique*, 44, 2 (1994), pp. 294–307.

20 In 'Il faut défendre la société', p. 80. Cf. 'Polemics, politics, and problemizations', in P. Rabinow (ed.), *The Foucault Reader* (Pantheon, New York, 1984), p. 383 (his remarks that political, judicial and religious practices invoked polemically involve a kind of theatre).

21 Michel Foucault, 'Nietzsche, genealogy, history', in D.F. Bouchard (ed.), *Language, Counter-Memory, Practice: Selected Essays and Interviews by Michel Foucault* (Cornell University Press, New York, 1977), pp. 150–1. Foucault also refers to the 'rights' exercised by a polemicist (compared to the 'serious play of questions and answers') which allow him to 'wage war' on the other, 'an enemy who is wrong, who is harmful, and whose very existence constitutes a threat' (Foucault, 'Politics and ethics: an interview' in Rabinow (ed.), *Foucault Reader*, p. 382). See below in section I and III for further discussion.

22 Thus I am taking a different tack from a challenge to Foucault's conception of law by Gillian Rose; see *The Dialectic of Nihilism: Post-Structuralism and Law* (Basil Blackwell, Oxford, 1984), especially chapter 9. She claims that Foucault sets out to replace 'politics' by warfare, or

at least that warfare – and its accompanying metaphors of tactics, strategies, etc. – is the most appropriate conception of power for understanding the relation between civil society and the state: 'the Roman army in place of Roman law, as it were'. In doing so, Foucault 'destroy[s] the question of the specific relation between civil society and the state', or at least renders their connections 'redundant', missing the fact that 'war' is itself a political concept (pp. 192–3). I am claiming that Foucault does indeed take these questions seriously, that he does try to make a distinction between 'actual war' and civil society, and that he even invokes (if only implicitly and obscurely) a sense of the political in the midst of this relation. But it remains to be seen whether he is successful in doing so.

23 See Foucault, 'What is Enlightenment?', in Rabinow (ed.), *Foucault Reader*, pp. 32–50, at p. 48.

24 Michel Foucault, *Discipline and Punish*, trans. A. Sheridan (Pantheon, New York, 1977), pp. 137–8; *The History of Sexuality, Vol. 1: An Introduction*, trans. R. Hurley (Penguin, London, 1978), p.139.

25 H.L. Dreyfus and P. Rabinow (eds), *Michel Foucault: Beyond Structuralism and Hermeneutics* (University of Chicago Press, Chicago, 1983), pp. 192–3.

26 Foucault, *Discipline and Punish*, p. 194.

27 Michel Foucault, 'Lecture two, 14 January 1976', in *Power/Knowledge*, p. 105 (emphasis added).

28 Ibid., p. 108 (emphasis added).

29 Ibid.

30 Foucault, *History of Sexuality*, p. 144 (emphasis added).

31 Foucault, 'Lecture two', p. 98.

32 Michel Foucault, 'Technologies of the self', in Luther H. Martin, Huck Gutman and Patrick H. Hutton (eds), *Technologies of the Self: A Seminar with Michel Foucault* (Amherst University Press, Amherst MA, 1988), p. 15.

33 Michel Foucault, 'Face aux gouverments, les droits de l'homme', *Libération* (30 June–1 July 1984), p. 22; and in D. Eribon, *Michel Foucault*, trans. B. Wing (Harvard University Press, Cambridge MA, 1989), p. 279; and in Keenan, 'Reading Foucault on a bias', pp. 20–1.

34 'Polemics, politics, and problemizations: an interview', in Rabinow (ed.), *Foucault Reader*, pp. 381–2.

35 For Foucault on liberalism, see 'Governmentality', trans. Colin Gordon, in G. Burchell, C. Gordon and P. Miller (eds), *The Foucault Effect: Studies in Governmentality* (Harvester, Wheatsheaf, Brighton, 1991); *Résumé des Cours* (University of Paris, Paris, 1989); *Annuaire Collège de France* (University of Paris, Paris, 1978–9); 'War in the filigree of peace, course summary', trans. Ian McLeod, *Oxford Literary Review*, 4 (1980), pp. 15–19 (the complete manuscript – Il faut défendre la société – along with other lectures from this period, can be consulted at the Centre Michel Foucault in Paris); 'Faire vivre et laisser mourir: la naissance du racism', *Les Temps Modernes*, 46 (Fevrier 1991), pp. 37–61 (1976 lecture); 'Qu'est ce que la critique?', *Bulletin de la Société Française de Philosophie*, 84 (April/June 1990) (1978 lecture); and Pasquino, 'Political theory of war and peace', pp. 77–88. It is interesting to read Foucault's lectures on early modern political thought and contemporary liberalism alongside his 'ethical' studies of the different constitutive practices of self, which occupied so much of his efforts towards the end of his life. It is certainly more interesting than insisting that Foucault was converted to a kind of conservative neo-liberalism – for that see Andre Glucksmann, 'En horreur de la servitude', *Libération*, 30 June–1 July 1984, p. 22; and more generally L. Ferry and A. Renault, *La pensée 68: essai sur l'anti-humanisme contemporain* (Gallimard, Paris, 1985). Cf. Duncan Ivison, 'Liberal conduct', *History of the Human Sciences*, 6 August 1993, pp. 25–60.

36 See Joel Feinberg, *Rights, Justice, and the Bounds of Liberty* (Princeton University Press, Princeton NJ, 1980).

37 H.L.A. Hart, 'Are there any natural rights?', in J. Waldron (ed.), *Theories of Rights* (Oxford University Press, Oxford, 1984), pp. 77–90.

38 Hart, 'Are there any natural rights?', pp. 77–8.

39 See the lucid discussion in A. John Simmons, *The Lockean Theory of Rights* (Princeton University Press, Princeton NJ, 1992), especially chapters 1–2.

40 It might be that there are situations where even these basic capacities cannot emerge, for example in the case of the mentally handicapped. This is not to say they do not have rights, but that another kind of justification is required. This is an important issue, though I can't pursue it here.

41 See, for example, Annette Baier, *Moral Prejudices: Essays on Ethics* (Harvard University Press, Cambridge MA, 1994).

42 Simmons, *Lockean Theory*, p. 112. See also Joseph Raz, 'Rights and individual well-being', *Ratio Juris*, 5 July 1992, pp. 127–42.

43 See, for example, J. Habermas, 'Towards a communication-concept of rational collective will-formation: A thought-experiment', *Ratio Juris*, 2 July 1989, pp. 144–54; and more recently, *Between Facts and Norms: Contributions to a Discourse Theory of Law and Democracy*, trans. William Rehg (MIT Press, Cambridge MA, 1996).

44 Habermas, 'Towards a communication-concept', pp. 153–4.

45 Ibid., p. 154.

46 Foucault, 'Powers and strategies', in *Power/Knowledge*, pp. 140–1.

47 Foucault, 'The subject and power' in Dreyfus and Rabinow (eds), *Beyond Structuralism and Hermeneutics*, pp. 210–11.

48 'The ethic of care for the self as a practice of freedom', in J. Bernauer and D. Rasmussen (eds), *The Final Foucault* (MIT Press, Cambridge MA and London, 1988), p. 12.

49 Foucault, 'Ethic of care', pp. 12–13. Cf. 'The subject and power', p. 220 on distinguishing a relationship of power from one constituted essentially by violence.

50 Foucault, 'Politics and ethics', in Rabinow (ed.), *Foucault Reader*, p. 380.

51 Foucault, 'What is Enlightenment?', p. 44; Foucault, 'The subject and power', p. 216. Hence at p. 208: 'My objective . . . has been to create a history of the different modes by which, in our culture, human beings are made subjects.'

52 Michel Foucault, 'On the genealogy of ethics: an overview of work in progress' in Dreyfus and Rabinow (eds), *Beyond Structuralism and Hermeneutics*, p. 237; cf. *The History of Sexuality Vol. 2: The Use of Pleasure* (Viking, Harmondsworth, 1984), pp. 6–13; and 'The return of morality', in L. Kritzman (ed.), *Michel Foucault: Politics, Philosophy, Culture* (Routledge, London, 1988), pp. 243, 257.

53 Foucault, 'The subject and power': 'Where the determining factors saturate the whole there is no relationship of power . . .' (p. 221).

54 Cf., for example, in Locke's *Essay Concerning Human Understanding*, P. Nidditch (ed.) (Oxford University Press, Oxford, 1975), at 3.11.16.

55 For doubts about Foucault's interpretation of Hellenistic ethics, see Martha Nussbaum, *The Therapy of Desire: Theory and Practice in Hellenistic Ethics* (Princeton University Press, Princeton NJ, 1994).

56 Foucault, 'Space, knowledge and power', in Rabinow (ed.), *Foucault Reader*, p. 245.

57 Foucault, 'Ethic of care', p. 20.

58 Ibid., p. 4.

59 See, for example, Nancy Fraser's well-known 'Foucault on modern power: empirical insights and normative confusions', in her *Unruly Practices* (University of Minnesota Press, Minneapolis, 1989). For a lucid discussion of some of these issues see Richard Bernstein, 'Foucault: critique as a philosophical ethos', in Axel Honneth, Thomas McCarthy, Claus Offe and Albrecht Wellmer (eds), *Philosophical Interventions in the Unfinished Project of Enlightenment* (MIT Press, Cambridge MA, 1992), pp. 280–310.

60 Foucault, 'Questions of method', in Burchell et al. (eds), *Foucault Effect*, pp. 84–5.

61 Cf. Keenan, 'Reading Foucault on a bias', p. 29.

62 Foucault, 'War in the filigree of peace', p. 17 (emphasis added). This is strikingly similar to Nietzsche's line in *Daybreak*, pp. 66–7.

63 Ibid. See also his Howison Lectures, University of California, Berkeley, 1980; and 'Inutile de soulever?' (Is it useless to revolt?), *Le Monde*, 11 May 1979, p. 12.

64 'Qu'est ce que la critique?', *Bulletin de la Société Française de Philosophie*, 84, 2 (April–June 1990) (lecture delivered on 27 May 1978). Also 'Faire vivre et laisser mourir: la naissance du racisme', *Les Temps Modernes*, 46, 535 (1991), pp. 37–61. Cf. the last chapter of *The History of Sexuality Vol. 1*, trans. Robert Hurley (Random House, New York, 1976).

65 Cf. the discussion in Keenan, 'Reading Foucault on a bias', pp. 26–9.

66 Foucault, *History of Sexuality*, p. 145 (emphasis added).

67 As Richard Tuck has so ably shown in his *Natural Rights Theories* (Cambridge University Press, Cambridge, 1979). Cf. David Wootten, 'Leveller democracy and the Puritan revolution', in J.H. Burns with Mark Goldie (eds), *Cambridge History of Political Thought 1450–1700* (Cambridge University Press, Cambridge, 1990), pp. 412–42, especially at pp. 412–13: 'The levellers were a political movement united around the program of the first Agreement of the People. That agreement is the first proposal in history for a written constitution based on inalienable natural rights . . . [They] were not merely seeking to establish in England freedom that existed elsewhere . . . but to establish for the first time freedom which (outside a mythical historical past, that of Anglo-Saxon England) never had existed, and were not to come into existence for over three centuries.'

68 Foucault, 'Politics and ethics', pp. 382–3.

69 See *Power/Knowledge*, especially at pp. 27–8, where he talks of how the forms of 'state apparatus' to do with justice that would be inherited from the 'bourgeois apparatus' could not serve any post-revolutionary organization. The common categories of bourgeois courts to do with 'its' justice must be treated with 'the very greatest of suspicion'. The court is the 'bureaucracy of the law', and 'the masses' have suffered too much over the centuries from this judicial system. So how should justice be regularized? – 'it remains to be discovered. . . . The masses will discover a way of dealing with the problem of their enemies . . . methods of retribution which will range from punishment to reeducation, without involving the form of the court which . . . is to be avoided.'

70 Note also that as late as his interview on 'Ethic of care' Foucault still talked of giving oneself 'the rules of law' (p. 18) in his discussion of ethics and the 'practices of self' which would allow for a minimal play of domination.

71 Foucault construes 'juridical' government very narrowly, mainly in terms of absolutist natural law theory. This does not exactly exhaust the horizons of natural law theory. A more careful consideration of early modern 'juridical' theorists would make the distinction between the two representations of law – as norm or as sovereign command – more difficult to maintain, or at least more porous than Foucault thinks. A lucid account of 'the juridical' in early modern political thought is found in James Tully, *An Approach to Political Philosophy Locke in Contexts* (Cambridge University Press, Cambridge, 1993). A good treatment of the law's different modes of expression that builds on Foucault's distinction is François Ewald, 'Norms, discipline, and the law', *Representations*, 30 (Spring 1990), pp. 138–61.

72 Gunther Teubner, 'Juridification: concepts, aspects, limits, solutions', in G. Teubner (ed.), *Juridification of Social Spheres* (de Gruyter, Berlin, 1987), pp. 3–40; François Ewald, 'A concept of social law', in G. Teubner (ed.), *Dilemmas of Law in the Welfare State* (de Gruyter, Berlin, 1986), pp. 41–75.

73 'Faire vivre', p. 39. See the helpful discussion by Pasquino, 'Political Theory', p. 84; and more specifically in relation to Hobbes in 'Thomas Hobbes et la condition naturelle', *passim*.

9

Foucault, Rawls and Public Reason

Jeremy Moss

Foucault once wondered in an interview why the dominant political organizations of his day had never addressed the general questions that he raised. He complained that all too often his focus on localized problems meant that people ignored the larger framework presupposed by his analyses. After all, he argued, what could be more general than the way in which a society defines its relation to madness, or to truth for that matter?[1] His response was prompted by a question from his interviewer, Duccio Trombadori, which suggested a focus on the local obscured more general historical problems. This apparent conflict concerned Trombadori because even local problems pose the need to find political solutions, which in turn meant being able to arrange the many different political solutions into one coherent political approach. While this is not a new concern for Foucault's critics, it does point to the problem of how one might best appreciate the significance of his work in the political arena. Of course, in a general sense, there is an abundance of political writing that both uses or is inspired by Foucaultian themes. But there are certain types of question and topic that are rarely raised in connection with Foucault's work. So while there are numerous Foucault-influenced works on political issues such as the body, reason or the possibility of critique, there are few that take up problems such as justice, democracy or citizenship. No doubt this has something to do with what Foucault had to say on the role of intellectuals in society, and with his insistence that he was not interested in a 'theory' of power or society.[2]

However, I do not think that Foucault meant that questions about democracy could not be posed, only that they be posed in a different way. It is not that issues such as human rights or justice do not matter, it is just that our understanding of them should not be tied to, for instance, an idea of sovereign power. Indeed, there are many insights in Foucault's work that, if they are accurate, should be incorporated into our understanding of political concepts such as democracy and justice. For example, his understanding of the embedded nature of human subjectivity and the possibilities for human freedom both have much to offer democratic theory. The last phase of his work is particularly interesting for political philosophy in that it outlines his account of government and gives new life to the traditional philosophical terms 'freedom' and 'autonomy', two concepts which are central to contemporary political philosophy.

In order to see the possible connections of Foucault's thought with political philosophy when it concerns itself with issues such as democracy and justice, I have chosen to compare Foucault with John Rawls. On the face of it, this might seem like an odd choice and certainly needs some justification. In the Anglo-American tradition, Rawls is probably the most important post-war political philosopher, chiefly through the influence of his book, *A Theory of Justice*. Opening *Theory* at any page is enough to make one realize not only that Rawls's subject matter is different from Foucault's, but also that his style is very different. In *Theory* Rawls was interested in a conception of justice that was applicable for any group of rational individuals. His model of justice is argued for in a manner typical of post-war analytical philosophy. Nonetheless, some of Rawls's central concerns touch on the subject-matter of Foucault's last studies. Indeed, Rawls's later work, *Political Liberalism*, is notable for its clarification of his conception of a person and its role in political philosophy, as well as the 'scope' of the political domain. It is on these two issues that Foucault's work has considerable bearing.

My aim in comparing Foucault with Rawls is not to somehow provide a support for the type of liberalism argued for by Rawls, or for liberalism in general. On the contrary, I think the sorts of issues which dominate Foucault's later thinking make him more egalitarian than Rawls. While I will offer an interpretation of some of Foucault's key concepts, on the whole, I am interested chiefly in the significance of some of these concepts for political philosophy. Specifically, Foucault's thoughts on power as 'government', and the process whereby a person becomes a subject, are the key differences that he introduces to Rawls's model of political philosophy. While these two insights complicate the picture of democracy that Rawls paints, their accounts share a common concern with freedom and autonomy. Using this common concern as a starting point, I will argue that Foucault's understanding of some of the fundamental ideas of political philosophy leads to an expanded idea of democracy, which shows the relevance of the self to political theory. It is to these ideas that I now turn.

Political Liberalism

In contrast to *A Theory of Justice*, in *Political Liberalism* Rawls thinks of his project as justifying and articulating elements of a specifically Western conception of democracy.[3] He assumes that there are a variety of what he calls 'reasonable comprehensive doctrines' (different ethical, religious or philosophical doctrines), which combine to make society ethically and politically irreducibly plural. In addition, individuals holding these views should be regarded, in a political sense, as free; that is, we should assume that they have the capacity to form a conception of the good, have a sense of justice, and take moral responsibility for their decisions.[4] Given the fact of pluralism and reasonable disagreement on the one hand, and the difficulty of finding a workable conception of justice on the other, Rawls asks, 'How is it possible that there may exist over time a stable and just society of free and equal citizens profoundly divided by reasonable though incompatible religious, philosophical, and moral doctrines?'.[5] Rawls's answer to this question is the 'political conception' of justice, which regulates the basic structure of society.

The political conception, which is the linchpin of Rawls's theory of justice, has three distinguishing features. First, what Rawls calls the basic structure of society (economic, political and social institutions) is to be regulated by this conception. In addition to the institutions themselves, Rawls includes the principles that govern the institutions as well as the norms embodied by the citizens who live in the society.[6] Importantly for Rawls, the political conception of justice is also what he terms a 'freestanding' view.[7] This second point is a vital element in the justification of the theoretical results of the political conception, because, if we assume with Rawls the fact of reasonable pluralism, it would be inappropriate for a theory of justice to reflect the moral framework of any one perspective in society. While justice as fairness, as a rule, should not embody any particular moral theory of the good, Rawls maintains that the political conception can have particular goods so long as they are goods that can apply to every citizen.[8]

The third distinguishing feature of this conception is that political liberalism is expressed in terms of the traditions that form part of 'our' political heritage. The aim, therefore, of justice as fairness is practical: a conception that will be shared by all citizens. One example of 'our' heritage is the idea of society as a fair system of cooperation. The idea here is that citizens have publicly available a system of principles that specify rights and duties which regulate the functioning of the society's basic structure so as to benefit everyone. Political liberalism looks for a political conception of justice that can gain the acceptance of all reasonable doctrines. This is the insight that guides public conduct of institutions for Rawls. Much depends on Rawls's claim that people be reasonable in his special sense. For Rawls, a person is reasonable if he or she is moved by a desire for 'a social world in which they, as free and equal, can cooperate with others on terms all can accept'.[9] People must also accept the 'burdens of judgement'; that is, people should be able to disagree without it impinging on their being reasonable. These are the two characteristics that a person needs in order to be a reasonable citizen. If we apply these criteria to moral beliefs, we can see that people might subscribe to a plethora of moral positions, hence the importance for Rawls of establishing an overlapping consensus concerning principles of justice.

With these considerations before him, Rawls is able to say that his theory of justice is a political conception and not a comprehensive moral one. Indeed, Rawls claims that, 'the full significance of the political conception lies in its connection with the fact of reasonable pluralism and the need for a democratic society to secure the possibility of an overlapping consensus on its fundamental political values'.[10] One can see why this has been such an appealing idea in contemporary political philosophy. On the one hand, we have an acknowledgement of the plurality of moral views in society, while at the same time there is an attempt to find common ground on which to construct a theory of justice that has few references to particular moral doctrines. The whole project is guided by a practical imperative: to find a conception of justice that can be held by – and benefit – all citizens, while leaving them with basic freedoms.

The Two Moral Powers

As we have seen, the political conception of justice is justified without reference to any comprehensive doctrine. It also refers to a tradition of political philosophy that is part of what is supposedly 'our' political culture, according to Rawls. Whatever problems there are in interpreting our culture, Rawls is correct to stress that his conception of political liberalism is based on fundamental ideas that are themselves not subject to the same scrutiny as, for instance, the arguments for the two principles of justice.[11] Thus, there is a family of ideas that function in what we might call a 'constitutive' way for Rawls. What Rawls calls the 'two moral powers' fall under this heading. By the two moral powers Rawls means, one, the capacity to have a conception of the good, apply it, revise it and so on, and, two, the ability to understand, apply and act from a 'public conception of justice which characterizes the fair terms of social cooperation'.[12]

Closely associated with the moral powers is the idea of freedom. Having a conception of the good is also one of the three things that makes a person free in political liberalism. In addition, Rawls considers a person free in that he or she is the self-authenticating source of moral claims and can take moral responsibility for his or her actions. It is on the basis of these powers and capacities that Rawls considers persons morally equal.[13] When Rawls first speaks of these capacities he assumes, for the sake of the argument, that everyone has them in full measure.[14] Of course he realizes that there are constraints like accidents and illnesses which prevent the exercise of capacities. However, there is a range of limitations which he does not cover and which Foucault's work on government shows to be important.

If citizens are free in Rawls's three senses, then he also considers them to be rationally autonomous. Being rationally autonomous consists of two things: the ability 'to form, to revise, and to pursue a conception of the good, and to deliberate in accordance with it'.[15] People are also rational if they show a willingness to enter into agreement with others. On this story, a person's autonomy is modelled in the original position by making it an example of 'pure procedural justice',[16] thus ensuring that whatever principles are chosen in the original position are just. In short, freedom and the two moral powers rely on citizens having the power to develop their capacities in a way that they have reflectively chosen. Rawls thus appeals to a notion of autonomy that is not very far removed from the one I will claim is present in Foucault's later work. This is a sense of autonomy which is built on the idea of self-development of capacities in a context of relative freedom from oppression.

The final point to which I want to draw attention in this admittedly brief summary is the stage on which the drama of political liberalism unfolds. The capacity which citizens have to discuss matters of political importance and the context of their discussion is society's public reason. What can be discussed is constrained by what Rawls calls the 'liberal principle of legitimacy'.[17] The principle of legitimacy limits discussion to (a) the structure of democratic institutions and (b) the basic rights and liberties which each citizen is said to have, rights such as freedom of conscience, association and movement.[18] This list of constitutional essentials seems to cover a wide range of society's institutions and resources, as well as many of the political processes with which we are familiar. However, what it does not cover is just as interesting and important. Rawls is anxious to stress that of course the *public* use of reason does not exhaust the use of reason; community bodies and families are all examples of contexts in which reason is used in a way that may not be immediately relevant to public reason.[19] Many economic decisions are not immediately relevant to public discussion either. Issues such as taxation or the environment are relevant to the public, but better suited to the legislative phase of the decision-making process.

It is interesting to note that the principle of legitimacy itself is used in conjunction with a family of ideas that forms part of 'our' political tradition. As we saw, one of the goals of justice is to allow citizens to maximize their capacities in ways that they take to be important. To do this they need to be autonomous in Rawls's sense. However, while Rawls is correct to stress the importance of being autonomous, he fails to properly conceive of the barriers to autonomy present in modern society and the important differences these make to the boundaries of public reason and, ultimately, to the conception of the political itself. Foucault's work on the threats to autonomy brings this problem into focus. I want now to look at Foucault's work on the twin ideas of government and autonomy so as to understand some of the problems with Rawls's work, as well as to appreciate Foucault's own contribution to political philosophy.[20]

Autonomy and Government in Foucault

Autonomy

Autonomy is not a word that is usually associated with Foucault's writings. Yet there have been a number of authors over the past few years who have suggested that a conception of autonomy is present in the later work.[21] Much of what we might interpret as being concerned with autonomy is found in the interviews Foucault gave later in his life, especially those concerned with ethics. For example, the 'work on the self' that Foucault writes of in his discussion of Ancient Greek ethics is part of his overall characterization of the self's relation to itself in Antiquity. However, he does employ a similar idea of work on the self (with normative implications) in discussing contemporary society in some of the other works from this period. For instance, in the essay 'What is Enlightenment?', Foucault argues that we need to create ourselves as autonomous beings; that is, while recognizing that the development of our capacities is a product of our historical circumstances, we nonetheless have (and ethically need) the ability to perform work on ourselves. In this essay, Foucault tells us that an analysis of ourselves will be 'oriented toward the "contemporary limits of the necessary" that is, what is not or is no longer indispensable for the constitution of ourselves as autonomous subjects'.[22] What is important in this analysis for Foucault is that subjects have the ability to choose autonomously a course of action or set of goods. Foucault argues in his later work that subjects are well served by the ability to critique, reflect on and ultimately adopt one of a range of alternative modes of existence, or, indeed, what Rawls might call a different conception of the good. Work on the self is, in Foucault's sense, an autonomous act requiring the use of moral and intellectual capacities to determine a course of action.

The ability of subjects to act in this autonomous manner also has normative implications. As Patton has argued, the capacity for autonomy operates as a meta-capacity necessary for the development of other capacities.[23] Patton also suggests that it is in the capacity for autonomy that we find part of the answer to the question of what normative criterion Foucault could use to distinguish between different forms of power. On Patton's account, if a power relationship limited the capacity for autonomy, we would have grounds for condemning it, because it would prevent the appropriate exercise or development of a person's capacities. This understanding of the role of autonomy in Foucault's thought seems to me to be borne out by the efforts, described above, that Foucault made to articulate a space for work on the self in his later writings.

Earlier I claimed that there was a sense in which Rawls employed a conception of autonomy similar to Foucault's. I am now in a position to say more about the similarity. For both authors, their conceptions of autonomy depend on their accounts of freedom. In Foucault's case, it is the freedom that subjects have in relation to a regime of power that allows them to exercise autonomy. While on Rawls's account, autonomy ('rational' as distinct from 'full' autonomy at least) rests on a person's moral and intellectual powers.[24] In both cases there is a requirement that, in order for agents to be called autonomous, they have to use their capacities reflectively to choose a type of good, whether it is the final shape of one's capacities (Foucault) or a conception of the good life (Rawls). On each account the autonomous agent is someone who uses his or her moral and intellectual powers (his/her capacities) to choose a conception of the good for which he or she can be held responsible. It is on these last points that the two accounts of autonomy are similar.

There are clearly many impediments to autonomy as I have outlined it here, and Rawls's emphasis on having primary goods is one attempt to deal with these threats. However, I want to focus on the sense in which Foucault perceives threats to autonomy through his understanding of power as government, as Rawls seems only to address threats to autonomy of a particular kind. Moreover, if what Foucault says about how autonomy can be undermined is plausible, then it will alter how we think of public reason and the scope of the political.

Government

Foucault's thinking about power follows a radically different path from Rawls's. For Foucault, the sense in which power threatens autonomy is less direct than for Rawls. While Foucault of course recognizes that threats to autonomy still arise from disturbances such as wars, government repression, violence and the like, his own work has focused on a different sort of threat. In a way, Foucault's concern was similar to Kant's, in that he tried to uncover how it is possible that people are prevented from using their own 'understanding', to use Kant's term.[25] Foucault's version of this inquiry involves comprehending the process whereby subjects are shaped by power. He says: 'To put the matter clearly: my problem is to see how men govern (themselves and others) by the production of truth.'[26] This passage captures nicely two of the key interests in Foucault's later work: government and ethics. It is the concern with the government of others that interests us here.

To be sure, as a term for how power operates, Foucault's use of the word 'government' does not become common until the later writings. However, the term had its genesis in the work of the 1970s. The best examples that Foucault gave of government are still to be found in *Discipline and Punish*. There one can find described in detail the operations of power at a minute level. For example, in the section on 'The means of correct training', there is a description of how a soldier is led through a series of drills in order that he become a certain type of person, a person whose capacities are, in the above sense, governed by a disposition that is embodied in his actions without the aid of his will.[27] This is, of course, an extreme case, and one chosen by Foucault to make the point that it is possible to intervene at the level of a person's capacities. What this example and others in *Discipline and Punish* indicate is how power can harness and transform the body and its forces such that the conscious actions of a person follow an acceptable pattern, and come to embody an ideal. The success of this subjectivization occurs when the model of behaviour becomes part of an individual identity. To govern, in this sense, is to 'structure the possible field of action of others', not simply by intervening by force to prevent an action, but by restructuring the types of action open to a subject by restricting him or her at the level of his or her capacities. Indeed, this is precisely what he thinks he has been revealing in his books, the way in which various types of subject – the insane, prisoners, sexual subjects – have had their actions modified at the level of capacities. The threat to capacities, in this instance, is one where an agent's potential to perform a range of actions is reduced. This is not to say that subjects' identities are fixed forever. One of the things that Foucault sought to clarify in the later work was how the process of government operated against a backdrop of human freedom.[28]

Where an agent's capacities are transformed in the above way their ɾstanding of how they can act also changes. Such a process will alter how ɕ think of agents as choosing their actions. In a sense the prisoner in Foucault's discussion in *Discipline and Punish* chooses to do a certain action. However, that choice is one that has been made for him in advance because his identity and preferences have been structured so as to make it normal to choose a certain range of actions. To the extent that this occurs, it is a form of internal constraint on the agent, one that operates on the very capacities and images that an agent possesses. As such the operation of governmental power could significantly alter the extent to which an individual is the author of his or her own life.

To relate this back to Rawls, recall that the two moral powers are essentially capacities or combinations of capacities. Given that they play a vital role in according people moral equality and in deciding on conceptions of the good, the sense in which they are present in a citizen is, or rather should be, an important question for Rawls. To be fair, Rawls shows an awareness of threats to the exercise of moral powers when he talks of everyone having enough income, yet he ignores the type of threat that is posed by practices that undermine the development and exercise of moral powers through the government of action. It is this assumption concerning a citizen's capacities that Foucault's idea of autonomy and governmentality place in doubt, because the threat that is posed by this type of power is a threat precisely at the level of an agent's capacities.

When we assess the impact of the threats to autonomy we are led, ultimately, to the question of how deeply the idea of government intrudes into Rawls's conception of justice as fairness, in particular, to the question of whether the *content* of public reason is sufficient for a discussion of justice at all. For example, one consequence is that we might have to include governmentality, and the loss of autonomy that often accompanies it, as fixtures of contemporary political life. So, in the same way that Rawls argues that political democracy (seen as a type of positive freedom) is necessary, we could say that economic and social democracy is necessary to prevent governmental power curtailing people's ability to use their capacities effectively. In order to see how we might argue for the inclusion of the economic and social into public reason, it will be useful to understand Rawls's reasons for the importance of political democracy.[29]

As we saw above, the content of public reason is defined by the constraints of the political conception. Rawls's argument for a political conception which is freestanding has as its subject matter our considered convictions and the basic structure of society, and stems, in part, from the fact of reasonable pluralism and the belief in a society organized as a fair system of cooperation. Rawls's insistence on the diversity of religious, philosophical and moral doctrines as a permanent feature of public life means that citizens have a moral duty and a practical imperative to participate in politics so as to determine which principles will govern the regulation of the basic structure. In this sense, the participation of citizens in the political arena is a practical or instrumental good. Citizens participate in order to explain their own views and understand the views of others, and thus fairly exercise coercive public power. As Rawls writes:

> Democracy involves, as I have said, a political relationship between citizens within the basic structure of the society into which they are born and within which they normally lead a complete life; it implies further an equal share in the coercive political power that citizens exercise over one another by voting and in other ways. As reasonable and rational, and knowing that they affirm a diversity of reasonable religious and philosophical doctrines, they should be ready to explain the basis of their actions to one another in terms each could reasonably expect that others might endorse as consistent with their freedom and equality. Trying to meet this condition is one of the tasks that this ideal of democratic politics asks of us.[30]

This type of positive freedom is conferred on free and equal citizens as a means of allowing them to govern their own lives, which would not be possible if the democratic process excluded those over whom it had coercive power.

Another reason why participation in the democratic forms is to be desired, for Rawls, is because it forms part of the tradition of 'our' public political culture. He says:

> In a democratic society there is a tradition of democratic thought, the content of which is at least familiar and intelligible to the educated common sense of citizens generally. Society's main institutions, and their accepted forms of interpretation, are seen as a fund of implicitly shared ideas and principles.[31]

One can reasonably assume that participation in democratic forms is one of these shared ideas to which Rawls refers. In this sense, democratic participation is an intrinsic good. While Rawls does not discuss this in *Political Liberalism*, he does mention it in *A Theory of Justice*. He writes there that political participation is 'an activity enjoyable in itself that leads to a larger conception of society and to the development of his [the citizen's] intellectual and moral faculties'.[32] However, the sense in which a political liberty, such as participation in public life, is an intrinsic good is not confined to strengthening the intellectual and moral capacities of citizens. Participation is also a good because 'it lay[s] the basis for a sense of duty and obligation upon which the stability of just institutions depends'.[33] These two quite separate reasons form the basis of the intrinsic worth of participation in democratic political institutions.

With this brief discussion as background, we can now comment on the significance of Rawls's argument for the connection between autonomy and political participation (defined here as self-determination). On both the intrinsic and instrumental story, there is a need for participation in political institutions. Where citizens participate for instrumental reasons, it is because they need to have the opportunity to explain, and to have explained, the views of others. Participation in democratic forms also stems from the idea of the irreducible plurality of persons and the consequent need to negotiate the different opinions citizens might have. Some of society's basic goods would be jeopardized by the exclusion of political institutions from the public domain. The threat to the intrinsic value of autonomy is simpler to articulate because the connection between autonomy and freedom as self-determination is less mediated. It concerns the denial of what is really a basic liberty, albeit a political one.

If Rawls can argue for participation in the political sphere on the basis of its necessity for autonomy, then why not apply the same argument to the inclusion of economic and social areas into a society's public reason? Consider the intrinsic goodness of participation in public political life as understood by Rawls. First of all, there is the development of moral and intellectual capacities. Foucault's work on embodiment in both *Discipline and Punish* and *The History of Sexuality Vol. 1* show how the capacities of subjects are limited and shaped by the practices of everyday institutions. Take, for instance, the example of the workplace, which can involve a loss of control over the use and development of capacities. If a person has no influence over how his or her capacities are utilized, there would be just as great a threat to autonomy here as when he or she has a lack of access to political institutions. This issue is most clearly focused in situations where the economic circumstances of a community or country force citizens into work where there is little control over conditions.

The government of individuals occurs in the workplace, but it also occurs in society's institutions and in everyday practices. This type of government is closer empirically to the examples that illuminate Foucault's historical studies. The unacceptable government of actions might occur through normalizing social processes such as images stereotyping different communities, for example the gay community, or, through everyday discrimination against a racial or ethnic group. A great deal of work has been done on this area in the last decade which it is impossible to consider here.[34] However, this form of government is what some have called 'structural oppression'. Oppression in this sense is the denial of self-development as a consequence of social norms, customs and images, and the consequences of putting these into operation in people's daily lives.[35]

The type of power that Foucault describes as governmental and the way in which this produces subjects are the key differences between Rawls and Foucault. In describing the *process* of action on the action of others, of how people become subjects, and in describing the process as one which often operates outside the usual political structures, Foucault's work insists on a different model of power from Rawls's model. Foucault's work on power also suggests the relevance of a conception of how the self is formed in contemporary society, which Rawls's political philosophy seems keen to avoid; a conception which is both 'metaphysical' *and* 'political'.[36]

Public Reason and the Political

Our discussion of the necessity of expanding the range of areas considered in a theory of justice brings us back to the idea of public reason and with it the question of the scope of the political. Recall that, according to Rawls, a society's reason is its way of 'formulating its plans, of putting its ends in an order of priority, and of making its decisions accordingly'.[37] There is a restriction, however, in just what those ends and priorities might be, because the content of public reason is formulated by the political conception of justice. One of the key constitutional essentials is the basic political process – how one is to participate in the institutions of government. But, as we saw above, the intrinsic and instrumental reasons Rawls gives for political participation could also be used to argue that there are other things, such as economic and social matters, that should also be included on the list of constitutional essentials. This is because, in the same way that it is necessary to make a minimal redistribution of wealth in order to give citizens the means to exercise their capacities,[38] there is reason to ensure that there are not practices that threaten those capacities, which, as we saw, leads to the lessening of autonomy. If this last point is true, then clearly the scope of public reason is too narrow to accommodate the types of argument made in favour of economic democracy. However, it is not just public reason that is altered by this argument, but the whole idea of the political.

The change in the scope of the political occurs because there is a need, on my account, to include participation in the areas of the workplace as well as in certain social and cultural practices that significantly threaten the use of autonomy. Recall that one of the things that the political conception was supposed to cover was the basic structure of society. With the inclusion of economic and social domains, the basic structure is much larger than it was for Rawls. However, the additions to the scope of the political are not just additions to the Rawlsian story; they make qualitative changes as well.

Understood as a consequence of the threats to autonomy, the expansion of the public sphere has as its correlate the expansion of the role of democratic participation in many areas of the social. So, if participation is seen as a good in both intrinsic and instrumental senses for subjects (seen as bearers and exercisers of capacities), then they will seek to exercise their capacities in all the areas where fulfilment of those capacities matters – in the social, economic and political spheres. When we combine this condition with the injunction to participate in the expansion of the basic structure, we end up with a picture of democracy which is substantially different from the one presented by Rawls. Obviously there is not the space here to outline how a Foucaultian-inspired analysis would issue in a full-blown theory of democracy. However, as a minimum, the demands placed on an account of democracy would include a structure where much of what threatened the development of autonomy and people's capacities would come under some sort of democratic control. As I have argued, the expansion of public reason into areas such as the economy necessitates a much fuller conception of democracy than the one supported by Rawls. This expanded model of democracy draws on a political tradition that is in some respects closer to socialism than to liberalism.

A further worry for Rawls is that the political conception looks less like a freestanding view. Rawls characterized what he meant by the political conception by contrasting it with general and comprehensive moral views. Each of the latter has a wider scope than the political conception in that they cover virtues and values in all aspects of human life – familial, associational, and so on. While the considerations I have put forward do not mean that justice is to cover every social act, they do broaden the basic structure sufficiently to bend the freestanding view out of shape. If the content of public reason is expanded to include the economic and social aspects, then justice takes on more of the features of a moral view. In truth, it is probably somewhere in between, as justice, on my account, still does not apply to every value, only those that have significant influence over the development of a person's capacities in a political sense.

Recall that the third feature of the political conception was that its content was expressed in terms of 'certain fundamental ideas seen as implicit in the public political culture of a democratic society'.[39] Rawls refers to a fund of 'shared ideas' that provides, it seems, constitutive ideas for political philosophy. However, there are all sorts of reasons why a certain political tradition has come to dominate debate. This process might have involved the exclusion of other traditions, or might not be open to the emergence of new traditions. Foucault has sought to reverse the process of exclusion in other areas such as health or sexuality, through a genealogical focus. While I have not the space to go into it here, I think a critical attitude should be kept towards political traditions such as the ones Rawls draws upon. By doing so, we might become aware of the 'birth' and 'descent' of the liberal tradition as well as being aware of different constituting values. For instance, while one of the ideas that Rawls draws on is society as a fair system of cooperation, there are many other ideas that are part of 'public culture'.

These last two points are bound to raise questions about the suitability of Foucault's ideas for political theory as I have understood it. I am thinking here of Foucault's many remarks to the effect that his analyses show the undesirability of providing theories ('totalizing' or otherwise) of political ideas or morality.[40] Again, what Foucault had to say on theory is a large topic and cannot be dealt with here. We should note, however, an important point that Foucault often drew attention to in his work, namely, that, as far as he was concerned, he was interested in historical problems which were *general* in their scope.[41] These problems might well be different from the ones investigated by other political writers, but that is not to say there are not general problems which have to be solved in a coordinated way.

These considerations powerfully suggest that political liberalism is sorely tested by the interaction with the concepts that a Foucaultian analysis introduces into political theory. The broad picture of the scope of the political that emerges after these considerations of the method and assumptions that Foucault introduces, is one where there is a greatly expanded scope for public authority. If we assume values such as moral equality between individuals, respect for persons and the desire to have society ordered as a fair system of cooperation, the picture of public reason developed would have a public authority that had greater scope for intervention in the social and economic spheres. Were this not the case one would be left with the situation where many of the threats to autonomy would remain untouched, leaving the idea of people's moral and non-moral freedom in jeopardy.

Conclusion: Foucault and Political Theory

The later Foucault gives us a vision of political practice which signals a close attention to the autonomous development of our capacities. This attention to the self was one of the dominant themes of Foucault's later research, as we can see in the last two volumes of *The History of Sexuality*. As such, it is easy to assume that there is a tendency in his later work towards introspection, a focus on individual self-creation. While this is a concern of Foucault's, it is not all that there is to Foucault in this period. I would argue that he always saw work on the self as possible only in relation to other subjects and to power. One only has to think of how, in one of his later interviews, he links both power and games of truth to the 'form' of subjectivity to realize that he never lost sight of the relation between the strategies of truth and power and the possibility of work on the self.[42] It is the effects of these relationships which necessitates the critical ontology of the self, and a critical approach to the world around us.

Obviously, the meaning of 'critique' here has a broader application than theories of justice. For Foucault it is a modern form of the Kantian question about knowledge. He writes:

> But if the Kantian question was that of knowing what limits knowledge has to renounce transgressing, it seems to me that the critical question today has to be turned back into a positive one: in what is given to us as universal, necessary, oblig-atory, what place is occupied by whatever is singular, contingent, and the product of arbitrary constraints?[43]

Another Kantian theme of the self as a chooser of ends provides a useful yardstick for an appreciation of some of the differences between Rawls and Foucault. Of course both authors approach the question of the person/subject from different methodological perspectives. Rawls's conception of a person is a normative one, which begins from our everyday understanding and is tai-lored to suit justice as fairness. Foucault, on the other hand, is interested first and foremost in the practices which shape individuals and how this process enables them to then reshape themselves. It is from this type of analysis found in his longer works that a concrete conception, relevant to political philoso-phy, emerges. The different route Foucault takes in pursuit of an understanding of modern subjectivity is one of the main reasons why his account is useful for political philosophy. It shows both the relevance of the self to political philosophy and what follows from acknowledging the partic-ular forms of constraint to which subjects are exposed in modern society. Indeed, it is Foucault's version of the Kantian chooser of ends – the autonomous subject – which allows him to do this. But as we saw, the autonomous subject is made up of capacities which are themselves devel-oped in ways that exhibit the signs of interaction with society; a subject's capacities are thus embodied in a way that reflects (though not passively) social and economic relationships. Rawls invites us to believe that there is a chooser of ends in the political arena who is able to develop his or her capacities in a way that is not threatened by the operation of governmental power. In contrast, Foucault's model of the choosing subject is sensitive to the twists and turns of relationships of power and their impact on the development of the very capacities that are needed for people to function as autonomous choosers of ends. It is this insight into how a subject is embodied that is Foucault's chief contribution to political philosophy.

Notes

For their helpful comments on earlier drafts of this chapter, I would like to thank Tony Coady, Len O'Neill, Marion Tapper and Steven Tudor.

1 Michel Foucault, 'The discourse on power', in D. Trombadori (ed.), *Remarks on Marx*, trans. R.J. Goldstein and J. Cascaito (Semiotext(e), New York, 1991).

2 Michel Foucault, 'Politics and ethics: an interview', in P. Rabinow (ed.), *The Foucault Reader* (Penguin, Harmondsworth, 1986).

3 J. Rawls, *Political Liberalism* (Columbia University Press, New York, 1993), pp. 11ff.

4 Ibid., p. 29ff.

5 Ibid., p. 4.

6 Ibid., pp. 11–12, 257ff.

7 Ibid., p. 12.

8 This is Rawls's own interpretation of the meaning of the priority of the right over the good and what it is for the state to be neutral in choosing between goods. See Rawls, *Political Liberalism*, p. 176.

9 Ibid., p. 50.

10 Ibid., p. 90.

11 J. Rawls, *A Theory of Justice* (Oxford University Press, Oxford, 1971), chapters II, III.

12 Rawls, *Political Liberalism*, p. 19.

13 Rawls, *Theory of Justice*, ss 77.

14 Rawls, *Political Liberalism*, p. 19.

15 Ibid., p. 72.

16 Ibid., p. 72ff.

17 Ibid., p. 136.

18 Ibid., Pt IV: 1, 2–3.

19 Ibid., p. 220.

20 Interestingly, Rawls does not use the public/private distinction here, preferring to call the reasoning that goes on outside public reason 'non-public', insisting that all reasoning must have certain standards of evidence and judgement if it is to count as reasoning and not just discourse. See Rawls, *Political Liberalism*, p. 220.

21 There have been several authors who have suggested that a concept of autonomy is present in Foucault's later work, often in response to the criticisms of Fraser and Taylor. In particular, L. NcNay, *Foucault: A Critical Introduction* (Polity Press, Cambridge, 1994), and J. Rajchman, *Michel Foucault: The Freedom of Philosophy* (Columbia University Press, New York, 1985), have developed a response to the problem of the lack of normative standards in Foucault's work along this line. The most thorough and interesting treatment of the question of autonomy in Foucault's work is provided by Patton in this collection. See also R. Hiley, *Philosophy in Question* (University of Chicago Press, London, 1988), p. 105, and P. Veyne, 'The final Foucault and his ethics', *Critical Inquiry*, 20 (1993).

22 Foucault, 'What is Enlightenment?', in Rabinow (ed.), *Foucault Reader*, p. 43.

23 See Patton in this collection.

24 Rawls, *Political Liberalism*, p. 72.

25 I. Kant, 'What is Enlightenment?', in H. Reiss (ed.), *Kant: Political Writings* (Cambridge University Press, Cambridge, 1991), pp. 54–5.

26 M. Foucault, 'Questions of method', in G. Burchell, C. Gordon and P. Miller (eds), *The Foucault Effect: Studies in Governmentality* (Harvester Wheatsheaf, Brighton, 1991), p. 79.

27 M. Foucault, *Discipline and Punish* (Vintage Books, New York, 1979), Pt III, chapter 2.

28 In this sense, Foucault's work suffers in the critical literature from some of the same difficulties that recent debates have brought to Marx's *Capital*, in that, while on one level we are dealing with texts that offer us descriptive and normatively neutral analyses of power, on another level there are clear normative judgements and assumptions in Marx's work (see N. Geras, 'The controversy about Marx and justice', in A. Callinicos (ed.), *Marxist Theory* (Oxford University Press, Oxford, 1989). As is well known Foucault was often accused of not having a clear normative position (see R. Hiley, *Philosophy in Question* (University of Chicago Press, London, 1990), chapter 4). But, as I said above, if, following Patton, we entertain the idea of autonomy as a necessary but not sufficient criterion for judging between forms of power, then it is possible to see the sense in which a position like Foucault's is normatively engaged, because it is precisely the loss of autonomy, through the restructuring of capacities and the consequent loss of choice, that is at issue in the example Foucault provides in *Discipline nad Punish*.

29 Rodney Peffer's account of the value of political democracy (to which my account is indebted) argues that the two reasons Rawls gives for the value of political democracy show that he does not see it as a particularly strong value. See R. Peffer, *Marxism, Morality and Social Justice* (Princeton University Press, Princeton NJ, 1990), p. 399ff.

30 Rawls, *Political Liberalism*, pp. 217–18.

31 Ibid., p. 14.

32 Rawls, *Theory of Justice*, p. 234.

33 Ibid.

34 See, for example, J. Caputo and M. Yount, *Foucault and the Critique of Institutions* (The Pennsylvania State University Press, Pennsylvania, 1993); and G. Burchell et al., *The Foucault Effect*.

35 I.M. Young, *Justice and the Politics of Difference* (Princeton University Press, Princeton NJ, 1990), p. 41.

36 See here Rawls's comments on avoiding assumptions on the nature and identity of persons in 'Justice as fairness: political not metaphysical', in *Philosophy and Public Affairs*, 14, 3 (1985), pp. 223–51.

37 Rawls, *Political Liberalism*, p. 212.

38 Ibid., p. 180.

39 Ibid., p. 13.

40 M. Foucault, 'Two lectures', in C. Gordon (ed.), *Power/Knowledge* (Pantheon Books, New York, 1980).

41 Foucault, 'What is Enlightenment?', p. 47ff.

42 M. Foucault, 'The ethic of care for the self as a practice of freedom', in J. Bernauer and D. Rasmussen (eds), *The Final Foucault* (MIT Press, Cambridge MA, 1988), pp. 6–9.

43 Ibid., p. 45.

10

Foucault and Modern Political Philosophy

Barry Allen

The failure of the major political theories nowadays must lead not to a non-political way of thinking but to an investigation of what has been our political way of thinking during this century.

—Foucault

Foucault does not seem to have set out to be a political philosopher. In his first works he appears more interested in existential or anthropological ideas; the usual themes of political philosophy have practically no prominence. When he does raise points explicitly linked to political topics they are nebulous, formulaic, and receive no elaboration. In fact, he scarcely has a 'political thought' to speak of prior to *Discipline and Punish* (1975). Thereafter, however, political questions acquire prominence in his work. I shall not speculate on the reasons for this change. The point is that he increasingly came to question the pieties and platitudes of the post-war European Left, and to develop a line of reflection on political topics which makes a worthwhile study.

In the first phase of the reception of Foucault's work among English-speaking scholars, the usual complaint was that it was unclear what normative assumptions lay behind his criticism of existing society, especially of its institutions of welfare and security.[1] In the second phase of that reception, the trend is to suggest that the missing normative premise has been there all along. For instance, according to Jon Simons, Foucault's ultimate normative recommendation, the long-missing normative premise, is his commitment to a 'project of potential liberation involved in promoting new forms of subjectivity'. Walter Privitera, while sympathetic to Habermas's criticism that Foucault's supposed 'obfuscation of the validity problematic' and 'stubborn refusal to provide the normative grounds of his theory . . . undermines his whole approach', suggests that Foucault's 'hidden normative conception' entails 'the social validity of a *self-produced* identity . . . in opposition to the compulsion . . . toward assuming forms of identity sanctioned by dominant social values'. On this reading the 'creativity of social actors' is supposed to provide 'the criterion whereby the productivity of normalizing and objectifying actions governed by the will to knowledge is to be distinguished from those actions that resist it'.[2]

Nihilistic aesthete or politics as aesthetic? It is unfortunate to see the scholarship on Foucault oscillate between these alternatives. Is there another option? I shall be suggesting that Foucault's work can best be related to one leading tendency of modern political thought. His 'normative assumption', or the stance from which he criticizes present practice, is one which, with qualification, he shares with an entire tradition of modern political philosophers, from Locke and Adam Smith to Bentham and Isaiah Berlin. We must not be misled by trendy clichés and suppose that since it is fashionable to refer to Foucault as a 'postmodern' thinker, his work must have little or nothing in common with this (or any other) modern tradition. This assumption obscures one of the few leads that can assist us in understanding what Foucault has accomplished in political theory.

One undeniable contribution is to have put 'small power' – the 'micropowers' he describes in discussing the rise of what he calls 'discipline' – on the agenda for both theory and practice. These forms of power are increasingly more significant to our experience of government than the 'big powers' which preoccupy modern political philosophy (Sovereign, State, Capital, Ruling Class). Yet disciplinary micropowers typically do not operate with the mechanisms of coercion that history and theory have accustomed us to expect from dominating powers. Because of the new centrality of disciplinary micropowers, and because of the key role of scientific or quasi-scientific knowledge in their operation and in their legitimacy, the relationship between knowledge and power acquires unprecedented political significance. To grasp both the effectiveness of disciplinary power and its high degree of legitimacy requires a theory capable of appreciating this relation better than can the traditions of pragmatism or *Ideologiekritik*. Here is where I locate Foucault's signal contribution to political philosophy.

What are Politics?

What is political philosophy *about*? Politics? Not exactly. The state? Certainly not. It is about social government, about the activity of governing and the experience of being governed. Modern political philosophy is implicitly a reflection on the experience of government in Europe and America since around 1500, and it is this even when, as is usual, authors present their conclusions as universally valid propositions concerning eternal notions of government and human nature. It is appropriate to speak of a 'modern' political thought, because however continuous history may ultimately be, it is difficult to deny that by the end of the sixteenth century, a new political condition had appeared in Europe, not like a bolt from the blue but as a gradual modification of medieval practice. When people with the leisure and inclination to reflect on their new and different experience of government did so, there began what in retrospect we can see is a new epoch in the history of Western political philosophy.

Four points stand out as characteristic of the political government of the early-modern period. Two of these concern differences in the exercise of social power: Political government is increasingly perceived as a sovereign activity, meaning that the authority to govern is single and supreme over other authorities, clerical, traditional, and so on; and, secondly, rulers now enjoy much greater resources of power, an enhanced capacity to control important things and to govern people's conduct. Two further points concern correlated changes in the way people experience the new conditions of government. By the sixteenth century, there were increasingly abundant opportunities to lead increasingly self-determined lives – should people wish to do so, as increasingly many did. But then as now many were uncomfortable with autonomy. Hence the subjects of modern political government divide into those who desire and are accustomed to make their own choices in belief and conduct, and those who do not enjoy the new opportunities for self-determination, who prefer security to liberty, solidarity to enterprise, equality to freedom. Perhaps any group of people will divide along the same lines, but the point is that the conditions of early-modern Europe offered increasingly numerous opportunities for increasingly many people to expand the range in which their lives were the result of self-determined choice or to refrain from self-determination and submit to authority. European modernity is not merely the birth of a new individualism but of *two* new and obliquely opposed moral dispositions: an ethos of individuality shared among those intent upon enjoying the new opportunities for choice, and an ethos of authority among those who not only did not want to chose for themselves but did not want anyone else to do so either, preferring the authoritative ordering of conduct over the 'chaos' of individual self-determination.[3]

To these different moral dispositions correspond two different ideas about what it is to govern and what makes government good. Those who participate in the ethos of individuality want arrangements that prevent people from colliding with each other as they pursue their chosen course. The best polity accommodates the largest number of different patterns of conduct. And since free and self-determining individuals are constantly engaging in new activities and forming new relationships, their government must be ready to recognize new rights and expand the field of legal protection to embrace a constantly changing ensemble of activities and expectations. The ethos of authority requires governments not only to expand the range of legal rights well beyond anything medieval rulers had either the authority or the resources to provide, but also to embrace wholly new projects in the name of some collective good that is supposed to take precedence over the merely individual. The enhanced coercive power of modern governments as well as their conspicuous innovations in the field of 'welfare' and 'security', are not a response to the needs of a flourishing ethos of individuality but for the sake of a closer regulation of conduct, especially in matters newly opened to individual choice.[4]

The opposition between an ethos of individuality and of authority, and the conception of political government each of these imply, provides a schematic grid for reading the history of modern political philosophy. Can Foucault's thought helpfully be described with this scheme? Despite dissent and reservations, it does not seem violently wrong to associate Foucault with the modern ethos of individuality and its affiliated conception of political government. Under the description of 'arts of the self' and 'aesthetics of existence', he reaffirms the ethos of individuality that has been the mainstay of this understanding of government, feeling his way towards a different conception of morality and politics in the light of a new experience of individuality characteristic of the late twentieth century. Why then dissent and reservations? They arise from some important differences between the experience of government in Foucault's lifetime and the experiences available to the contemporaries of, say, Bodin or Burke.

One source of reservation about modern individuality is theoretical and academic: the 'discovery' (if that is the right word) that the individual is not coextensive with consciousness and does not dispose of an unconditional freedom of choice, being subject to a variety of determinations which arise from the most fundamental biological and social conditions from which psychological individuality first emerges. Supposing there are such conditions, and supposing they are beyond the reach of political change, then individuality must be conceived as a product of circumstances rather than an original element in the circumstances of government. While Freud's conception of the unconscious is an obvious model of such determination, this idea is not unique to the school of Freud, being a theme in variation from Marx, Nietzsche, Freud and Saussure to Heidegger, Althusser, Lacan and Lévi Strauss, all of whom left a trace in Foucault's thought. But would this insight have modified the political theory and practice of the nineteenth century were it not supported by events, by a changed experience of government? What does it matter that ego is not master of its own house (as Freud put it) for the great majority of people, who have neither the inclination nor wealth to indulge in a course of psychotherapy or peruse the latest theoretical fashions from Paris? Does it make their circumstantially determined individuality less interesting to them or their unconsciously circumscribed choices less real? Of course not.

Beyond these esoteric academic references, however, is a series of historical events: the First World War and the economic slump which followed, the Second World War and the extraordinary affluence which followed it before things began to sour again, especially after the oil crisis of 1973. Foucault belongs to the first generation to live under the full-blown security- and welfare-state, born from the new experience of total war, the total mobilization of an entire society for the prosecution of an end at once military, political and ideological. His work is, in part, an effort to feel his way in a new milieu, searching for conceptions adequate to the experience of government on the other side of the historical watershed these events define. This point would benefit from some discussion of changes in the context and practice of political government, European and global, which characterize the last years of the century which recently ended, our 'short twentieth century' (1914–91).[5] These may be summarized under seven headings:

1   The Globalization of the Economy

The latter half of the twentieth century witnessed the emergence of transnational entities which have exposed the limits of national sovereignty. National
territory and state policy no longer provide the framework for economic
activity, being instead merely complicating factors in a global economy with
no specific territorial base and which limits what even large and powerful
states can do. Not only has the globe become a single operational unit; its
economy has become uncontrollable. Nobody knows what to do about the
vagaries of the world economy or has instruments to manage it.

2   The Weakening of the Nation-state

That is, its collapse, in the face of autonomous transnational entities with significant non-military power, as a principle of world order. Both by its
monopoly of coercive power and because for most purposes it constituted the
effective field of political and economic action, the nation-state has been the
central institution of modern politics. Yet by the end of our century the
nation-state is increasingly untenable, on the defensive against a global economy it cannot control, straining to maintain a budget of welfare services, and
even to maintain what had always been its major function: public law and
order.

3   Total War and its Aftermath

The two world wars were unprecedented in every dimension. Waging war on
this scale requires careful management and planning of production, distribution – of the entire economy and resources of the nation. States discovered
that they could manage their economies and their populations to a far greater
extent than had ever been tried or even suspected. The idea of political government as a comprehensive management of resources is an old one; the
tendency of European (or 'modern') states had been in this direction at least
since the eighteenth century. The experience of world war confirmed the tendency, accelerated its progress, and enlarged the scope and scale of
intervention. The lessons learned and the managerial skills and interests con-
solidated and legitimized by wartime experience were not set aside at the
conclusion of hostilities. Both wars, and especially the second, were followed
by efforts at far-reaching social and economic reforms, presupposing state
planning and management on an unprecedented scale, introduced by governments committed to them on principle.

4   The Welfare State

The Second World War did not cause the welfare state, whose genealogy is
much older (I discuss Foucault's ideas on this point later), but war was an
essential spur to its appearance and legitimacy, and without that experience
it is difficult to imagine the magnitude of present-day governmental preoccupation with issues of welfare and internal security. So vast is its reach and

popular legitimacy that it is easy to forget how recent the welfare state really is. If such a state may be defined as one in which welfare accounts for the greater part of total public expenditure and people engaged in welfare activities compose the largest body of public employment, then a full-blown welfare state did not exist before 1970.

5   Growth of Interconnections among Science, Technology, Economy and Administration

This also belongs to the aftermath of the Second World War, which convinced modern governments to commit unprecedented resources to scientific research. The war seemed to prove that there were no problems which the combination of big science and high-tech innovation could not solve, and in the post-war period this assumption was applied to every sector of the economy. One result was the greater penetration of advanced scientific technology, as evidenced by the rapidity with which the outputs of the laboratory spill over into the routines and usages of everyday life, spreading techno-scientific objects so deep and wide across society that we now share our community with things fabricated in a laboratory. Such promiscuous mixing of the quotidian and the ultra high-tech is now commonplace, though unheard of before the nineteenth century. Half of politics today is conducted in science and technology, half of what we regard as nature is a technical artefact sealing a social bond.[6]

6   The Intensification of Administrative Control

This is one major example of the trend mentioned in the previous point: the discovery of non-military applications for advanced technology, especially in the area of administration, public and corporate. In conjunction with statistical techniques developed since the nineteenth century, the new information and communications technologies of the computer age enable a system of disciplinary surveillance not unlike that of Bentham's Panopticon, but without its clumsy architectural constraints. Technology-assisted authority can be exercised remotely at multiple sites and at a fraction of the cost of physical presence, vastly enhancing administrative capacity (private and public) at the expense of individuals and unorganized sectors of society. The now routine use of such technology evinces a trend towards an actuarial conception of social control. Relying on high-speed sorting and analysis, individual records can be compared with statistically constructed normative 'profiles' and pre-emptive measures taken on the basis of *probable* deviancy, the would-be delinquents systemically 'predetected' before they have the opportunity to disobey. Under these conditions, civil law comes to be identified with the authoritative redistribution of social risk, and the administration of justice with a mechanism of social control. However efficient such innovations may seem, they cannot fail to corrupt the conceptions of responsibility, judicial punishment and rule of law which have been pillars of Western justice since the end of the middle ages.[7]

7   *The Bankruptcy of the Political Left*

A number of points belong under this one and merit separate discussion.

The End of World Revolution and 'Really Existing Socialism'   Foucault did not live to see the events of 1989 in the countries on the eastern side of the former 'iron curtain'. But it did not require supernatural foresight to observe three things: the intellectual bankruptcy of Marxism; the increasingly grievous economy of societies belonging to the community of 'really existing socialism'; and the hollowness of 'proletarian internationalism'. As it became obvious that socialism could not overtake Western economies (as modified after the depression of the 1930s and assisted by the new information and communication technologies of the 1970s), its legitimacy, staked on a predicted triumph over capitalism, became increasingly untenable. Since fear has never been a durable foundation of social order, the eminent collapse of these states was not difficult to foresee, however vague one had to be about the details. The end of the international communist movement, and with it any kind of socialist or world-revolutionary internationalism, preceded that collapse; it can be dated from the Soviet invasion of Czechoslovakia in 1968, if not from Stalin's pact with Hitler. While the enthusiasm of the Left was briefly captured by Third-Worldism and the student revolts of the 1960s, 'no single doctrine of revolution replaced the old revolutionary tradition of 1789/1917, nor any single dominant project for changing the world, as distinct from overthrowing it'.[8]

The End of Imperialism   By 1980 no territory of significant size with the exception of South Africa remained under the administration of the former colonial powers or their settler regimes. With the end of imperialism came the end of much that had mobilized the Left. Although new 'imperialisms' were discovered and denounced by academic leftists searching for a cause, who sententiously redescribed whatever they did not approve of in terms of 'imperialism', 'colonization', 'oppression', 'fascism', and so on, they generated no spark to reignite a revolutionary movement that had been reduced to irrelevance everywhere but in the schools.

The Dissolution of 'the Proletariat'   If the end of imperialism robbed the Left of one traditional concern, the demise of the industrial proletariat reduced it to a movement without a cause. Not that industrial production employs fewer people today than previously; on the contrary, the rate has remained constant or risen since the nineteenth century. But the industrial proletariat as a conspicuous and solidary class is a thing of the past. Partly this is due to changes in the nature of industrial employment in Europe and the Americas; for instance, the US steel industry now employs fewer people than McDonalds. Nor is it merely that these new employers have somehow been able to control the formation of class solidarity or fend off unionization; time and again the employees reject it themselves. Meanwhile the heavy industries which were the former hotbed of trade unionism are increasingly located in so-called Third

World countries where political governments tend to be hostile towards working-class activism and unimpeded in their effort to suppress it.

The Exhaustion of Modernism in the Arts That is, the demise of the avant garde, the end of the dream of a world transformed through a combination of modern art and radical politics. 'One must surrender to the evidence: art no longer contests anything, if it ever did. Revolt is isolated, the malediction "consumed".'[9]

The Decline of the Political Party As a means of educating and mobilizing large numbers of people, the idea of the party seems dead. Instead, its name, representatives and ideological polarities have become the clichés of the mass media, whose greatly enhanced political function makes it probably more important in shaping governmental policy than political parties or even the electoral process itself.

The Appearance of New Liberation Movements The American civil rights movement and the revived feminism of the 1960s are obvious examples, as are gay-rights, anti-psychiatry and ecology movements. As Foucault observed of these movements, they cut across national lines and are largely indifferent to the old shibboleths of the socialist Left: the target is not 'the state' or 'the ruling class', but more specific forms of power, such as the medical or legal professions, welfare administrations, or traditional relations between men and women. Nor is the goal utopian. Theirs are limited and realistic struggles against what Foucault calls the 'government of individualization', that is, the effort to govern people through and because of 'who they are' – because you are female, homosexual, black, mentally ill, HIV-positive, and so on, this is what you should do, how you should feel, what you should want. These movements assert the individual's right to be different against the power of a scientific and administratively determined identity.[10]

I do not want to suggest that on the other side of these events we live in a completely different world from the past. The continuities are as obvious as the changes, many of which are merely the rapid intensification of trends that had been mounting for centuries. The security- and welfare-state is an example of that, as is the extension of administrative control. Yet it cannot be denied that the activities of government and the experience of being subject to political rule are not now what they were in the nineteenth century, and the points I have mentioned touch the major differences. Neither can it be denied that philosophy, if it is to be something more than an academic pastime, must take the measure of these changes, and seek new conceptions for the understanding of political activity in light of this transformation of our experience.

Discipline and Modern Government

Foucault is capable of a caricature in order to make his own position stand out in sharper relief; his caricature of 'the tradition' in political philosophy offers an example. 'We can formulate the traditional question in political philosophy in the following terms: how is the discourse of truth, or quite simply, philosophy, as that discourse which *par excellence* is concerned with truth, able to fix limits to the rights of power? That is the traditional question.' In other words, the philosophers have supposedly been interested in nothing more than speaking truth to power, using their privileged knowledge to limit the ruler's power, *de jure* if not *de facto*, should he choose not to harken to their wisdom or recognize the visage of truth. As a claim about the history of political thought this does not bear taking seriously. Those philosophers who did want to 'speak truth to power' (Stoics and Platonists of late Antiquity would be prime examples[11]) made no recorded contribution to political philosophy, while those who did make such contributions were seldom so simple-minded as to think that by wrapping themselves in the mantle of Philosophy they could become the rulers of the rulers, governing power by their superior knowledge of truth. What political philosophy has been about over the centuries is more accurately described by Oakeshott as a history of efforts to consider the changing place of political activity on the map of our whole experience.[12] But caricature is useful to Foucault's purpose. Having travestied the tradition, he can formulate his own question, which, he says:

> is rather different. Compared to the traditional, noble, and philosophic question it is much more down to earth and concrete. My problem is rather this: what rules of right are implemented by the relations of power in the production of discourses of truth? Or alternatively, what type of power is susceptible of producing discourses of truth that in a society such as ours are endowed with such potent effects?[13]

This *is* an important question, significantly different from those which have preoccupied modern political philosophy, even if the difference is not quite as Foucault suggests. The question of what political governments should do with their power or whether they should acknowledge limits on their activity is not exactly 'traditional'; in fact, it aroused little reflection prior to the sixteenth century, largely because that power was already sharply limited by straitened circumstances. Up to that time the undertakings of government had changed little. There was scant latitude for choice about what range of activities were appropriate, and nothing to spare on innovative new ventures in policy or regulation. Yet while modern governments enjoy resources of power more considerable than their premodern predecessors, nearly all of the instruments of control now available were coming into use by the latter sixteenth century. Some were inherited from the medieval inquisitions, such as an entire apparatus of records, registers, files, dossiers and indexes. These, together with a probabilistic style of reasoning about the relationship between evidence and fact, which was also inherited from the inquisitions, enabled governments to maintain convenient and constantly updated information about their subjects and the resources of their territories. Other new instruments of control with which early-modern governments began to experiment include improved maps and more accurate means of measuring time, more reliable roads and communications, new sources of finance and techniques of accounting, settled and guarded frontiers, and readily mobilized military forces supplied with uniform, equipment and powerful weapons.[14]

Only after governments began to avail themselves of these enhanced resources could the question (which Foucault identified as 'traditional') arise of what they have 'the right' to do and where the limits of intervention lie. Yet even then the desire 'to fix limits to the rights of power' was scarcely the only matter to preoccupy modern political thinkers, and for some – Melanchthon, Bacon, Rousseau, Condorcet, Fourier, Owen, Marx, De Maistre or Carl Schmitt, to name a few – it was not even especially important. They were more concerned with advocating innovative uses for the new resources of the state, new enterprises to which political government might dedicate itself, new reasons to bring new regions of conduct under the aegis of governmental regulation and policy. Nor does it matter that these thinkers are not 'liberals', not friends of the modern ethos of individuality; for the ethos of authority which they represent is equally a child of modernity.

What Foucault describes as the leading question of 'traditional political philosophy' is in fact uniquely the concern of just one main line of *modern* political thought, that associated with the modern ethos of individuality. Rather than a simple mistake, however, I see this as an indication of Foucault's solidarity with that ethos and his interest in taking up its concerns. If he tries to press those concerns in a new direction, it is for the sake of renewing rather than rejecting their relevance at the end of the 'short twentieth century'. Foucault may caricature political philosophy by conflating its complex traditions to the question of foundations as it arises in the political theory of modern individualism. Yet he is right to dismiss the preoccupation with 'foundational' thinking, which is a constant motif in this tradition, whose authors invariably deduce the limits they favour on government from some putative insight into non-political reality, claiming that something about God or reason or nature entails a limit to government. Such arguments are always fallacious and convincing only to those who already accept their conclusions. By trying to prove too much they prove nothing at all, and invite the detractors of individuality to confuse the issue by quarreling with a metaphysical argument that should not have been made in the first place.

Not, of course, that we should accept, say, the redistributive welfare state merely because it has survived long enough to acquire legitimacy in the eyes of a large public. But the question whether such states *should* exist, whether they are 'legitimate' or 'rational' or have a 'right' to exist, is no longer a helpful one (if it ever was). The alternative is not to abandon political philosophy, but to modify its questions. One way in which to do so is to ask why the redistributive state – or more generally the concern with welfare and security – enjoy the high degree of legitimacy which they now do. Foucault poses the question of how our economy of knowledge – the patterns of its production and circulation, as well as what is excluded as false or as non-knowledge – contribute to this legitimacy and, consequently, to the corruption of the modern ethos of self-determination. This is very much a new question in political philosophy, and a timely one. Scientific or quasi-scientific knowledge enjoys a kind of political authority unlike ever before. An appreciation of this new relationship between knowledge and power seems necessary for a sound grasp of present-day political reality.

Foucault's ideas of 'discipline' and 'power/knowledge' are among his most well known; there is no need for me to paraphrase texts we have all read on these topics, but a brief summary would be helpful for my argument. The early-modern period witnessed the rise of a new form of power-relation which runs parallel to those familiar from state and law – sometimes antagonistic to these older powers, sometimes complementary, and capable of colonizing entire regions of everyday life which had not previously been within the reach of governmental power. To see this new form of power we have to look away from the sites where political theory has accustomed us to expect domination: the state, the law, the tyrant. We have to look at relatively new institutions, agents, practices, and forms of knowledge, such as the public school or modern hospital, the bureaucrats of the welfare state or the police, the practice of prenatal medicine or genetic counselling, and the knowledge of statistics, criminology or psychiatry. All of these were unknown before modern times, and are in some cases quite recent. These new forms of knowledge, roughly coextensive with the human sciences broadly construed, crossed the threshold of scientificity in the same historical moment when modern Europe 'discovered the body as an object and target of power'.

Every society surrounds the body with prohibitions, constraints and obligations, and all or nearly all have experience with some techniques of ascetic discipline. Yet these are usually practised either at the margins of society, where the number of people affected is small in comparison with the entire population (as in monasticism), or on rare and highly ritualized occasions. That changed in the seventeenth to eighteenth centuries in Europe. Disciplinary techniques long known in the history of Western asceticism become, as it were, portable, disembedded from the religious and medical contexts in which they were perfected and given meaning, liberated from their exclusion at the margins of society, made more precise and efficient, and generalized into purely instrumental methods capable of producing what Foucault calls a 'docile body', one that is simultaneously stronger and more obedient.[15]

In contrast to sovereign or law-making power, disciplinary power is exercised over bodies rather than territory, and by constant surveillance rather than ministerial agents or intermittent levies. Such power requires a tight grid of coercion capable of compelling conduct without threatening violence: the time clock and the factory whistle rather than the slave driver or the whip. The point of discipline is not to force people to do what you want, but to make them into the kind of people you want; not to make people do what you want them to do, but to make them want to do it, and to do it *as* you want them to, with the desired tools, efficiency and order. Discipline relies on what Foucault memorably called a 'political anatomy of detail'. No detail of conduct or context is unimportant, not for the meaning it reveals but for the occasion it provides for power to multiply its grip upon the body. Individual conduct is constantly monitored, differentiated and ranked in relation to group norms, as better than or below average, normal, deviant, and so on. Fussy inspection combines with an awareness of the value of such small things for the control of human beings. The interest is entirely in the body's mechanical force; discipline is no longer a means to spiritual freedom, health or self-mastery, but to efficient movements and appropriate attitudes. Supervision is uninterrupted and concentrates on the activity being taught and practised rather than on the effect it may have on the individual. The disciplinary instructor is no longer a spiritual master or director of souls but a drill sergeant, shop foreman, or time-and-motion consultant.

In a useful comment Foucault explains that

> what is to be understood by the disciplining of societies in Europe since the eighteenth century is not, of course, that the individuals who are a part of them become more and more obedient, nor that they set about assembling in barracks, schools, or prisons; rather that an increasingly better invigilated process of adjustment has been sought after – more and more rational and economic – between productive activities, resources of communication, and the play of power relations.[16]

During the last two hundred years the instrumental, despiritualized application of disciplinary technology has become an unproblematic, self-evident, normal feature of increasingly many people's everyday lives. A few easily transferable mechanisms spilt over the walls of the monastery and spread across the social body, to become organizing principles in factories, prisons, hospitals, armies and schools, gradually colonizing more and more regions of daily life, and forming disciplinary networks that run back and forth across the population. Here is the curious spectacle of an instrumental rationality operating locally yet producing effects with the appearance of a global strategy. Despite the absence of conspiracy or a master plan, discipline has been cut free of its former limitations and spread over broader and broader domains as if in response to the command to discipline the entire social body.

Discipline produces a docile body, more powerful yet easier to direct and subjugate, and also more calculable and easier to know, a predictable object for the quasi-scientific knowledge of the social or human sciences, which grow up in the same historical moment as the great growth period in the disciplining of European populations. In becoming a target for these new mechanisms of power – ascetic discipline generalized, instrumentalized, stripped of spiritual meaning – the body is also offered up to these new forms of knowledge. The same interventions which produce a docile body also make it possible to compile precise data on individuals and to study them comparatively under controlled conditions. At the same time, this new knowledge enhances the capacity for control. An effective reciprocity develops between the knowledge that discipline produces and the power which it exercises; 'the exercise of power itself creates and causes to emerge new objects of knowledge and accumulates new bodies of information', while conversely 'knowledge constantly induces effects of power'.[17]

Here is the origin of Foucault's conception of 'power/knowledge'. The point of this expression is not to assert that knowledge *is* power, or that there is nothing more to knowledge than service to power, or anything of the sort. The slash, backstroke or virgule in power/knowledge is not an equals-sign and does not mean identity; as Foucault put it, 'the very fact that I pose the question of their relation proves clearly that I do not *identify* them'.[18] The point is to emphasize the *reciprocity* that obtains between those specific forms of knowledge which generalized discipline made possible (the so-called human sciences) and the exercise of disciplinary power over conduct – the reciprocity of a knowledge that accumulates through the exercise of a power over conduct which is itself extended and refined though the growth of that knowledge. Political government is increasingly effected by power in this form and guise – power whose character it is to produce and perfect a quasi-scientific knowledge which feeds back into the disciplinary operations that produce it, to refine and extend their capacity for the government of conduct.

This knowledge, like the disciplinary government which makes its accumulation possible, has the quality of being at once individualizing and totalizing. It is individualizing in the sense that it represents 'the entry of the individual description, of the cross-examination, of the anamnesis, of the "file" into the general functioning of scientific discourse'. Individuals become describable, analysable objects of sciences whose new methods and discursive techniques register individual differences in development, aptitude, attitude, ability, and so on, yielding knowledge that preserves and even magnifies our individuality. Such knowledge is at the same time 'totalizing' in the sense that its production also produces knowledge of collective facts, permitting 'the calculation of the gaps between individuals, their distribution in a given "population"' and directing the exercise of power over useful new artificial collectives defined by scientific rather than moral judgement. The result is an improbable configuration of scientific knowledge and political power which realizes the effective government of collectivities by an effective knowledge of their individual members.[19]

The government of conduct happens differently than it did in the time of Machiavelli, Locke or Mill. The means by which political government is effected can no longer be accommodated by the alternative between consent and coercion. Commands backed up by threats of violence are no longer exemplary of power, which can be violent, of course, or coercive, or repressive, but that is not its essence or even its most common manifestation. Think of mandatory prenatal care for welfare mothers, or genetic screening of applicants for life insurance. Think of social workers, trained in the university and examined and licensed by boards of qualification, working in the administration of a prison or a welfare system. Think of economists, demographers, epidemiologists, statisticians or pollsters advising on bureaucratic policy, or of forensic psychiatry and other forms of expert witness in the courts. Nobody is threatened, no one's natural rights alienated. These disciplinary experts do not claim a sovereign right to lay down the law. Their power to define options and govern conduct derives from their position in our economy of knowledge, from their claim to special competence before which we often have little choice but to submit, their disciplinary credentials disqualifying lay reservations and reducing us to silence.[20]

Foucault suggests that what really defines a relationship of power is that it is a mode of action not directly or immediately upon the body of others, but upon their actions or, more precisely, upon their options for action, governing conduct by modifying people's understanding of the alternatives from which they must choose. An exercise of power is an action designed to govern someone's conduct by modifying their subjective representation of the practically possible future. Obviously the word 'government' must not be restricted to a conventional political structure like the state, for the activity it names concerns nothing less than the entire spectrum of ways in which conduct, individual or collective, can be directed. So conceived, the exercise of power has no essential connection to violence or threats, which are merely its most frustrated and graceless form. It is not something that *could* be monopolized by one agency (such as the nation-state), nor is it always bad. There will never be a human collectivity in which there are not innumerable asymmetries of power, innumerable opportunities for people to conduct the conduct of others, and there is no reason to deplore this fact or wish it were otherwise. Without government we could not raise children, settle disputes, undertake complex endeavours, or enjoy the advantages of a civilized, or even a merely social form of existence, which is not in any case an option for us. The 'problem' that the exercise of power raises is not how to get rid of it, how to free ourselves from power, but how to make the inevitable asymmetries compatible with the greatest personal liberty for subjective individuality. Ethical life requires such liberty, areas of choice where the government of our conduct is up to us. The frontier between ethics and politics is the constantly shifting line between ethical autonomy, or the liberties people can take, and political heteronomy, or the liberties that are taken from them and with them by others.[21]

Foucault's conception of power as government, or the capacity to conduct conduct, seems more useful than any which the social sciences have produced. Consider for instance Max Weber's definition: 'Power is the probability that one actor within a social relationship will be in a position to carry out his own will despite resistance, regardless of the basis on which this probability rests.'[22] Here is the old dichotomy of intellect and will, with power situated on the side of will against or beyond reason, nor can violence be far from any exercise of power as Weber conceives it. While not explicitly mentioning it, his definition does state that one who exercises power will triumph 'despite resistance', that is, one way or the other, and thus eventually by recourse to threats and ultimately violence. Weber's definition also assumes that power is only real or effective where it cannot be resisted, as if the mere fact that an action *elicits* another's resistance were not already proof of the power relation between them – proof that the action of one was capable of modifying, however slightly, the other's understanding of where his or her options lie. I do not have to triumph to establish the fact of a power relation between us. In part that is because power is not a substance or piece of property that I *have* and those over whom I exercise it *lack*, as Weber assumes when he supposes that those with power must, by definition, triumph. Power, as Foucault famously maintained, is relational, not substantial; it is not anybody's property but is rather a pattern of relations in an entire social formation – asymmetrical relationships in which there is a potential for governing, conducting, modifying another's understanding of options for action.

While for Weber there is power only where there is triumph and defeat, for Foucault power does not exist apart from the possibility – and actuality – of resistance.

> Should it be said that one is always 'inside' power, there is no 'escaping' it? This would be to misunderstand the strictly relational character of power relationships. Their existence depends on a multiplicity of points of resistance . . . present everywhere in the power network. . . . They are the odd term in relations of power.

Foucault is I think significantly right to see the mere fact that one is able to elicit a response from the other, and not only an eventual triumph, as proof of a relationship of power. The proper alternative to power is not defeat but indifference.[23]

One impediment to our capacity to perceive and appropriately conceive the relation between power and knowledge is an inherited conception of power which aligns it with 'will' against 'reason'. Another impediment is a conception of knowledge which aligns it with 'truth', enlightenment, and freedom against 'power'. For instance, Charles Taylor asserts that the term 'power' belongs 'in a semantic field from which "truth" and "freedom" cannot be excluded. Because it is linked with the notion of the imposition on our significant desires/purposes, it cannot be separated from the notion of some relative lifting of this restraint, from an unimpeded fulfilment of these desires/purposes. But this is just what is involved in a notion of freedom'. So, he concludes, the idea of power '*does not make sense* without at least the idea of liberation.' Indeed, he thinks, the concept of power 'not only requires for its sense the correlative notions of truth and liberation, but even the standard link between them, which makes truth the condition of liberation'.[24]

Foucault, of course, thinks otherwise, and it is his determination to think otherwise on this question that leads him to one of his most significant insights:

> The history of the West cannot be dissociated from the way its 'truth' is produced and produces its effects. We are living in a society that . . . produces and circulates discourse having truth as its function, passing itself off as such and thus attaining specific powers.[25]

Despite the intuitions of metaphysicians, the truth-value of a statement is not measured by nature itself, no more than the exchange-value of a commodity. It should be no more surprising that knowledge and truth are implicated in the exercise of power than that money is. Considered in abstraction from *what* truth is in question, *for whom* it is passing true, and to *what effect*, truth 'itself' has no more value than coins apart from their circulation. Whether this truth or that knowledge is good, or empowering, or useful, or the opposite depends on who more specifically you are, but nothing about the nature of knowledge or the essence of truth unconditionally precludes their complicity with tyranny and all the more so with tutelage, nor must such knowledge be some kind of pseudo-knowledge, or such truth a mere passing-for-true that is really false.

Consider some topical statements: 'Homosexuality is genetically determined'; 'Schizophrenia is a chemical imbalance in the brain'; 'Male and female brains are neurologically different'; 'We are in the midst of a process of global warming'. Whether these statements are 'really true', in the sense of corresponding with reality, is of no importance; all that matters is whether they pass for true and to what effect. It is the effects of their currency, not their correspondence with reality (or lack of it) which makes the only difference that matters. Metaphysicians may balk, but there is no practical difference between 'passing for true' and 'really being true'.[26] The production of knowledge and the circulation of truth cannot fail to penetrate people's practical reasoning, and the effects on how they envision their options and choose and act are precisely effects of government. Since we no longer assume that power is bad or government opposed to an ideal of emancipated autonomy – since we accept that differences of power belong to the human condition and that government is indispensable and, in principle, highly desirable – we should not assume that this reciprocity of power and knowledge is always bad, but neither should we persist in the Platonic assumption that knowledge and truth are over there with being and freedom, on the other side of an ontological chasm from will or power or the chains of sensuality.

Reasons of State, Police and Governmentality

Earlier I described a number of features which I claimed make the social world at the end of the 'short twentieth century' significantly different from the other side of a historical watershed defined by the wars and alternating depression and affluence of the years 1914–73. Three main points stand out: (1) the enhanced prestige of administrative planning and management, whether by corporate, local or national entities; (2) the increasingly compromised quality of the nation-state; (3) the bankruptcy of the Left, which is perhaps just as well, given the pre-eminence it accords to the state in its political theory and the record levels of administrative intervention by its regimes when in power.

'Governmentality' is a neologism Foucault introduced to combine the idea of *government*, or the power to direct conduct, with the idea of a peculiar *mentality* with which the activity of government has been approached in modern times: the presumption that 'everything' can, should, must be managed, administered, regulated by authority. This point should not be confused with a claim about the growth of the state or the rise of a disciplinary society, both of which are connected but ultimately distinct from our modern governmentality, which is a style of political reasoning more than a specific institution or practice. Behind the modern state and the disciplinary society, and capable of surviving both, is a comprehensive trend towards more resourceful, more intense, more intractable, more fine-grained government; not merely the growth of the state (though there has been that too), but the growth of demands, mechanisms, agencies, and occasions for conducting behaviour, setting options, ordering the field within which people have to choose and act. More and more of everyday life comes under the umbrella of some agency of government, whether of the nation-state or a petty local committee, the welfare bureaucracy or the administration of public schools and utilities; whether the requirement is for a licence, permit, certificate or credential, or the obligation to meet regulations, standards, ordinances, or codes which, despite a nominal rationale (protecting society or the consumer, say) seem driven mainly by the assumption that there is something scandalous about a possible activity that is not subject to authoritative control.

Foucault's last work was not exclusively concerned with the questions of sexual ethics he treats in the latter volumes of *The History of Sexuality*. He also posed the question of the origin of modern governmentality. His work on this question falls in two parts: the idea of pastoral power, which takes us back to the oldest historical roots of our govern-mentality; and his investigation of 'police' and the doctrine of 'reasons of state'. The ancient idea of pastoral care intersects with the secularizing trend of modern European history at the birth of the 'police state', the prototype of all modern welfare and security regimes.

The idea of pastoral care began in the deserts of Egypt among the first Christian monks in the third century. Their monastic rule, which included the practice of confession and recognized the pastoral office of a director of conscience, was eventually translated to Ireland and Wales, where it was codified in the so-called Celtic penitentials, which were later used to guide pastoral activity on the continent. Besides these monastic practices, the administration of charity by the first Christian bishops, which was a major instrument of episcopal power in the cities of the Roman empire, blended pastoral care of souls with worldly solicitude for the body. The Church was the source of charity and the director of consciences. The rule of pastoral care would eventually comprise both functions, and accustom Europeans to the ministrations of an institution dedicated to comprehensive care.[27]

The rationale for submitting to its gentle coercions is assurance of salvation in the next world. Unlike a prince, a pastor does not merely command; the office is oblative, the pastor must be prepared to sacrifice himself for even the least of his flock. Dedication to the community combines with concern for each separate individual, continuously, from cradle to grave. His office requires the director of souls to know his flock, all of them and each of them, intimately and thoroughly. A major work on pastoral care, the *Liber Regula Pastoralis* (591) of Pope Gregory the Great, defines its subject as 'the government of souls'. The director of conscience must govern the whole people by moving the minds of each one separately; knowing their singular differences the pastor plays them like the strings of a harp. 'For what else are the minds of attentive hearers but, if I may say so, the taut strings of a harp, which the skillful harpist plays with a variety of strokes. . . . And it is for this reason that the strings give forth a harmonious melody, because they are not plucked with the same kind of stroke.'[28]

The contribution of the inquisitions to the development of techniques of modern administration has not been widely appreciated. Inquisitors were the first great innovators in methods for accumulating discursive knowledge about individuals. Their system of records has been called 'a masterpiece of archival science'. They took care to know the soul of the accused, to discern the precise extent of deviation, and usually tried to lead heretics back to orthodoxy; for inquisitors were also spiritual physicians and inquisitions pastoral interventions. Heresy is a disease, heretics need care and curing. 'The Holy Office devotes itself only to the health and winning of souls.'[29]

The Roman Church is the paradigm of an institution that is both individualizing and totalizing, and its pastors prototypes of the 'helping professions' of the welfare state. Whether in its mildest form in the confessional, or in the more vigorous form of inquisitions, pastoral power defines its object (sin, guilt, heresy, concupiscence, perversion) by reference to special knowledge reserved to its practitioners and operates through the production of knowledge concerning a hidden state that these trained professionals alone can identify and treat. The Christian Church thus established the office of one who, by virtue of his religious quality and expert knowledge, cared for others body and soul. Those who enter a pastoral relationship are drawn into the play of a peculiar form of power: power that is oblative, continuous, coextensive with life, and putatively salvific, soliciting intimate knowledge which, despite its radically individualizing character, is cultivated for collective effects, for the government of all by the comprehensive care of each.

With the disintegration of Roman secular power, responsibility for local administration increasingly fell to the Church, which seems to have tried to adapt to the new purpose models of government with which it was already familiar. These models were monastic, pastoral and charitable. Confession provides an example. It was originally part of monastic routine and not practised with the laity; St Gregory, for instance, does not discuss it in his treatise on the pastoral office. Private confession by lay parishioners was first codified in the Celtic penitentials of the seventh century. A reading of these works strongly suggests that this once esoteric practice was adapted for the laity as a method of disciplining a populace still wedded to pagan practices and belief. Down to early-modern times, however, persons charged with care of souls were relatively few and clearly marked as priests. One aspect of European modernity is the assumption of pastoral responsibilities by secular governments. Pastoral claims to care for individuals, claims which for more than a millennium had been linked to the practice of a specific religion, spread and multiplied outside the ecclesiastical institution. Generalized, secularized, despiritualized, an ecclesiastical practice formerly reserved to the faithful climbed over the walls of the monastery, became portable, universal, a technique of political government. Politics replaces religion as the instrument of this-worldly salvation; mundane concern for health, welfare and security replace the religious aims of the traditional pastorate; the subjects of modern government become a predominantly urban population accustomed to comprehensive care by professional agencies with expert knowledge and benevolent intentions; and the modern state becomes 'both an individualizing and a totalizing form of power . . . a tricky combination in the same political structures of individualization techniques and of totalization procedures'.[30]

One of the earliest European books of advice for princes, written by an unknown author *circa* 1220, bears the title *Oculus Pastoralis*, the Pastoral Eye. Although the distinction between the apparatus of state and the person of the ruler did not become sharp until the later seventeenth century, this work and the 'mirror-for-princes' genre to which it belongs plays a key role in the genealogy of the modern state. Another significant link is the doctrine of 'reasons of state'. Before I discuss Foucault's thoughts on this idea, however, it will be useful to dwell a moment on the historical context in which it arises: the innovative political theory and practice of northern Italy in the sixteenth century. Many Italian political thinkers had become convinced of the deficiencies of traditional ideas about politics and of the need to question long-standing assumptions both about the forces at work in political life and the appropriate aims of government. The results of their effort to rethink the idea of political order can be summarized in a few points:

1 Political institutions are artificial contrivances that can be re-fashioned at will to suit their rulers.
2 Political order involves the whole of society, everything either strengthening or weakening the ruler, who depends for the stability and coherence of his rule on the capacity to harness every available resource.
3 Political administration requires special talent and knowledge – expertise which does not automatically accompany wisdom, learning or virtue.
4 The standards by which political institutions should be measured are rational criteria of efficiency and usefulness, which depend on the special circumstances that obtain in each society. Consequently, there is no one perfect form of political order, God-given and immutable, to which every society should conform.
5 Political government is an autonomous enterprise with its own rules and laws, the appropriateness of a ruler's action depending on the opportunities inherent in the political situation rather than on some external standard of virtue or duty.
6 Force, far from being one among many factors, is the decisive one in both foreign and domestic affairs. It gives princes security and stability and provides strength and coherence to the entire state.[31]

This new conception of political government was born of Florentine politics in the early decades of the sixteenth century. These ideas were not destined to remain parochial curiosities, but slowly gained influence throughout early-modern Europe until they practically define the intellectual context of 'modern' political thought. The overwhelming impression of this new conception of politics is its 'rationalistic' character. The old belief that humanity was in the hands of ultimately uncontrollable forces supported the conviction that the best government remains within the proven, time-honoured framework of custom and prescription. The new perspective exudes confidence in the capacity of reason to shape political life by inventing and imposing more efficient instruments of government. For the first time in our history, politics is disembedded from the wider cultural context of tradition, kinship and myth, regarded as an isolable field for instrumental action unencumbered by 'irrational' constraints, such as traditions of honour or customary prescription, or a religious conception of kingship and its obligations. To think 'rationally' about political government is to think instrumentally, unconstrained by such considerations except when political calculation reveals their 'Machiavellian' potential for being manipulated.

Karl Polanyi wrote incisively of the disembedding of the economy (production and exchange) during the industrial revolution in the early nineteenth century. Usually, the production and exchange of goods is submerged in the whole social system, embedded with kinship relations, political traditions, magic, myth, law and religion. The separation of politics and economics as distinct sectors is an outstanding characteristic of modern social perception. Polanyi calls the discovery of the economy 'an astounding revelation' which precipitated the 'avalanche of social dislocation' that we call 'economic modernization' and 'development'. Before the economy could be disembedded and 'developed', however, it had to become visible as a distinct dimension of reality and an isolable field for intervention. As Foucault argues in his 'Governmentality' lecture, that prior step was the result of a new idea of 'population' as a distinct and isolable field of intervention. 'Prior to the emergence of population, it was impossible to conceive the art of government except on the model of the family, in terms of economy conceived as the management of a family; from the moment when, on the contrary, population appears absolutely irreducible to the family, the latter becomes of secondary importance compared to population . . . in its larger sense; that is to say, what we now call the economy.' This idea of 'population' was itself a result of the prior and ultimately more fundamental rationalization and cultural disembedding of political government, which sought analytically to identify the resources upon which the success of states depends. It is assumed that deliberately contrived political inventions can take the place of the whole continuous cultural context of morality, education, tradition, prescription, religious belief, myth, law, and natural knowledge out of which political government is wrenched. No wonder that modern, that is, rationalistic politics, depends so much on ideology. Once politics is disembedded, isolated as a field of instrumental action, there is little left to guide rulers apart from convictions about what should work or what ends should be achieved. That is what ideology supplies – a political doctrine to take the place of a habit of political behaviour, a speculative abstraction to take the place of a moral tradition, rational instructions for rulers who have no tradition to trust.[32]

The expression 'reasons of state' did not enter the European political vocabulary until the late sixteenth century, although Guicciardini (1483–1540), who was a major contributor to the new political conceptions just outlined, may have been the first author to write of *ragione di stato*. According to the usual understanding, this idea, which is among the earliest of distinctly modern European political conceptions, is simply that there are actions that a ruler may have good reason to perform even though, in the words of Botero (1589), they 'cannot be considered in the light of ordinary reason'. Reduced to this simple form, the idea seems to be no more than that for which Machiavelli became notorious: the Prince may do anything to hold or enhance his power. And indeed, scholars commonly describe 'reasons of state' as a Machiavellian doctrine despite the fact that he did not use the expression.[33]

Foucault argues that this usual treatment overlooks what is novel and interesting about the idea of reasons of state, which he sees as a deliberately anti-Machiavellian conception, introduced to avoid the undesirable implications of Machiavelli's teaching without overlooking the indisputable logic which it seemed to contain. In Foucault's view, 'reasons of state' implies a conception of political government significantly different from that of Machiavelli, for whom the problem of the ruler is one of keeping a territory free from rivals. Such an approach to the problems of government preserves a distinction between state and prince which the conception of reasons of state dissolves. 'Reason of state is a milestone in the emergence of an extremely different type of rationality from that of the conception of Machiavelli. The aim of this new art of governing is precisely not to reinforce the power of the prince. Its aim is to reinforce the state itself.'[34] He views Machiavelli as tied more closely than later sixteenth century 'art of government' authors to a feudal conception of sovereignty. Three features of Machiavelli's analysis reveal this heritage. First, he is concerned to draw the line between the power of the prince and other forms of power, as it were constitutionally to define the prince's sovereignty, on the assumption (which is indeed characteristic of medieval political thought) that the prince is unique in his principality, transcending what he rules. Secondly, Machiavelli adapts 'a juridical principle which from the middle ages to the sixteenth-century defined sovereignty in public law: sovereignty is not exercised on things but above all on a territory . . . territory is the fundamental element both in Machiavellian principality and in juridical sovereignty'. Finally, there is in Machiavelli more than a trace of the medieval rationale for sovereignty, according to which the end of a political state, while nominally the common good, actually becomes nothing more than the exercise of sovereignty itself, since that good cannot be defined apart from saying that the people obey wise laws. Hence the end of feudal sovereignty is simply the submission to and continuous exercise of that sovereignty. Foucault sees Machiavelli as very close to this conception in his view that the primary aim of the prince is to retain his principality.[35]

The 'art of government' authors of the sixteenth and early seventeenth centuries take strong exception to all three ideas. The ruler is part of the state, a temporary office-holder in charge of a political apparatus which is distinct from his person, while his rule concerns not merely a territory but everything on or in it that might contribute to the stability and strength of the state. The rationale of government is the right disposition of things – all things, everything that informed judgement reveals as material to a durable political order. There is no *one* aim or end of government but a plurality of ends, as there is not *one* essential instrument of government – the law – but rather a plurality of tactics, with law itself becoming merely one of a number of political instruments and tactics.

The difference between Machiavelli and the 'art of government' authors corresponds with two different concerns visible in the history of Western political reflection. One is constitutional, its focus on the correct composition and rationale of political authority. How is kingship correctly instituted? What is the proper relation between king and clergy? What makes a king a king, and what rights and privileges does monarchical sovereignty entail? Such questions preoccupy medieval political reflection. A second sort of question concerns the activities to which a government may turn its hand. What is the appropriate degree or level of enterprise for government? What kinds of activity may we expect governors to do and which should they refrain from? Medieval political philosophy had little to say about these questions, largely because there were so few choices open to rulers. There was agreement about their major responsibilities and how they should be pursued, but few resources left over with which to expand the horizons of government by engaging in wholly new enterprises or opening new domains of authority. Towards the end of the fifteenth century that began to change. Governments began to enjoy an access of power that gave them the resources with which to be enterprising, and the question of *what* it is proper for government to do first acquires some point and urgency.[36]

The 'art of government' and 'reason of state' literature of the sixteenth century offers the first clear evidence of a shift from one concern to the other. In response to Machiavelli – who poses the question of governmental enterprise (what the prince can or should do), yet in terms that retain the assumptions of the medieval constitutional problematic – the 'art of government' thinkers pose the problem of enterprise more starkly and consistently, as that of what the *government* or *state* should do, through the agency of a ruler, perhaps, but not one whose *own* 'state' (status) transcends the polity. What is original in the 'reasons of state' conception is the conceptual distance its theorists insert between ruler and state. According to Botero, political government requires 'a perfect knowledge of the means through which states form, strengthen themselves, endure, and grow'. Another thinker defines reasons of state as 'a rule or an art enabling us to discover how to establish peace and order within the republic', while a third explains that reasons of state comprise any considerations 'required of all public matters, councils, and projects, whose only aim is the state's preservation, expansion, and felicity, to which end the easiest and the promptest means are to be employed'.[37]

It is evident that these thinkers take a significant step – greater than they have been given credit for – towards the modern idea of the state as an autonomous political entity with its own immanent priorities. Its 'sovereignty' consists in its control of everything that 'political arithmetic' identifies as material to its strength. The sovereign state (that is, the state in so far as it *is* a state) therefore requires current, exhaustive and exact information about its strengths and weaknesses, making government a technical field for expert knowledge. Of course people are the political resource *par excellence*, so the state must know its subjects, individually and collectively, each of them and all of them. The calculations of political arithmetic include the individual not as citizen but as resource, as a factor in the state's marginal utility. That requires detailed and accurate information about individuals, and providing it is the task of a new adjunct to government, deploying a battery of new techniques and methods of knowledge. In the language of the day, the name for both the agency and the knowledge it produced was *police*.

Before its semantic range shrunk to its present narrow and almost entirely negative connotations, *police* designated the entire spectrum of ways 'by which a government in the framework of the state was able to govern people as individuals significantly useful for the world'. For Beccaria, 'the sciences, education, good order, security, and public tranquillity [are] objects all comprehended under the name of police'. According to another theorist, 'the object of police is everything that has to do with maintaining and augmenting the happiness of its citizens, *omnium et singulorum*'. Police seek to know and utilize everything that can

> consolidate and augment, through the wisdom of its regulations, the internal power of the state; and since this power consists not only in the Republic in general, and in each of the members who constitute it, but also in the faculties and talents of those belonging to it, it follows that the police must concern themselves with these means and make them serve the public welfare. And they can only obtain this result through the knowledge they have of those different assets.

Delamare defines the object of police as simply to 'see to living'. As Foucault explains,

> The police deal with religion, not, of course, from the point of view of dogmatic orthodoxy but from the point of view of the moral quality of life. In seeing to health and supplies, the police deal with the preservation of life. Concerning trade, factories, workers, the poor, and public order, the police deal with the conveniences of life. In seeing to the theatre, literature, and entertainment, their object is life's pleasure. In short, life is the object of the police. The indispensable, the useful, and the superfluous: Those are the three types of things that we need, or that we can use in our lives. That people survive, that people live, that people do even better than just survive or live: That is exactly what the police have to insure.[38]

This may sound like the old idea that the proof of good government is the happiness of the people, but it is not. The point is not to reaffirm happiness as the end or criterion of good government, but to make the rather different point that the happiness of individuals 'is a requirement for the survival and development of the state. It is a condition, it is an instrument, and not simply a consequence. People's happiness becomes an element of state strength.' The object of police, the instrument of this insight, is the population as a whole, all of them and each of them, while the *raison d'être* of the state attains new clarity: 'to take care of men as a population. It wields its power over living beings as living beings, and its politics, therefore, has to be a biopolitics.'[39]

As this last remark indicates, 'police' as a form of knowledge and practice adjutant to the state is the matrix from which emerges what Foucault calls 'biopower' or 'biopolitics'. In the course of the sixteenth and early seventeenth centuries, as the reformation of Christianity developed from a parochial insurrection to a European crisis, the principal objective of government changed. The obligation to defend the true faith and inculcate virtue is dropped, and the problem of the preservation of the population in all its multifarious aspects becomes paramount.[40] Not until our century, however, did the sheer existence of human beings as a species or even in substantial numbers (as a race or territorial population) enter the political field as a possible object of policy. As infectious disease was staunched and famine no longer one poor harvest away, after medicine mutates into a branch of the welfare state and the mechanism of descent gives up its secret, phenomena peculiar to life itself finally enter the reach of political calculation. That is what Foucault calls *biopolitics*. Governments acquire capacities equal to their ambition to work political effects at the level of entire populations, arrogating to themselves the task of administering life itself – the life of the fetus, the life of the cod on the Grand Banks, the life of the biosphere – conceived as a resource requiring 'responsible' management. Biopolitics is the culmination of a four-hundred-year fantasy of modern governmentality.

Why this Western govern-mentality? Why does our civilization have this passion to control things, to conduct people's lives for them, to administer and bureaucratize? Foucault was notoriously averse to 'explain' the apparently discontinuous historical changes he describes. He seemed content to confine his attention to the identification of genealogical prototypes of the phenomena under study (penitentiaries, clinics, and so on), even though no mere sequence of prototypes can explain why the thing itself came together when and as it did. While it is true that the category of cause is usually worthless in history, that does not mean history cannot explain, but only that its explanations are usually not causal explanations. We do not have to choose between the myth of historical causation and Foucault's austere refusal to explain the changes he documents.[41]

Why then Western governmentality? Perhaps it is not so 'Western'. Every civilization seems to be characterized 'by a seemingly inexorable trend toward higher levels of complexity, specialization, and sociopolitical control'. The history of civilization, whether in the ancient Near East or Egypt, Greece, China or Rome, or medieval Europe or modern America, is a history of the appearance of 'more parts, different kinds of parts, more social differentiation, more inequality, and more kinds of centralization and control'. This may in part be due to the fact that 'complexity is the base of civilization', and that 'a common trend among human organizations is to respond to problems by developing specialized administrators, and by increasing the proportion of the population engaged in administrative tasks'.[42] Or it may be due to people's love of comfort, of being cared for, their fear of change, of disruption, of anything different from what is accustomed and long prescribed. These are human emotions; it is not surprising that they should move men and women of far-flung cultures widely separated in time. Nor is it surprising that some people, especially those who have a lot to lose, want to make their society static, to ensure that things remain as they are, to take what works and freeze it, insulate it from innovation, even when (sometimes *especially* when) change might improve the efficiency, ease and excellence of the work. Institutions and especially bureaucracies, with their proliferating rules and regulations, offer massive resistance against change. Ever since there have been patent laws, for instance, they have been used at least as often and effectively to resist innovation as to encourage it. In 1623 the Privy Council of England ordered the destruction of a machine for making needles. In 1686 the importation of cheap Indian calico was forbidden, as were inexpensive and easily fashioned cloth buttons, a rival to bone, which was more expensive to work but more profitable. By 1730, French craft codes required seven volumes of 2,200 pages to prescribe every detail of established craft techniques, effectively proscribing innovation and retarding industrial production in France down to the Revolution.[43]

Is Western governmentality merely an example of a universal trend in complex societies towards higher levels of administration? Or of a generic anxiety before change and a desire for stability? Or human-all-too-human greed and the fear of competitive innovation? No doubt these play a part in our history as they do elsewhere. We have also to take account of the reciprocal, looping effect of bureaucratic complexity: the more there is, the more we need of it; for the more there is, the less scope for personal initiative and political leadership, which then intensifies the need for administrative agencies to fill the gap – the political vacuum – they themselves create. But there is more to Western governmentality than these universal factors can explain. There *is* something peculiar about the Western passion for government. It arises from, or at least is constantly reinforcing and reinforced by, the idea we have cultivated as to what it means to be 'rational' in matters of political government.

Writing in 1982, Foucault said, 'the failure of [present-day] political theories is probably due neither to politics nor to theories but to the type of rationality in which they are rooted'.[44] And what are its characteristics? Most of them were present or intimated in the new political thinking initiated in northern Italy at the beginning of the sixteenth century: political institutions are human inventions that can be refashioned according to will, the sole criteria of success being efficiency and utility; political order is autonomous, disembedded from the rest of society, though it mobilizes (and therefore must know and administer) the totality, each thing and everything, each and all individuals; government is a field of technical knowledge about such 'objects' as the economy, the population, welfare and security, entailing such actions as planning and management, and requiring obligatory credulity about the possibility of economic forecasting or the value of opinion-polling. Thus it is not merely that modern societies govern densely, deeply, in detail. That much may be a characteristic of complex societies anywhere. Our passion for government bespeaks the rationalism that has corrupted European politics since the beginning of modern times. A peculiarly irrational rationalism, which is evidenced in all of our distinctive strategies of political control. It is there, in the *how* of government, the strategies of control, the techniques and modalities, that we have to seek the peculiarity of Western governmentality. To mention some of the more important ones:

- Imputed and hybrid needs. Any society must provide for its people's needs, even if the precise content of those needs is highly variable. But Western societies have a peculiar history of *implanting* needs for the express purpose of giving someone the job of fulfilling them or regulating those who do – needs the like of which we would otherwise not dream of, such as the need for a sacrament, a life insurance policy, a psychoanalysis, a diversity facilitator, or 500 channels of television. And only in the West do we grow hybrid needs, so that what used to satisfy no longer does, not because we have something better, but because the need has been deliberately modified just enough that what used to satisfy does so no longer.
- The welfare state, and behind it the whole idea of benevolent, tutelary public authority is another probably unique strategy for the open-ended expansion of governmental control. Our contemporary welfare system and the whole apparatus of caring industries is a ghastly corruption of the Samaritan act, a secular perversion that would probably be incapable of rationalizing actions by anyone untouched by the history of Christian conscience.
- Generalized discipline. Most societies are acquainted with some form of ascetic discipline, but modern Western societies are exceptional in the manner in which we have disembedded and generalized discipline, stripping it of spiritual or ethical meaning and reducing it to a set of all-purpose techniques for training the body and rendering it tractable.
- Disembedding of political government from the wider cultural milieu. As I argued, this political disembedding is presupposed by the later disembedding of economy, of production and exchange. It entailed a reinterpretation of the wisdom traditionally required of a good ruler in terms of information – current, exhaustive, factual, objective – and the development of new forms of disciplinary knowledge to produce and analyse such information: economics, demographics, epidemiology, statistics of all kinds. As Foucault points out, these historically new disciplines provide 'knowledge of the state in all its different elements, dimensions, and factors of power, questions which were termed precisely "statistics", meaning the science of the state . . . a *savoir* of state that could be used as a tactic of government'.[45]
- Making people up. Among its techniques, Western power/knowledge

governs by producing new and tractable forms of subjectivity, reforming and refashioning people. Western social and psychological sciences subtly deconstruct the ancient philosophical connection between truth and freedom, and refashion the pursuit of enlightened self-knowledge as a tactic of subjugation. Our subjectivity, in so far as it is the knowable object of sciences, is the product 'of a certain technology of power over the body' – power exercised on those we punish, supervise, train, and correct; power over the mad and the sick; over those employed in factories and offices, and the unemployed recipients of welfare services.[46] Hacking's research on multiple-personality syndrome is a cogent illustration of a larger pattern.[47] Our 'human sciences' do far more than merely report on the objective facts of social reality: they contribute to the fabrication of those facts; their knowledge is a power in the world, a power to *make up* the people that they describe. If people's economic behaviour is predictable, it is in part because we have made them predictable, inculcating by discipline habits that correspond to what economic theory says should happen, making people who are calculating and therefore calculable. The same sort of process goes on in psychiatry and psychology, medicine and pedagogy, criminology and even linguistics. The normativity we experience in language is an artefact of discipline at the level of tongue and ear, speech patterns induced and sustained by differences of social power, above all around the pedagogic institution. Rather than language being 'by nature' a regular system capable of representation in a recursive list of rules, we *make* people's use of language fit this privileged model, *making* speech systematic, regular, rule-like, by social discipline.[48]

What conclusions should we draw from this account of modern governmentality? Perhaps that there is a trend of Western history towards the government 'of all and of each', towards forms of political power whose concern is at once to totalize and to individualize, to care for us as individuals and as a population, not for *our* sake, but for 'social security'. There is now a more or less permanent contest among political forces over the way in which the state should best minister to the socioeconomic needs of a society exposed to the cycles of economic boom and bust. How we see ourselves, individually and collectively, is increasingly set by our politicians' and administrators' catalogue of problems to be dealt with by (more) government.[49]

But is that all? Or the most significant? What good is this genealogy, this diagnosis or history of the present? What are we supposed to do with its insights? In what normative context can they be situated, and what philosophical conclusions do they support? As I see it, this late work of Foucault's on governmentality is an effort to specify the most significant forces now aligned against the modern ethos of individuality, and to reaffirm, if in an unexpected way, the traditional message of modern political individualism: that political government is properly subordinate to ethical ends, to the ethos of individuality, to what makes *individual* life worth living, rather than to collective ends imposed on individuals for whatever reason, in the name of whatever stirring ideal (social justice, democracy, progress, and so on).

It has been said before, but it is worth saying again; for the forces aligned against individual freedom are not less but greater than in the past. And from Foucault the message comes without the baggage with which it has been overburdened, whether by economic arguments purporting to demonstrate that the state governs better by governing less (von Mieses, Hayek), or moral and metaphysical argument intended to prove that an enterprising social-welfare state is immoral or unjust (De Jouvenel, Nozick). Foucault follows a different tack. He does not show us state and society as they ought to be, nor does he moralize or play dialectical games with academic abstractions. He provides an historical perspective on the govern-mentality or governmental rationalism of modern politics, offering an incisive description of the present plight of individuality, exposing the forces that threaten it and the source of their legitimacy, without encouraging an intemperate confidence that anything can be done about it.

Liberty and Politics

It is tempting to call Foucault a liberal, but that is an equivocal and misleading term. The distinction between the ethos and political theory of individuality and that of authority and the priority of collective over individual goals is more useful. For if Foucault is a liberal, he is in the tradition which spurns the authority of collective goals – the tradition of Spinoza, Locke, Smith and Kant – rather than the line that leads to social-democratic or socialist ideology – the tradition of Mill, Marx, Keynes, Habermas and Rawls.[50] If the description of Foucault as a liberal or a friend of modern individuality sounds paradoxical, or if it seems surprising to put him in the company of Locke and Smith, that is in part because, of course, he does not merely repeat what they have said or try to reoccupy their position unmodified. For instance, he has no use for the notion of human nature or the dogma of *laissez-faire* on which exponents of this political philosophy have relied. But their use of those ideas was extravagant in the first place, unnecessary and distracting baggage for a philosophy which is better without it.

For another difference, the early theorists of liberal individualism conceived political government as a means of ruling individuals in a way that would encourage and strengthen the ethos of individuality. The office of government is to be an umpire, administering the rules of a game in which it is not a player. Government is not a manager of collective action or an enterprising leader with goals of its own.[51] From our vantage point at the end of the 'short twentieth century' it is not difficult to criticize their notion of 'civil society' or the assumption that arbitrary domination by a juridical sovereign power (king, state) is the most substantial threat to individual freedom. Rather than preserve an original individuality that flourishes in civil society prior to the heavy-handed tampering of the state, it seems more needful to *recuperate* individuality, to *regain* a freedom of self-determination from the *imposed* individuality of the welfare state and its 'helping professions'. The exigent threat to the ethos of individuality does not lie in arbitrary state action or a misguided effort to manipulate the economy; it is deeper, more intractable, also more self-evident, unquestioned, legitimate, and probably capable of surviving the collapse of the nation-state. It lies not in the unto-ward power of the state but in the peculiar 'political rationality' under which we live and act, the political rationalism of modern governmentality, with the steep *rise* it has brought in the resources, occasions, agents, provocations, instruments, ingenuity, rationalizations and effectiveness of government.

In a famous sentence Foucault writes, 'the body is directly involved in a political field; power relations have an immediate hold on it; they invest it, mark it, train it, torture it, force it to carry out tasks, to perform ceremonies, to emit signs.' That does not make the individual 'a mere screen onto which disciplinary and objectifying practices are projected'.[52] Foucault never claimed that the subject is *utterly* the product of forces that objectify it; objec-tification, whether by disciplinary training or (pseudo)scientific knowledge, is but one axis of modern subjectivity. Of course in opposition to the mysticism of the self or the idea of consciousness as an originary fount of meaning or intentionality (as in Bergson, Sartre, phenomenology, existentialism, and so on), Foucault regards the self as an artefact not, however, exclusively of exter-nal social forces, but also of individual choice and aesthetic self-selection. If there is no original, primordial, pre-social self, the conclusion to draw is not that individuality is a mere farce with no basis in reality. 'There is', Foucault writes, 'only one practical consequence: we have to create ourselves as a work of art.' So far is he from denying the reality of such self-creation or the free-dom it presupposes that he makes it the basis for his conception of ethical life as an aesthetic 'work on the self'.[53]

Instead of dismissing this idea with a mere label, as some sort of dissolute postmodern 'aestheticism',[54] wiser critics would see that Foucault restates, in terms more realistic for the present day, the claim that has always been asso-ciated with the ethos of modern individuality and the politics of liberal individualism: That political government is a second-order pursuit, which owes its rationale to the fact that there are other, more significant things to do with life than politics, whose purpose is to preserve the free space of individ-ual choice. It says something about our times that Foucault should find it necessary to suggest we should 'get rid of [the] idea of an analytical or neces-sary link between ethics and other social or economic or political structures'.[55] Personal identity is not wholly a social construction, nor is it merely the result of anonymous forces operating on a pliant and indifferent body. The self as work of art is elaborated in the free space which, despite constantly shifting contours, it is the business of political government to pre-serve so that we can enjoy something more important than politics, something that politics is *for*. Precisely because the drift of modern politics is away from this limitation and acknowledgement of proper bounds, with the presumption consistently in favour of higher levels of administration and the integration of individuals into ever greater corporate totalities, Foucault deems 'the problems of governmentality and the techniques of government' to be 'the only political issue, the only real space for political struggle and contestation'. Of course the idea that 'we' might 'do something', that a new programme, new instructions, new controls diligently implemented might reverse the modern trend towards more intense and pervasive government is extremely naive. Yet does Foucault's idea of ethical life as a work on the self or an aesthetics of existence offer a real alternative? I think not.

It is not difficult to understand the attraction of an aesthetics of the self for Foucault or for any philosopher who agrees with Nietzsche's judgement that European ethical thought has been corrupted by what Nietzsche called the morality of pity. Ethics is reduced to a universal pattern, a claim about how everybody ought to be but unfortunately is not, and therefore are to be pitied – which is not incompatible with 'forcing them to be free'. It seems clear that the attraction of Stoic ethics as Foucault interpreted or misinterpreted it was that it did not present a universal pattern that everyone was expected to follow.[56] His suggestion that one approach life as a problem of art, working its indifferent material into a beautiful, uniquely personal form, is quite intelligible as a reaction against Christian ethics from St Paul to Kant. But it is a mistake to confuse the admirable idea that people should be free to take up this aesthetic attitude towards their lives, with *ethics*, as if the one might substitute for the other.

Few who think carefully would want to live in a world where the *only* 'ethical' constraints were those freely chosen by devotees of self-cultivation. That is not a bold new approach to the problem of ethics in a post-Christian world; it is the description of a world without ethics, and such a world is not sustainable. The fabric of social relations that supports cooperative emotions and durable human relationships can take various forms, but it is not infinitely flexible. Not *anything* we may have the wit to invent and the force to impose on social life is necessarily viable. A social world in which people self-consciously view their lives as works of art in the making is humanly impossible without an appropriate framework of ethical self-restraint and political government. But that simply means it is bootless to look to Foucaultian 'aesthetics of existence' for insight into the ethical framework that such a conception of personal life *presupposes*.

My point is not to claim once again the irreducibility of ethics to aesthetics; for that supposed irreducibility presupposes Christian–Kantian conceptions of both ethics and art which I think we have to overcome. Instead of asserting the irreducibility of ethics to aesthetics, we have to ask whether we really have any idea of what an aesthetics of existence would be like that was not informed by a substantial *ethical* conception of the difference between good and bad lives. What content can we give to the suggestion that people approach their lives aesthetically unless we have some idea of the difference between success and disaster, between ethical art and monstrosity? What Foucault does not explain is where we are supposed to get such ideas, or with what right we should enforce them on those who may choose (doubtless in the name of the self) to reject them as incompatible with their idea of a beautiful life.

Aesthetic conceptions are no help in elucidating ethical conceptions because when aesthetic conceptions are applied to life itself, we have no idea of the difference between excellence and failure except by referring back to our *ethical* ideas of what makes life excellent, beautiful, happy. What does the idea of a 'beautiful life' presuppose in the way of aesthetic judgement, and how is such judgement to be cultivated? Is an aesthetic 'work on the self' merely the effort to impart a form or set of formal qualities? Such qualities are unlikely to imply much self-restraint, yet the ethos of individuality cannot flourish without it. How would the concern for 'beautiful form' guide us in deciding what, in a real case, it would be best, or right, or even beautiful to do? Is such beauty an inexplicable, know-it-when-we-see-it *je ne sais quoi*? Or might something be said about what makes a thing a work of art, about how such things differ from natural objects or inept or indifferent artefacts? Does excellence enter into 'aesthetics' and therefore into the question of ethics and of what makes a life good? If so – and I do not see how to avoid this implication – then before we can say whose life merits distinction as a work of art and why, we have to know what makes life excellent.

Foucault's idea of ethical life as a work on the self therefore does not take us very far. He discusses the 'aesthetics of existence' as if 'beautiful' or 'work of art' could be the basic concepts in terms of which ethics might be elucidated. They cannot be. An aesthetics of existence *presupposes* and cannot explicate the ethical idea of a good life. Rather than claim the irreducibility of ethics to aesthetics, my point is the inseparability of the two. We have no idea of a *good life* that is not the most complete synthesis of aesthetics and ethics, beauty and morality. Foucault's 'aesthetic of existence' is not this synthesis, for he is still opposing, polemically, art to morality, particularity to universality, a Kantian conception of aesthetics to a Kantian conception of ethics. The result is a monstrosity that cannot possibly offer a workable solution to the real problem it tries to address.

If, as Oakeshott said of J.S. Mill, his work amounts to a muddled and unconfident exploration of the political theory of collectivism under cover of the rhetoric of individualism, one might say of Foucault, conversely, that his comprises a muddled and unconfident exploration of the political theory of individualism under cover of the rhetoric of radicalism. By way of apology, however, one may add that his muddle is largely our muddle – the muddle in which friends of the ethos of individuality find themselves at the end of the short twentieth century. We have so far circumvented the administrative equivalent of entropic heat-death, though that probably proves the immaturity of governmental technics in the past rather than the capacity of an ethos of individuality to overcome any enhancement of the forces which authority and the Western will to power throw against it.

In one of his late reflections on the Kantian question, What is Enlightenment? Foucault writes:

> The question which arises at the end of the eighteenth century is: What are we in our actuality? . . . I think a new pole has been constituted for the activity of philosophizing, and this pole is characterized by the question, the permanent and ever-changing question, 'What are we today?'[57]

Perhaps the best that political philosophy can do without degenerating into ideology is to seek conceptions which yield the greatest insight into where we are now, what we have become, whether as modern Europeans or as human beings. Foucault sought concepts adequate to our ambiguous and confusing experience of political government at the end of the twentieth century. He did not offer a shiny new ideal, or another excuse for believing in the revolutionary future. One reason his work resonates for us is because we are weary of the radical agenda. His achievement in political philosophy is to have contributed to the concepts we have to use to elucidate the present, even if we cannot descry in it the obscure lineaments of a future we can believe in.

Notes

1 See Charles Taylor, 'Foucault on freedom and truth', in D.C. Hoy (ed.), *Foucault: A Critical Reader* (Blackwell, Oxford, 1986); and Nancy Fraser, 'Foucault on modern power: empirical insights and normative confusions', *Praxis International*, 1 (1981), pp. 272–87.

2 Jon Simons, *Foucault and the Political* (Routledge, London, 1995), p. 66. Walter Privitera, *Problems of Style: Michel Foucault's Epistemology*, trans. J. Keller (State University of New York Press, Albany, 1995), pp. 65, 128, 64, 110; compare Simons, *Foucault*, p. 114. Privitera's book elaborates Jürgen Habermas's critique of Foucault in *The Philosophical Discourse of Modernity*, trans. F. Lawrence (MIT Press, Cambridge MA, 1987).

3 Michael Oakeshott, *Morality and Politics in Modern Europe* (Yale University Press, New Haven CT, 1993), pp. 32–5, 27, 23, 24.

4 Ibid., pp. 24, 48–9, 91, 92, 109.

5 See Eric Hobsbawm, *Age of Extremes: The Short Twentieth Century 1914–1991* (Michael Joseph, London, 1994). My discussion of the points that follow is indebted to this work.

6 Bruno Latour, *We Have Never Been Modern*, trans. C. Porter (Harvard University Press, Cambridge MA, 1993), pp. 7, 21, 37, 139, 144.

7 See O. H. Gandy, Jr, *The Panoptic Sort: A Political Economy of Personal Information* (Westview Press, Boulder CO, 1993); and F. Ewald, 'Insurance and risk,' and R. Castel, 'From dangerousness to risk', both in G. Burchell, C. Gordon and P. Miller (eds), *The Foucault Effect: Studies in Governmentality* (University of Chicago Press, Chicago, 1991).

8 Hobsbawm, *Age of Extremes*, p. 455.

9 Jean Baudrillard, *For a Critique of the Political Economy of the Sign*, trans. C. Levin (Telos Press, St Louis, 1981), p. 110.

10 Foucault, 'The subject and power', in H. Dreyfus and P. Rabinow (eds), *Michel Foucault: Beyond Structuralism and Hermeneutics*, 2nd edn (University of Chicago Press, Chicago, 1983), pp. 210–12.

11 'The scenario of the philosopher who tamed the heart of the emperor remained important in the political imagination of the later empire. It explained why the worst did not always happen.' Peter Brown, *Power and Persuasion in Late Antiquity* (University of Wisconsin Press, Madison WI, 1992), p. 66.

12 M. Oakeshott, *Rationalism in Politics and Other Essays* (Methuen, London, 1962), p. 132.

13 Foucault, *Power/Knowledge: Selected Interviews and Other Writings 1972–1977*, C. Gorden (ed.) (Pantheon, New York, 1980), p. 93.

14 Oakeshott, *Morality and Politics*, pp. 10, 34. On inquisitions and probabilistic reasoning, see James Tully, 'Governing conduct', in Edmund Leites (ed.), *Conscience and Casuistry in Early Modern Europe* (Cambridge University Press, Cambridge, 1988), pp. 27–9.

15 Foucault, *Discipline and Punish: The Birth of the Prison*, trans. Alan Sheridan (Vintage Books, New York, 1979), pp. 135–41. Foucault's tendency sometimes to treat law as if it were essentially a medieval concept and practice at odds with the normalizing trend of modern

discipline is plausibly criticized in Alan Hunt and Gary Wickham, *Foucault and Law: Toward a Sociology of Law as Governance* (Pluto Press, London, 1994).

16 Foucault, 'The subject and power', p. 219.

17 Foucault, *Power/Knowledge*, pp. 51–2. For a historical example of the reciprocity of power and knowledge worked out in some detail, see my 'Demonology, styles of reasoning, and truth', *International Journal of Moral and Social Studies*, 8 (1993), pp. 95–122.

18 Foucault, *Politics, Philosophy, Culture: Interviews and Other Writings 1977–1984*, L.D. Kritzman (ed.) (Blackwell, Oxford, 1988), p. 43. As this is still a common misunderstanding, a fuller citation may be worth while: 'when I read – and I know it has been attributed to me – the thesis "Knowledge is power", or "Power is knowledge", I begin to laugh, since studying their *relation* is precisely my problem. If they were identical, I would not have to study them and I would be spared a lot of fatigue as a result. The very fact that I pose the question of their relation proves clearly that I do not *identify* them.' The same point is made again on pp. 264–5.

19. Foucault, *Discipline and Punish*, pp. 190–1; 'The subject and power', p. 213; and 'The political technology of individuals', in L.H. Martin, H. Gutman and P.H. Hutton (eds), *Technologies of the Self: A Seminar with Michel Foucault* (University of Massachusetts Press, Amherst MA, 1988), pp. 161–2.

20 I discuss the disabling power of expert knowledge at more length in 'Disabling knowledge', in G.B. Madison and M. Fairbairn (eds), *The Ethics of Postmodernity* (Northwestern University Press, Evanston IL, 1998).

21 Foucault, 'The subject and power', pp. 219–21. It should be clear that Foucault has little use for Nietzsche's idea of 'will to power'. The uncritical assumption that there is some significant connection between Foucault's contribution to the conception of social power and Nietzsche's dark musings about *Wille zur Macht* is perhaps the most misleading of entrenched presuppositions in the critical literature on Foucault. For further discussion of their relationship, see my 'Government in Foucault', *Canadian Journal of Philosophy*, 21 (1991), pp. 421–40.

22 Max Weber, *The Theory of Social and Economic Organizations*, T. Parsons (ed.) (Free Press, New York, 1964), p. 152.

23 Foucault, *History of Sexuality, Vol. 1: Introduction*, trans. R. Hurley (Vintage Books, New York, 1980), pp. 95–6; and 'The subject and power', p. 221.

24 Taylor, 'Foucault on freedom and truth', pp. 91–2, 93.

25 Foucault, *Politics, Philosophy, and Culture*, p. 112.

26 See my *Truth in Philosophy* (Harvard University Press, Cambridge MA, 1993).

27 On ancient asceticism, see Foucault, 'The battle for chastity', *Western Sexuality*, P. Ariès and A. Béjin (eds), trans. A. Forster (Blackwell, Oxford, 1985); and Peter Brown, *The Body and Society: Men, Women, and Sexual Renunciation in Early Christianity* (Columbia University Press, New York, 1988). On episcopal charity, see Brown, *Power and Persuasion in Late Antiquity*, chapter 3. On the Celtic penitentials and their influence, see J.T. McNeill, *A History of the Cure of Souls* (Harper & Brothers, New York, 1951), and J.T. McNeill and H.M. Gamer (eds), *Medieval Handbooks of Penance* (Columbia University Press, New York, 1990).

28 St Gregory the Great, *Pastoral Care*, trans. H. Davis (Neuman Press, New York, 1950), I, 1, p. 21; III prologue (p. 89). St Columban received a copy of this work in Ireland where, with Cassian's writings, it influenced the development of the Celtic penitential. St Benedict's son took Gregory's codex to England, and in the ninth century King Alfred translated it into West Saxon. Charlemagne instructed his bishops to follow it, leading to its description as the book that made the bishops who made the modern nations.

29 Archbishop of Sarno, 1588; cited in N. Davidson, 'The Inquisition and the Italian Jews', in S. Haliczar (ed.), *Inquisition and Society in Early Modern Europe* (Croom Helm, London, 1987), p. 20. G. Henningsen, 'The archives and the historiography of the Spanish Inquisition', in G. Henningsen and J. Tedeschi (eds), *The Inquisition in Early Modern Europe* (Northern Illinois University Press, Dekalb, 1986), p. 56. Heresy was interpreted by the semantic chain of *disease, pestilence, leprosy, cancer* and *plague*, words 'used of almost every significant outbreak of heresy in the twelfth century', R.I. Moore, 'Heresy as disease', in W. Lourdaux and D. Verhelst (eds), *The Concept of Heresy in the Middle Ages* (Louvain University Press, Louvain, 1976), p. 2. The penitential handbooks constantly reiterate the comparison of the pastor to a physician; see

McNeill and Gamer, *Handbooks of Penance*, pp. 148–9, 221–3, 323, 347–8, 413–14. Ladurie describes the activities of inquisitor Jacques Fournier (later Pope Benedict XII): 'He proceeded, and succeeded, essentially through the diabolical and tenacious skill of his interrogations; only rarely did he have recourse to torture. He was fanatical about detail. . . . What drove him on was the desire . . . to know the truth. For him, it was a matter first of detecting sinful behavior and then of saving souls.' E. Le Roy Ladurie, *Montaillou: Cathers and Catholics in a French Village 1294–1324*, trans. B. Bray (Scolar Press, London, 1978), pp. xiii, xv.

30 Foucault, 'The subject and power', pp. 213–15. On secular care and the welfare state, see Ivan Illich, 'Useful unemployment and its professional enemies', *Toward a History of Needs* (Heyday, Berkeley CA, 1978); 'The war against subsistence', *Shadow Work* (Marion Boyars, London, 1981); and 'Disabling professions', in Ivan Illich, Irving Zola, John McKnight, Jonathan Caplan and Harley Shaiken (eds), *Disabling Professions* (Marion Boyars, London, 1977). Critical steps in the secularization of pastoral care are recounted in Michel Mollat, *The Poor in the Middle Ages*, trans. Arthur Goldhammer (Yale University Press, New Haven CT, 1986).

31 Felix Gilbert, *Machiavelli and Guicciardini: Politics and History in Sixteenth-Century Florence* (Princeton University Press, Princeton NJ, 1965), pp. 84, 94–6, 101–4, 119–20, 129, 131, 138–9, 150, 299. On the development of the modern concept of 'state', see Quentin Skinner, 'The state', in T. Ball, J. Farr and R. Hanson (eds), *Political Innovation and Conceptual Change* (Cambridge University Press, Cambridge, 1989); and J. Anderson, 'The modernity of modern states', in J. Anderson (ed.), *The Rise of the Modern State* (Harvester Wheatsheaf, Brighton, 1986).

32 Karl Polanyi, *The Great Transformation* (Beacon, Boston, 1957), pp. 40, 46, 54–5, 68, 119, 195; and H.W. Pearson (ed.), *The Livelihood of Man* (Academic Press, New York, 1997), pp. 55, 57. Foucault, 'Governmentality', *Foucault Effect*, pp. 99–100. Oakeshott, *Rationalism in Politics*, p. 25. On 'development' and economic modernization, see also Wolfgang Sachs (ed.), *The Development Dictionary: A Guide to Knowledge as Power* (Zed Books, London, 1992).

33 Quentin Skinner, *The Foundations of Modern Political Thought, Vol. 1: The Renaissance* (Cambridge University Press, Cambridge, 1978), pp. 248–9; citing Giovanni Botero, *The Reason of State* (1589). Skinner repeatedly identifies Machiavelli with the idea of reasons of state: 'Machiavellian defenders of *ragione di stato*'; 'Machiavellian conception of reason of state'; 'the pure Machiavellian doctrine of *ragione di stato*'; 'Machiavelli's doctrine of reason of state,' and so on (pp. 250–4).

34 Foucault, 'Political technology of individuals', p. 150.

35 Foucault, 'Governmentality', pp. 91, 93, 95.

36 St Thomas Aquinas, *On Kingship*, trans. G.B. Phelan (Pontifical Institute of Mediaeval Studies, Toronto, 1949). Walter Ullmann, *A History of Political Thought: The Middle Ages* (Penguin, Harmondsworth, 1965). Oakeshott, *Morality and Politics*, pp. 9–12.

37 Giovanni Botero, *The Reason of State* (1589); Palazzo, *Discourse on Government and True Reason of State* (1606); Chemnitz, *De Ratione Status* (1647); all cited in Foucault, 'Political technology of individuals', p. 148.

38 Foucault, 'Political technology of individuals', p. 154. Beccaria, *Elementi di Economia Pubblica* (1769); P. von Hohesntal, *Liber de Politia* (1776); Johann von Justi, *Éléments généreaux de police* (French trans., 1769); Delamare, *Traité de la Police* (1705). Cited in Pasquale Pasquino, 'Theatrum politicum', *The Foucault Effect*, pp. 105–18; Foucault, *History of Sexuality*, p. 25; and 'Political technology of individuals', pp. 157, 160. Pasquino notes that a bibliography limited to German publications on the 'science of police' lists 3,215 entries between 1600 and 1800. Adam Smith used the English word 'police' in this older sense in the title of his *Lectures on Justice, Police, Revenue and Arms* (1763).

39 Foucault, 'Political technology of individuals', pp. 158, 160. On biopower, see Foucault, *History of Sexuality*, pp. 137–42. See also Ivan Illich, 'The institutional construction of a new fetish: human life', *In the Mirror of the Past: Lectures and Addresses 1978–1990* (Marion Boyars, New York, 1992).

40 'This modern political project, where life itself is wagered on our political technology, is the informing principle of mercantile practice.' Tully, 'Governing conduct', p. 15.

41 For a convincing critique of causal explanation in history and an alternative narrative conception, see M. Oakeshott, *Experience and its Modes* (Cambridge University Press, Cambridge, 1933), chapter 3; and 'Historical events', in his *On History and Other Essays* (Barnes and Noble, Totowa NJ, 1983).

42 J.A. Tainter, *The Collapse of Complex Societies* (Cambridge University Press, Cambridge, 1988), pp. 3, 37, 41, 115.

43 Carroll Quigley, *The Evolution of Civilizations* (Liberty Fund, Indianapolis, 1979), p. 378.

44 Foucault, 'Political technology of individuals', p. 161.

45 Foucault, 'Governmentality', pp. 96–8.

46 Foucault, *Discipline and Punish*, p. 29.

47 See Ian Hacking, *Rewriting the Soul* (Princeton University Press, Princeton NJ, 1995).

48 I expand on this argument in 'The historical discourse of philosophy', *Reconstructing Philosophy: New Essays in Metaphilosophy, Canadian Journal of Philosophy*, (suppl.) 19 (1994), pp. 127–58. See also Roy Harris, *The Language Machine* (Duckworth, London, 1987), and *The Language Makers* (Cornell University Press, Ithaca NY, 1980).

49 See Colin Gorden, 'Governmental rationality', *Foucault Effect*, pp. 19, 34–5.

50 Oakeshott plausibly sees Mill as ultimately favouring the priority of collective aims. 'Rhetorically, Mill's writings may be said to belong to the political theory of individualism; but substantially they compose a rather muddled and unconfident exploration of the political theory of collectivism . . . under cover of the rhetoric of individualism, Mill shuffled his way toward a collectivist theory of government. . . . In the final analysis, the individual for Mill is not an end in himself: he is an instrument and a servant of racial progress. . . . His last thoughts on government are bureaucratic rather than democratic. He understood mankind to be engaged in a cooperative enterprise to discover the true character of human well-being; and he understood government to have a part to play in organizing and controlling the pursuit of this enterprise. And it was only when collectivism spelt "collective mediocrity" that he feared and disapproved of it'. *Morality and Politics*, pp. 79, 82, 83.

51 Oakeshott, *Morality and Politics*, pp. 48–9.

52 Foucault, *Discipline and Punish*, p. 25. Privitera, *Problems of Style*, p. 87.

53 Foucault, 'On the genealogy of ethics', in H.L. Dreyfus and P. Rabinow (eds), *Beyond Structuralism and Hermeneutics*, p. 237, and 'What is Enlightenment?' in P. Rabinow (ed.), *The Foucault Reader* (Pantheon, New York, 1984), pp. 41–2.

54 For examples of such criticism, see the chapter on Foucault in Alan Megill, *Prophets of Extremity* (University of California Press, Berkeley CA, 1985); and Simons, *Foucault*, pp. 101–4.

55 Foucault, 'Genealogy of Ethics', p. 236.

56 On Foucault's misinterpretation of Stoic ethics, see Pierre Hadot, 'Reflections on the idea of the "cultivation of the self"', *Philosophy as a Way of Life: Spiritual Exercises from Socrates to Foucault*, A.I. Davidson (ed.), trans. M. Chase (Blackwell, Oxford, 1995).

57 Foucault, 'Governmentality', p. 103; 'Political technology of individuals', p. 145.

Index